MW00804220

Undergraduate Research Experiences for STEM Students

SUCCESSES, CHALLENGES, AND OPPORTUNITIES

Committee on Strengthening Research Experiences
for Undergraduate STEM Students

James Gentile, Kerry Brenner, Amy Stephens, *Editors*

Board on Science Education
Division of Behavioral and Social Sciences and Education

Board on Life Sciences
Division on Earth and Life Studies

A Report of

The National Academies of
SCIENCES · ENGINEERING · MEDICINE

THE NATIONAL ACADEMIES PRESS
Washington, DC
www.nap.edu

THE NATIONAL ACADEMIES PRESS 500 Fifth Street, NW Washington, DC 20001

This study was supported by a contract between the National Academy of Sciences and the National Science Foundation. Any opinions, findings, conclusions, or recommendations expressed in this publication do not necessarily reflect the views of any organization or agency that provided support for the project.

International Standard Book Number-13: 978-0-309-45280-9
International Standard Book Number-10: 0-309-45280-5
Digital Object Identifier: https://doi.org/10.17226/24622
Library of Congress Control Number: 2017937426

Additional copies of this publication are available for sale from the National Academies Press, 500 Fifth Street, NW, Keck 360, Washington, DC 20001; (800) 624-6242 or (202) 334-3313; http://www.nap.edu/.

Copyright 2017 by the National Academy of Sciences. All rights reserved.

Printed in the United States of America

Suggested citation: National Academies of Sciences, Engineering, and Medicine. (2017). *Undergraduate Research Experiences for STEM Students: Successes, Challenges, and Opportunities*. Washington, DC: The National Academies Press. doi: https://doi.org/10.17226/24622.

The National Academies of
SCIENCES · ENGINEERING · MEDICINE

The **National Academy of Sciences** was established in 1863 by an Act of Congress, signed by President Lincoln, as a private, nongovernmental institution to advise the nation on issues related to science and technology. Members are elected by their peers for outstanding contributions to research. Dr. Marcia McNutt is president.

The **National Academy of Engineering** was established in 1964 under the charter of the National Academy of Sciences to bring the practices of engineering to advising the nation. Members are elected by their peers for extraordinary contributions to engineering. Dr. C. D. Mote, Jr., is president.

The **National Academy of Medicine** (formerly the Institute of Medicine) was established in 1970 under the charter of the National Academy of Sciences to advise the nation on medical and health issues. Members are elected by their peers for distinguished contributions to medicine and health. Dr. Victor J. Dzau is president.

The three Academies work together as the **National Academies of Sciences, Engineering, and Medicine** to provide independent, objective analysis and advice to the nation and conduct other activities to solve complex problems and inform public policy decisions. The National Academies also encourage education and research, recognize outstanding contributions to knowledge, and increase public understanding in matters of science, engineering, and medicine.

Learn more about the **National Academies of Sciences, Engineering, and Medicine** at www.national-academies.org.

The National Academies of
SCIENCES · ENGINEERING · MEDICINE

Reports document the evidence-based consensus of an authoring committee of experts. Reports typically include findings, conclusions, and recommendations based on information gathered by the committee and committee deliberations. Reports are peer reviewed and are approved by the National Academies of Sciences, Engineering, and Medicine.

Proceedings chronicle the presentations and discussions at a workshop, symposium, or other convening event. The statements and opinions contained in proceedings are those of the participants and have not been endorsed by other participants, the planning committee, or the National Academies of Sciences, Engineering, and Medicine.

For information about other products and activities of the National Academies, please visit nationalacademies.org/whatwedo.

COMMITTEE ON STRENGTHENING RESEARCH EXPERIENCES FOR UNDERGRADUATE STEM STUDENTS

James Gentile (*Chair*), Hope College, Holland, MI
Ann Beheler, Collin County Community College, Frisco, TX
Janet Branchaw, University of Wisconsin–Madison, WI
Deborah Faye Carter, Claremont Graduate University, Claremont, CA
Melanie Cooper, Michigan State University, East Lansing, MI
Edward J. Coyle, Georgia Institute of Technology, Atlanta, GA
Sarah C.R. Elgin, Washington University in St. Louis, St. Louis, MO
Mica Estrada, University of California, San Francisco, CA
Eli Fromm, Drexel University, Philadelphia, PA
Ralph Garruto, State University of New York, Binghamton, NY
Eric Grodsky, University of Wisconsin–Madison, WI
James Hewlett, Finger Lakes Community College, Canandaigua, NY
Laird Kramer, Florida International University, Miami, FL
Marcia C. Linn, University of California, Berkeley, CA
Linda A. Reinen, Pomona College, Claremont, CA
Heather Thiry, University of Colorado Boulder, CO

Kerry Brenner, *Study Director*
Jay Labov, *Senior Scientist/Program Director for Biology Education*, Board on Life Sciences
Amy Stephens, *Program Officer* (since December 2015)
Michael Feder, *Senior Program Officer* (until October 2015)
Miriam Scheiber, *Program Assistant*
Charles Morgan, *Christine Mirzayan Science and Technology Policy Fellow* (Spring 2016)

BOARD ON SCIENCE EDUCATION

Adam Gamoran (*Chair*), William T. Grant Foundation (president), New York, New York
Melanie Cooper, Department of Chemistry, Michigan State University
Rodolfo Dirzo, Department of Biology, Stanford University
Rush Holt, Jr., American Association for the Advancement of Science, Washington, DC
Matthew Krehbiel, Achieve, Inc., Washington, DC
Michael Lach, Urban Education Institute, University of Chicago
Lynn S. Liben, Department of Psychology, The Pennsylvania State University
Cathy Manduca, Science Education Resource Center, Carleton College
John Mather, NASA Goddard Space Flight Center, Greenbelt, MD
Tonya Matthews, Michigan Science Center, Detroit, MI
Brian Reiser, School of Education and Social Policy, Northwestern University
Marshall "Mike" Smith, Carnegie Foundation for the Advancement of Teaching, Stanford, CA
Roberta Tanner, Retired Physics Teacher, Thompson School District, Loveland, Colorado
Suzanne Wilson, Neag School of Education, University of Connecticut

Heidi Schweingruber, *Director*

BOARD ON LIFE SCIENCES

James Collins (*Chair*), School of Life Sciences, Arizona State University
Nancy Connell, Department of Medicine, New Jersey Medical School
Joseph Ecker, Genetics and Plant Biology Laboratory, Salk Institute for
   Biological Studies, La Jolla, CA
Sarah C.R. Elgin, Department of Biology, Washington University in
   St. Louis, St. Louis, MO
Linda Griffith, Biological and Mechanical Engineering, Massachusetts
   Institute of Technology
Richard Johnson, Global Helix LLC, Bethesda, MD
Judith Kimble, Biochemistry and Molecular Biology and Medical
   Genetics, University of Wisconsin–Madison, WI
Mary Maxon, Lawrence Berkeley National Laboratory, Berkeley, CA
Jill Porter Mesirov, Bioinformatics and Computational Biology,
   Massachusetts Institute of Technology
Karen Nelson, J. Craig Venter Institute, Rockville, MD
Claire Pomeroy, Albert and Mary Lasker Foundation, New York,
   New York
Mary Power, Department of Integrative Biology, University of California,
   Berkeley, CA
Margaret Riley, Department of Biology, University of Massachusetts,
   Amherst, MA
Lana Skirboll, Academic and Scientific Affairs, Sanofi, Washington, DC
Janis Weekes, Department of Biology, University of Oregon, Eugene, OR

Frances Sharples, *Director*

Preface

I have had the privilege and honor to be involved in undergraduate research throughout my more than 50-year career in science. I did research as an undergraduate, and I was fortunate to be a research mentor to more than 100 undergraduate students as a professor at a liberal arts college. As a departmental chair and academic dean, I hired and mentored faculty colleagues, assisting them in developing their own undergraduate research mentoring talents. As a foundation president, I was charged with leading an organization whose mission included sustaining and creating programs that supported institutions, faculty, and students engaged in undergraduate research.

As an undergraduate student at a small liberal arts college, I was initially focused on "fast tracking" toward medical school and a career as a practitioner of the healing arts. Along the way I met an outstanding professor who convinced me to take the opportunity to work with him and a team of a few other students on an ecology-focused research project. The summer research experience and science adventure involving hands-on science learning was eye opening and motivating for me. That adventure in science—and the amazing empowerment of discovering something known by no one else at that time and discussing those results with faculty both on and off campus in a collegial and professional manner—empowered and convinced me to pursue graduate school (instead of medical school) and look toward a career as a science educator and scholar.

The value of research is not merely intuitive, and it goes well beyond the fact that undergraduate laboratory work encourages graduate work. Undergraduate research is in itself the purest form of both faculty teaching and student learning. The research involvement not only deepens student learning in both the content and context of science but also promotes collaborations with faculty members and other student colleagues in a manner that builds and sustains a community of scholars who have the confidence to both ask the "What if?" questions in science and then engage in the exciting journey to find the answers.

The evolution, interest in, and adaptation of undergraduate research experiences (UREs) by all types of institutions (two- and four-year colleges and universities) have grown substantially, particularly so in the past two decades. Furthermore, expansion of UREs beyond the sciences to the broader academic community has grown significantly, adding to a new ecology of teaching, learning, and research that is currently embraced by increasing numbers of institutions across our nation. A report published by the Project Leap Project (under the auspices of the American Association of Colleges and Universities [AAC&U]) notes that many of the benefits of undergraduate research are aligned with three of the essential learning outcomes espoused by the AAC&U: intellectual and practical skills, personal and social responsibility, and integrative and applied learning. Undergraduate research embraces and promotes precisely the suite of experiences that have the potential to transform the way students perceive and understand what they are learning and how it is applied in authentic, real-world situations.[1]

Faculty at all categories of academic institution are working to improve mechanisms and pathways for embedding UREs into science, technology, engineering, and mathematics (STEM) courses, as well as expanding undergraduate research opportunities to students. These efforts cut across disciplines and include both mentored experiences with professors and course-embedded research that is a more formal part of the curriculum. Multiple benefits have been noted or claimed for students engaged in undergraduate research—both personal and professional. Personal benefits may include increased self-confidence, independence, readiness for the next level of challenge, and ability to tolerate obstacles. Professional benefits may include gaining both experience that will advance career opportunities and skills such as enhanced critical thinking. UREs may provide opportunities for developing intellectual tools that encourage students to always ask questions as they seek to understand, and these experiences may allow students to build upon the answers in ways that enhances their education. This report provides perspective and insight into impact on students engaged in apprentice-style undergraduate research with faculty mentors, as well as educational impacts for students who participate in course-embedded UREs.

---

[1] See https://www.aacu.org/publications-research/periodicals/research-and-discovery-across-curriculum [December 2016].

UREs can add an important dimension to undergraduate STEM education, in particular providing students with an opportunity to test and reaffirm their interest in a STEM career. This report by a committee appointed by the National Academies of Sciences, Engineering, and Medicine provides unique and informed insight into the "educational value-added" that accrues to students engaged in undergraduate research either through a faculty-mentored research experience in a laboratory or in the field, through active engagement in research that was embedded within a course, or other forms of UREs.

James Gentile, *Chair*
Committee on Strengthening Research Experiences
for Undergraduate STEM Students

Acknowledgments

This report represents the work of thousands of individuals, not only those who served on the committee, wrote papers for it, and participated in the committee's open sessions, but also those who conducted and were the subjects of the research on which the committee's conclusions and recommendations are based. We recognize their invaluable contributions to our work.

This report was made possible by the important contributions of the National Science Foundation (NSF). We particularly thank our program officer Dawn Rickey and Susan Singer (division director, NSF Division of Undergraduate Education).

Members of the committee benefited from discussion and presentation by many individuals who participated in our three fact-finding meetings.

- At the first meeting, different perspectives were presented on undergraduate research experiences (UREs), existing work to build upon, sources to evaluate, and the changing URE landscape. Presenters included Beth Ambos (Council on Undergraduate Research), David Asai (Howard Hughes Medical Institute), and Jo Handelsman (Office of Science and Technology Policy).
- At the second meeting, the following topics were explored:
  — Institutional-level data gathering and analysis. Presenters included Stephany Hazel (George Mason University), Marco Molinaro (University of California, Davis), and Bethany Usher (George Mason University).

- Institutional change. Presenters included Paul Hernandez (West Virginia University) and Mitch Malachowski (University of San Diego).
- Additional perspectives and commentary on presentations. Presenters included Erin Dolan (The University of Texas at Austin) and Tuajuanda Jordan (St. Mary's College of Maryland).

• The third meeting included three panels of subject matter experts:
  - Panel 1 discussed UREs in mathematical sciences. Panelists included Michael Dorff (Brigham Young University), Suzanne Weekes (Worcester Polytechnic University), and Michal Wolf (Rice University).
  - Panel 2 discussed faculty perspectives on undergraduate research. Panelists included Ariel Anbar (Arizona State University), Tracy Johnson (University of California, Los Angeles), and Sandra Laursen (University of Colorado Boulder).
  - Panel 3 discussed engineering perspectives on undergraduate research. Panelists included Lisa Benson (Clemson University) and Ann Saterbak (Rice University).

The committee is very grateful for the efforts of the three authors who prepared background papers on specific topics for the committee's use in drafting the report:

• Erin Dolan, on current knowledge and future directions of course-based UREs;
• Christine Pfund, on the role and impact of mentoring on UREs; and
• Linda Blockus, on the co-curricular model of the URE.

This report has been reviewed in draft form by individuals chosen for their diverse perspectives and technical expertise. The purpose of this independent review is to provide candid and critical comments that will assist the institution in making its published report as sound as possible and to ensure that the report meets institutional standards for objectivity, evidence, and responsiveness to the study charge. The review comments and draft manuscript remain confidential to protect the integrity of the deliberative process. We thank the following individuals for their review of this report: Cristina H. Amon, Mechanical Engineering, University of Toronto; Gita Bangera, RISE Learning Institute, Bellevue College; Sara E. Brownell, School of Life Sciences, Arizona State University; Thomas R. Cech, BioFrontiers Institute, University of Colorado Boulder; Michael Dorff, Department of Mathematics, Brigham Young University; Paul R. Hernandez, Department of Learning Sciences and Human Development, College of Education and Human Services, West Virginia University; Cathy

A. Manduca, Science Education Resource Center, Carleton College; Maria Ruiz-Primo, School of Education and Human Development, University of Colorado Denver; David W. Schaffer, Department of Educational Psychology, University of Wisconsin–Madison; Gabriela C. Weaver, Center for Teaching and Faculty Development, University of Massachusetts Amherst; and Huntington F. Willard, Marine Biological Laboratory, Woods Hole, Massachusetts.

Although the reviewers listed above provided many constructive comments and suggestions, they were not asked to endorse the content of the report nor did they see the final draft of the report before its release. The review of this report was overseen by Joseph Krajcik, Department of Teacher Education, Michigan State University, and Bruce Alberts, Department of Biochemistry and Biophysics, University of California, San Francisco. They were responsible for making certain that an independent examination of this report was carried out in accordance with institutional procedures and that all review comments were carefully considered. Responsibility for the final content of this report rests entirely with the authoring committee and the institution.

Thanks are also due to the project staff. Kerry Brenner of the Board on Science Education directed the study and played a key role in the report drafting process. Amy Stephens (program officer for the Board on Science Education) stepped in to help with the study in the middle and was immensely helpful with organizing the report and revising the writing. Joanna Roberts managed the administrative tasks associated with getting the project started. Mary Ghitelman managed the first meeting's logistical and administrative needs. Miriam Scheiber managed the rest of the study's logistical and administrative needs, along with manuscript preparation. Jay Labov (senior advisor for education and communication with the Teacher Advisory Council) contributed to the writing and provided guidance throughout the course of the project. Michael Feder (former program officer with the Board on Science Education) helped to get the project started on the right foot. Heidi Schweingruber (director of the Board on Science Education) provided thoughtful advice and many helpful suggestions throughout the entire study. We are also grateful to two Christine Mirzayan Science and Technology Fellows: Charlie Morgan provided many helpful and enthusiastic contributions during the initial report writing process, and Ryan Stowe assisted with information gathering at the start of the project.

Staff of the Division of Behavioral and Social Sciences and Education also provided help: Robert Katt substantially improved the readability of the report; Kirsten Sampson Snyder expertly guided the report through the report review process; and Yvonne Wise masterfully guided the report through production.

Contents

Summary

Undergraduate research has a rich history, and many practicing researchers point to undergraduate research experiences (UREs) as crucial to their own career success. One of the most prominent opportunities for undergraduate research has been through the National Science Foundation's Research Experiences for Undergraduates program, but many other funders (large and small) have contributed to the opportunities available. Organizations such as the Council on Undergraduate Research and the National Conferences on Undergraduate Research have provided a showcase for undergraduate work and a network for faculty to learn from each other about UREs.

There are many ongoing efforts to improve undergraduate science, technology, engineering, and mathematics (STEM) education that focus on increasing the active engagement of students and decreasing traditional lecture-based teaching. UREs have been proposed as an opportune way to actively engage students and may be a key strategy for broadening participation in STEM. Multiple reports have focused on the potential high impact of UREs and the often limited availability of the experiences.[1] These reports often call for an expansion in UREs to allow for greater access

---

[1]Three important examples of such reports are *Engage to Excel: Producing One Million Additional College Graduates with Degrees in Science, Technology, Engineering, and Mathematics* from the President's Council of Advisors on Science and Technology; *High-Impact Educational Practices: What They Are, Who Has Access to Them, and Why They Matter* from the Association of American Colleges and Universities; and *Science in Solution: The Impact of Undergraduate Research on Student Learning* by David Lopatto and published by the Research Corporation for Science Advancement.

to a wider array of students. Current efforts are working to increase the number of students participating in UREs and to increase the diversity of those participants.

The National Science Foundation commissioned this study by the National Academies of Sciences, Engineering, and Medicine to examine what is known about UREs and, if possible, to identify best practices that should be applied to future UREs. The committee was also asked to discuss the needs of involved faculty and administrators, to examine costs and benefits, and to provide recommendations for research and practice. The committee approached its analysis of UREs by considering them as part of a learning system that is shaped by forces related to national policy, institutional leadership, and departmental culture, as well as by the interactions among faculty, other mentors, and students. The committee also considered UREs in the context of the goals for students and what research on learning says about how such experiences should be designed to reach those goals. Many existing studies that provide information on how students learn can inform URE designers.

DIVERSITY OF URES

The classic image of a URE is a student spending the summer working directly with a faculty member on a project related to that faculty member's research, but UREs have diversified beyond this traditional apprentice model. Course-based undergraduate research experiences are becoming increasingly common. Students also participate in research via internships and co-ops, where they do academically relevant work outside of academia. In addition, undergraduate research can be part of wrap-around programs that may offer combinations of mentoring, scholarships, courses in study skills, and courses in research approaches and ethics. As well as these variations in structure, UREs can also differ in location (on campus or off campus, in a variety of settings) and rewards to students (e.g., academic year course credit, service credit, stipends). A discussion of the great variety of UREs and a definition of URE is provided in Chapter 2.

College students today are more diverse than in the past, and faculty and administrators implementing UREs need to consider how they include historically underrepresented students, first generation college students, STEM majors, non-STEM majors, beginning students, students enrolled in capstone experiences, and pre-service teachers.[2] Many of the more extensive

---

[2] Capstone experiences are large projects done by upper-level students that bring together multiple aspects of their undergraduate education. First generation students are the first generation in their family to attend college. Pre-service teachers are undergraduates preparing to become teachers in grades from kindergarten through 12th grade.

studies of UREs have focused on participation by historically underrepresented groups of students in a comprehensive program. Further research is needed to see whether the conclusions drawn from those studies can be applied more widely to other student populations and other types of UREs.

IMPLEMENTATION OF URES

The culture and values of campuses and departments affect how UREs are implemented and perceived. On some campuses, UREs are a prominent feature of undergraduate education for all students, whereas on other campuses, they are known (and hence available) only to a small pool of students. There are wide variations across departments and institutions in the degree to which faculty are expected to include undergraduates in research. Incentives for faculty to participate can be tied to traditions and attitudes, as well as to the potential for their participation to be considered in promotion and tenure decisions. These expectations and attitudes can influence the level of administrative support available to help faculty develop, implement, refine, and study UREs. Campus culture also impacts many more-practical issues, such as the availability of resources (e.g., space, equipment, libraries and journal access). The availability of external and internal funding can also affect the creation and sustainability of UREs. National networks, including disciplinary and educational societies, can play an important role in connecting faculty members with others with similar interests in a supportive "community of practice." New UREs are often modeled on or adapted from existing UREs, and this raises issues about the best ways to learn from the experiences of others. These networking connections can be very important on campuses where teaching expectations are high and few faculty members have maintained an active research program of their own.

Mentoring is a key aspect of the research experience for many undergraduates. In addition to the mentoring done by faculty members, undergraduates are frequently mentored by instructors, postdoctoral fellows, graduate students, and even fellow undergraduates. Faculty engage in UREs in many ways. In addition to serving as mentors they generally make decisions about the structure and design of the URE, including making decisions about goals and evaluation. A URE program has the potential to drive faculty research and create synergy between the teaching and research responsibilities of individual faculty members. Faculty incentives and rewards for engaging in UREs vary across departments and institutions. The opportunity for faculty and other mentors to engage in relevant professional development also varies. Little research has been done on how working with undergraduates doing research or establishing a URE program impacts the professional life of the faculty.

WHAT IS KNOWN ABOUT URES

Studies of UREs have examined many potential outcomes of participation in UREs. They have looked at the impact on persistence and retention of students in a STEM major or STEM career, promoting understanding of STEM, and integration into the STEM culture. From the available evidence, the committee concludes that UREs impact graduation rates and retention in STEM, and they may increase students' feelings of belonging and their confidence in understanding STEM content, data analysis, and the nature of experiments. In addition, there is a large body of literature available on how people learn that can be applied to UREs. However, the extent to which those designing and implementing UREs have explicitly relied upon the studies about UREs or on the knowledge of how students learn is unclear.

As the focus on UREs has grown, so have the questions about their impact. There is an emerging body of literature describing specific UREs and surveys of student participants, as well as unpublished evaluations that provide additional information about UREs. Although these sources provide a rich description of UREs, they do not currently answer questions about the ways that UREs lead to benefits to students and which aspects of UREs are most powerful. In addition, it is difficult to evaluate the costs of UREs because many schools seek to leverage already available resources or use in-kind donations, such as nonmonetized (uncompensated) faculty time, in building their URE program.

Taken together, there are many unanswered questions and opportunities for further investigation of the role of UREs in the undergraduate learning experience and the mechanisms by which UREs might support various student, faculty, and institutional goals. Different types of questions rely on different research methodologies, and attention to study design as UREs are planned will facilitate research on them. Carefully designed studies can enable the community to develop a more robust understanding of how UREs work for different students, why they work, and how to evaluate the reported outcomes for URE participants. Such studies need to be based on sound research questions and use valid methods to measure outcomes. The committee's research agenda in Chapter 7 proposes specific areas where additional studies would be particularly informative.

To maximize the return on the investment in URE programs, it will be useful to collect additional data comparing programs to ascertain those design features that contribute to student success. Student success includes many different aspects, such as learning important content of a discipline, understanding practices of STEM researchers, and gaining a sense of belonging to the STEM enterprise; markers of success can be measured in both the short term (e.g., by grade point averages) and the long term (e.g., by career choice). Despite this need for additional research, much is known that can inform the decisions and actions of the many interacting people and administrative units influencing UREs.

Practitioners designing or improving UREs can build on the experiences of colleagues and learn from both the literature about UREs and the research on how students learn. During the design process, practitioners should consider the goals of the students, goals of the program, goals of the faculty member, and goals of the campus. Other factors to consider include the available resources, how the program or experience will be evaluated or studied, and how to build in opportunities to improve the experience over time, based on new evidence. Analysis of the current offerings on campus can inform decisions and help create a culture of improvement in which faculty are supported in their efforts to continually refine UREs based on the evidence currently available and evidence that they and others generate in the future.

CONCLUSIONS AND RECOMMENDATIONS

Following its analysis of the available information, the committee reached consensus on a set of conclusions and recommendations. The conclusions and recommendations discussed in Chapter 9 are included in this summary. In addition, Chapter 7 identifies five additional recommendations for future research about UREs.

Conclusions

Conclusion 1: *The current and emerging landscape of what constitutes UREs is diverse and complex. Students can engage in STEM-based undergraduate research in many different ways, across a variety of settings, and along a continuum that extends and expands upon learning opportunities in other educational settings. The following characteristics define UREs. Due to the variation in the types of UREs, not all experiences include all of the following characteristics in the same way; experiences vary in how much a particular characteristic is emphasized.*

- *They engage students in research practices including the ability to argue from evidence.*
- *They aim to generate novel information with an emphasis on discovery and innovation or to determine whether recent preliminary results can be replicated.*
- *They focus on significant, relevant problems of interest to STEM researchers and in some cases a broader community (e.g., civic engagement).*
- *They emphasize and expect collaboration and teamwork.*

- *They involve iterative refinement of experimental design, experimental questions, or data obtained.*
- *They allow students to master specific research techniques.*
- *They help students engage in reflection about the problems being investigated and the work being undertaken to address those problems.*
- *They require communication of results, either through publication or presentations in various STEM venues.*
- *They are structured and guided by a mentor, with students assuming increasing ownership of some aspects of the project over time.*

Conclusion 2: *Research on the efficacy of UREs is still in the early stages of development compared with other interventions to improve undergraduate STEM education.*

- *The types of UREs are diverse, and their goals are even more diverse. Questions and methodologies used to investigate the roles and effectiveness of UREs in achieving those goals are similarly diverse.*
- *Most of the studies of UREs to date are descriptive case studies or use correlational designs. Many of these studies report positive outcomes from engagement in a URE.*
- *Only a small number of studies have employed research designs that can support inferences about causation. Most of these studies find evidence for a causal relationship between URE participation and subsequent persistence in STEM. More studies are needed to provide evidence that participation in UREs is a causal factor in a range of desired student outcomes.*

Taking the entire body of evidence into account, the committee concludes that the published peer-reviewed literature to date suggests that participation in a URE is beneficial for students.

Conclusion 3: *Studies focused on students from historically underrepresented groups indicate that participation in UREs improves their persistence in STEM and helps to validate their disciplinary identity.*

Conclusion 4: *The committee was unable to find evidence that URE designers are taking full advantage of the information available in the education literature on strategies for designing, implementing, and evaluating learning experiences. STEM faculty members do not generally receive training in interpreting or conducting education research. Partnerships between those with expertise in education research and those with expertise in implementing UREs are one way to strengthen the application of evidence on what works in planning and implementing UREs.*

Conclusion 5: *Evaluations of UREs are often conducted to inform program providers and funders; however, they may not be accessible to others. While these evaluations are not designed to be research studies and often have small sample sizes, they may contain information that could be useful to those initiating new URE programs and those refining UREs. Increasing access to these evaluations and to the accumulated experience of the program providers may enable URE designers and implementers to build upon knowledge gained from earlier UREs.*

Conclusion 6: *Data at the institutional, state, or national levels on the number and type of UREs offered, or who participates in UREs overall or at specific types of institutions, have not been collected systematically. Although the committee found that some individual institutions track at least some of this type of information, we were unable to determine how common it is to do so or what specific information is most commonly gathered.*

Conclusion 7: *While data are lacking on the precise number of students engaged in UREs, there is some evidence of a recent growth in course-based undergraduate research experiences (CUREs), which engage a cohort of students in a research project as part of a formal academic experience.*

Conclusion 8: *The quality of mentoring can make a substantial difference in a student's experiences with research. However, professional development in how to be a good mentor is not available to many faculty or other prospective mentors (e.g., graduate students, postdoctoral fellows).*

Conclusion 9: *The unique assets, resources, priorities, and constraints of the department and institution, in addition to those of individual mentors, impact the goals and structures of UREs. Schools across the country are showing considerable creativity in using unique resources, repurposing current assets, and leveraging student enthusiasm to increase research opportunities for their students.*

Recommendations

Recommendation 1: *Researchers with expertise in education research should conduct well-designed studies in collaboration with URE program directors to improve the evidence base about the processes and effects of UREs. This research should address how the various components of UREs may benefit students. It should also include additional causal evidence for the individual and additive effects of outcomes from student participation in different types of UREs. Not all UREs need be designed to undertake* *this type of research, but it would be very useful to have some UREs that are designed to facilitate these efforts to improve the evidence base.*

Recommendation 2: *Funders should provide appropriate resources to support the design, implementation, and analysis of some URE programs that are specifically designed to enable detailed research establishing the effects on participant outcomes and on other variables of interest such as the consequences for mentors or institutions.*

Recommendation 3: *Designers of UREs should base their design decisions on sound evidence. Consultations with education and social science researchers may be helpful as designers analyze the literature and make decisions on the creation or improvement of UREs. Professional development materials should be created and made available to faculty. Educational and disciplinary societies should consider how they can provide resources and connections to those working on UREs.*

Recommendation 4: *Institutions should collect data on student participation in UREs to inform their planning and to look for opportunities to improve quality and access.*

Recommendation 5: *Administrators and faculty at all types of colleges and universities should continually and holistically evaluate the range of UREs that they offer. As part of this process, institutions should:*
- *Consider how best to leverage available resources (including off-campus experiences available to students and current or potential networks or partnerships that the institution may form) when offering UREs so that they align with their institution's mission and priorities;*
- *Consider whether current UREs are both accessible and welcoming to students from various subpopulations across campus (e.g., historically underrepresented students, first generation college students, those with disabilities, non-STEM majors, prospective kindergarten-through-12th-grade teachers); and*
- *Gather and analyze data on the types of UREs offered and the students who participate, making this information widely available to the campus community and using it to make evidence-based decisions about improving opportunities for URE participation. This may entail devising or implementing systems for tracking relevant data (see Conclusion 4).*

Recommendation 6: *Administrators and faculty at colleges and universities should ensure that all who mentor undergraduates in research experiences* *(this includes faculty, instructors, postdoctoral fellows, graduate students, and undergraduates serving as peer mentors) have access to appropriate professional development opportunities to help them grow and succeed in this role.*

Recommendation 7: *Administrators and faculty at all types of colleges and universities should work together within and, where feasible, across institutions to create a culture that supports the development of evidence-based, iterative, and continuous refinement of UREs, in an effort to improve student learning outcomes and overall academic success. This should include the development, evaluation, and revision of policies and practices designed to create a culture supportive of the participation of faculty and other mentors in effective UREs. Policies should consider pedagogy, professional development, cross-cultural awareness, hiring practices, compensation, promotion (incentives, rewards), and the tenure process.*

Recommendation 8: *Administrators and faculty at all types of colleges and universities should work to develop strong and sustainable partnerships within and between institutions and with educational and professional societies for the purpose of sharing resources to facilitate the creation of sustainable URE programs.*

1

Introduction

I hear and I forget.
I see and I remember.
I do and I understand.
—Confucius

Undergraduate research experiences (UREs) are a meaningful opportunity for undergraduates to learn about the work and perspectives of science, technology, engineering, and mathematics (STEM) researchers. Many faculty members and other scientists recall that their own research experiences as an undergraduate were pivotal to their career success. Today, there are various forms of UREs available to students at a wide variety of institutions. However, while many students report that they enjoy the experiences and learn a lot from them (Harsh et al., 2011), there has been little analysis of which types of UREs might best serve students at different academic institutions and with diverse career aspirations.

Attention to UREs has grown significantly in the last few years as policy actions have promoted their expansion. In 1998, the Boyer Commission on Educating Undergraduates in the Research University considered a capstone research experience as an essential element in the reinvention of undergraduate education (Miller, 2013). However, the most prominent call was from a committee of the President's Council of Advisors on Science and Technology (PCAST). The second recommendation of its 2012 report, *Engage to Excel: Producing One Million Additional College Graduates with Degrees in STEM*, is to "advocate and provide support for replacing standard laboratory courses with discovery-based research courses"

(President's Council of Advisors on Science and Technology, 2012, p. 25). Specifically, the report discussed how undergraduates working on faculty projects can allow students to experience real discovery and innovation and to be inspired by STEM subjects. The PCAST report recommended that all relevant federal agencies examine their programs and make changes in an effort to decrease any policy or practice that creates barriers to early engagement of students in research. It also called on the agencies to "encourage projects that establish collaborations between research universities and community colleges or other institutions that do not have research programs" (President's Council of Advisors on Science and Technology, 2012, p. v).

As efforts have been made to expand opportunities for UREs, many questions have arisen. This report provides a comprehensive overview of and insights about the current and rapidly evolving types of UREs, in an effort to improve understanding of the complexity of UREs in terms of their content, their surrounding context, the diversity of the student participants (including the educational pathways of those students), and the opportunities for learning provided by a research experience. The report discusses the various types of UREs and the crosscutting characteristics that most UREs exhibit. The type and level of evidence available on the efficacy of UREs and how the evidence base might be strengthened are examined. The way that UREs currently fit with the educational "ecosystem" in higher education is discussed, as well as the problems that designers and implementers of such programs often encounter within the current structures for governance and funding of higher education. Recommendations are presented on how such barriers might be overcome in the future by rethinking how academic departments, institutions, and funding agencies might support UREs and how UREs could be assessed and evaluated more effectively and comprehensively.

As noted in Chapter 2 and discussed throughout the report, the authoring committee has examined many varieties of UREs. Students engage in research during capstone experiences, co-ops,[1] and internships; as part of community engagement projects; and as part of bridge programs to assist with transitions between high school and college or between college and graduate school. Traditionally, two general categories of UREs are most often discussed and analyzed in the literature: the apprentice model and the course-based undergraduate research experience (CURE). Other variations of UREs exist and will also be discussed throughout this report. In an *apprentice model experience,* one or a small number of students work with

---

[1] Undergraduate co-ops are full-time paid educational experiences designed to provide an opportunity for students to apply knowledge and skills from their coursework while working in a professional setting such as in industry. They are particularly common for students in engineering programs.

an individual or small group of established scientists, technologists, engineers, or mathematicians on a research or design problem, typically outside of the classroom. Individual students may play different roles depending on the wishes and needs of the sponsoring individual and the background of the student. In a *CURE*, small to large groups of students enrolled in a formal course or sequence of courses participate in a discovery-based project designed to engage them in the use of STEM practices, discovery, collaboration, iteration, and pursuit of broadly relevant or important work (Auchincloss et al., 2014; Brownell and Kloser, 2015; Litzinger et al., 2011). These course experiences may be offered over part of an academic term/semester, for full semesters, or for multiple semesters in a sequence of courses. Some CUREs are developed by individuals, while others are part of large national consortia. CUREs appear to have increased in popularity in recent years and are the subject of several new studies (discussed in Chapter 4).

HISTORY OF URES

Undergraduate research is sometimes thought to be a relatively recent development in higher education. However, faculty-mentored, apprentice-based undergraduate research has a long and rich history, dating back more than 200 years to Wilhelm von Humboldt (Zupanc, 2012). Many U.S. institutions of higher education adopted the "Humboldtian Ideal" of an unceasing process of inquiry that unified teaching and research (Kinkead, 2012). In keeping with this ideal, the National Science Foundation launched a program supporting undergraduate research participation in 1958. The program was canceled in 1981 but relaunched in its current form as Research Experiences for Undergraduates in 1987 (Bennett, 2015).

The Council on Undergraduate Research (CUR), founded in 1978, is a national organization that helps connect faculty and college administrators across institutions engaged with undergraduate research. Many of the first participants involved with CUR were faculty from liberal arts colleges who saw undergraduate research as good pedagogy that could expand horizons for the students while furthering basic or applied research being undertaken by faculty members themselves.

Many different types of academic institutions have now explored and established strong undergraduate research programs; the types of offerings have varied depending on the academic environment, the research infrastructure available, and the culture of the particular institution or discipline. With new avenues of funding through public and private foundations to support these efforts, programs have been replicated, modified, and expanded. As discussed in Chapter 4, the reported benefits of UREs include increasing the number of students who choose to major in STEM disciplines, continue throughout the program, and subsequently graduate with a STEM degree, in addition to helping students develop an interest and identity as a STEM researcher. They may also encourage more faculty members and other academic personnel to engage in some kind of basic or applied research.

The committee chose to take an inclusive view of the individual disciplines included in the definition of STEM by considering the social sciences, natural sciences, engineering, and mathematics. We attempted to find examples and identify literature from all of these fields that would provide evidence to inform the discussion of UREs. However, the relevant literature is limited for many of these specific disciplines, so examples and references cited in the report are not evenly distributed across all intended STEM disciplines. In particular, the discipline of engineering received attention in the committee's discussions and review of the literature. Engineering has a long history of capstone courses and other opportunities for undergraduate students to engage in work done by engineers (Rowles et al., 2004). However, much of the work on UREs has focused on examining the ways that students learn science. Therefore, throughout the report where those studies are discussed, the language may appear to be ignoring the engineering perspective.

As research has become a more institutionalized component of undergraduate education, faculty members have created links with colleagues at other campuses. In addition to CUR, other national groups that have joined the conversation on UREs include the National Conferences on Undergraduate Research, which started in 1987 and merged with CUR in 2010, and Project Kaleidoscope (PKAL). PKAL began in 1969 under the auspices of the Independent Colleges Office, and is now operating as a component of the American Association of Colleges and Universities (AAC&U). Founded on the principle of "discovering what works," PKAL has focused on catalyzing professional development for STEM faculty in ways that will enhance their success as scholar-educators who can then promote undergraduate student learning through hands-on approaches and through research in the classroom, laboratory, engineering design environment, or field.

Many professional and disciplinary societies have initiatives to fund student research or engage faculty in discussions about improving undergraduate research. For example, the Mathematical Association of America works to provide avenues for undergraduate students to engage in research and hosts a special interest group devoted to research in undergraduate mathematics education. Moreover, the American Society for Engineering provides access to programs that sponsor undergraduate research. Individually and collectively, these national organizations have played a significant catalytic role by bringing a strong and professional framework and culture to the affirmation and expansion of undergraduate research in all types of institutions across the nation.

Although initial efforts emphasized the classic apprenticeship model, often based on a summer experience in the lab, recent years have seen an expansion of CUREs in which undergraduate students are engaged in research as part of a formal course. The creation of a CURE is often driven by a desire to provide research experiences for a larger group of students than can be accommodated in a faculty member's research environment (the member's laboratory or field site). Alternatively, it can be part of the fieldwork for a given course. Some institutions see CUREs as a way to further engage students and encourage them to pursue and continue their education in a particular major or to continue their studies at that institution (Rodenbusch et al., 2016). These courses often have been developed by individual faculty members and are sometimes based on the faculty member's own research. Some CUREs have served as models and have been adapted or replicated at other institutions, including two-year colleges—for example, the Center for Authentic Science Practice in Education (Weaver et al., 2006). The Course-Based Undergraduate Research Experiences Network was initiated in 2012 to help faculty address challenges inherent to integrating research experiences into undergraduate courses in the biological sciences.[2]

CONTEXT OF THE STUDY

In the past decade, discussions of undergraduate research have intensified among various national and regional groups across campuses, in response to the need to better prepare an increasingly diverse student population to face 21st century challenges (Auchincloss et al., 2014; Bangera and Brownell, 2014; Brownell et al., 2015; Litzinger et al., 2011). Conversations have centered not only on student outcomes such as fostering students' learning and other psychosocial factors (e.g., engagement, belonging, interest in research) and how these may influence retention, but also on the costs inherent in expanding the availability of UREs. Recent years have also seen an increase in the numbers of students from underrepresented groups who are enrolled in undergraduate courses and programs (Bangera and Brownell, 2014; National Academies of Sciences, Engineering, and Medicine, 2016), thereby increasing the need to ensure that students from all groups are considered in the design of UREs. More discussion of student demographics and inclusion follows later in this section.

Multiple national reports have both stimulated and captured these discussions and called for expanding UREs. AAC&U reports that address

---

[2]For more information, see http://www.lifescied.org/content/13/1/29.full [November 2016].

undergraduate research include *College Learning for the New Global Century*; *High Impact Educational Practices: What They Are, Who Has Access to Them, and Why They Matter*; and *The LEAP Vision for Learning: Outcomes, Practices, Impact, and Employers' Views* (respectively, Association of American Colleges and Universities, 2007, 2008, 2011). These reports present UREs as one of the high-impact practices that can dramatically influence undergraduate education. Another report, *Vision and Change in Undergraduate Biology Education* (American Association for the Advancement of Science, 2011), called for integrating UREs into curricula. Follow-on activities prompted by that report have included formation of the PULSE (Partnership for Undergraduate Life Science Education) online community, conferences, and sharing of resources.

As discussed earlier in this introduction, the PCAST report *Engage to Excel: Producing One Million Additional College Graduates with Degrees in STEM* (President's Council of Advisors on Science and Technology, 2012) specifically highlighted the potential of UREs to improve the nation's undergraduate STEM education during the first 2 years of college and recommended their expansion so that eventually *all undergraduates are afforded this kind of learning opportunity*. The report recommended that current and future STEM faculty learn about and incorporate effective teaching methods into their STEM courses, particularly including the opportunity for students to generate or apply knowledge through research. The National Science Foundation has taken the lead in many aspects of implementing the PCAST report because enhancing the quality of STEM education is a high priority for that agency. However, questions remain about how best to achieve this goal, and some of those questions motivated this study.

The emphasis on UREs is part of a larger effort to improve and broaden participation in undergraduate STEM education, which has been the focus of numerous efforts and projects by a range of groups. In addition to the organizations mentioned above (American Association for the Advancement of Science, AAC&U, PCAST), work has been done by the American Association of Universities through its Undergraduate STEM Initiative, including the Framework for Systemic Change. Funding from the National Science Foundation, the National Institutes of Health, Howard Hughes Medical Institute, and numerous other funding entities has also driven efforts in undergraduate STEM education that have increased undergraduate opportunities to participate in research.

Consensus studies and other activities of the National Academies of Sciences, Engineering, and Medicine (the National Academies) have addressed the topic in multiple ways over the past 6 years. The 2011 report *Expanding Underrepresented Minority Participation: America's Science and Technology Talent at the Crossroads* (National Research Council, 2011) examined the role of diversity in the STEM workforce and called for efforts to increase demand for and access to postsecondary STEM education and technical training by historically underrepresented students. *Community Colleges in the Evolving STEM Education Landscape* (National Research Council, 2012a) reported on a summit that addressed the relationships between community colleges and four-year institutions, with a focus on partnerships and articulation processes that can facilitate student success in STEM. It also considered how to expand participation of students from historically underrepresented populations in undergraduate STEM, as well as how subjects such as mathematics can serve as gateways or barriers to college completion. The 2012 report *Discipline-Based Education Research: Understanding and Improving Learning in Undergraduate Science and Engineering* (National Research Council, 2012b) studied the new field that combines knowledge of teaching and learning with deep knowledge of discipline-specific science content. It analyzed empirical research on undergraduate teaching and learning and the extent to which the resulting evidence influences undergraduate instruction. *Reaching Students: What Research Says About Effective Instruction in Undergraduate Science and Engineering* (National Research Council, 2015) presented information from *Discipline-Based Education Research* and additional examples in a format designed to be more practical for faculty and instructors.

The recent report *Barriers and Opportunities for 2-Year and 4-Year STEM Degrees* (National Academies of Sciences, Engineering, and Medicine, 2016) addressed the changing demographics of college students and the multiple pathways they take in their education. It also described the challenges of needing to take developmental courses before being able to enroll in credit-earning courses, as well as the complications of transferring credits. This report includes recommendations about ways policy makers and institutions can learn more about students' varied pathways to better support them in reaching their goals and completing their degrees.

The National Academies publication most closely related to this project is the report of a convocation on *Integrating Discovery-based Research into the Undergraduate Curriculum*, convened to explore aspects of recommendation #2 of the 2012 PCAST report. The convocation report presents efforts to improve instruction through engaging students in research, with a focus on the opportunities and challenges of CUREs (National Academies of Sciences, Engineering, and Medicine, 2015).

As mentioned above, another important aspect of the study context is the changing demographics of today's undergraduate students, including more historically underrepresented students, first generation college students,[3] and nontraditional (e.g., part-time, delayed start, financially independent, and caregiver) students. Many private and publicly funded

---

[3] First generation students are those who are the first in their families to attend college.

programs have focused specifically on providing UREs to historically under-represented minorities, women, and first generation students because members of these groups are less likely to persist in STEM fields once they enter their undergraduate education and CUREs are proposed as a mechanism for broadening access to research for members of underrepresented groups (Bangera and Brownell, 2014). Although students from historically under-represented groups express greater interest in pursuing a STEM degree now compared with 30 years ago, there has not been a corresponding increase in the overall completion rates in STEM degrees, nor has there been a decrease in the notable disparities among historically underrepresented groups (Eagan et al., 2013, 2014; Estrada et al., 2016; Hurtado et al., 2012; National Science Foundation, 2014). Data on different participation rates of various groups are presented in Appendix A.

Overall, enrollment by women in STEM majors has increased in recent years; however, this change is not consistent across all disciplines. Of students pursuing STEM degrees in 1971, 62 percent were men and 38 percent were women. In 2012, 48 percent of those pursuing STEM degrees were men and 52 percent were women (Eagan et al., 2014). However, within specific STEM disciplines, there is still evidence of a gender gap. Men are more likely than women to pursue a degree in engineering (79 percent men versus 21 percent women) or in math or computer science (75 percent men versus 25 percent women). However, the pattern is reversed for the biological sciences (60 percent women versus 40 percent men) and the social sciences (70 percent women versus 30 percent men). In addition, even in fields with roughly equal numbers of women, concerns still remain with respect to discrimination in the selection of students to participate in UREs, discrimination during a URE, and the potential for sexual harassment (Clancy et al., 2014; Eddy and Brownell, 2016; Moss-Racusin et al., 2012).

Faculty and administrators at community colleges face additional or enhanced challenges compared to other types of institutions, particularly with respect to resources, including lower levels of funding for research and lack of appropriate facilities. This can make it difficult to implement and support UREs. In addition, the student populations at community colleges are generally quite diverse. Community colleges are more likely to serve first generation students and students who are slightly older, have families, or are working. Notably, students from Hispanic/Latino backgrounds were more likely to be enrolled in community college compared to students from other racial/ethnic backgrounds. Moreover, students in community colleges were on average less prepared than those in four-year institutions, often requiring some form of developmental education in their first year, especially in mathematics (Van Noy and Zeidenberg, 2014).

Although data exist on the demographics of students attending colleges and universities today, there is very limited information on how many students from historically underrepresented groups or at particular types of institutions participate in UREs. That is, there is currently no standardized metric used at educational institutions to track the type and duration of undergraduate research engagement for students. Programs that receive federal funding collect and maintain some information regarding the students involved in such UREs, but this represents only a fraction of the undergraduate research programs available to students. Thus, these data provide an incomplete picture of the demographics of students participating in UREs.

CHARGE TO THE COMMITTEE

In response to a request from the National Science Foundation, the National Academies of Sciences, Engineering, and Medicine convened a 16-member expert committee to evaluate the state of knowledge on the current broad array of UREs. The committee charge was to recommend ways to design, evaluate, and study UREs, based on a review of the available research evidence and taking into account the needs and resources of colleges and universities (see complete Statement of Task in Box 1-1). Membership on the committee included faculty from various STEM disciplines who have been involved in research opportunities for undergraduates at two- and four-year institutions, experts in education research and policy, and those with experience in higher education leadership.

Interpreting the Charge

The committee met five times over a 10-month period in 2015 and 2016 to gather information and explore the range of issues associated with UREs. In addition to reviewing published materials pertaining to the committee's charge, committee members heard from many experts and commissioned three papers during the information-gathering phase of the committee process (see below).

The committee spent a great deal of time discussing the charge and the best ways to respond to its call. We gathered evidence from literature reviews and presentations, by contacting faculty and administrators at numerous colleges and universities, and by sharing the members' own experiences and expertise. The conversations with faculty and administrators provided information about the range of UREs offered, examples of how students and faculty are compensated, and various examples of institutional support mechanisms, among other topics. The literature reviews searched for information on UREs, undergraduate research opportunities, research experiences for undergraduates, CUREs, mentors, apprentices, advisors, identity, and persistence. We also searched for evaluations of URE programs. Although some evaluations were found in the literature, the committee

BOX 1-1
Charge to the Committee

A committee will synthesize the broad range of literature on models for providing undergraduate students with authentic research experiences in STEM disciplines or professions. The committee will define what qualifies as "authentic undergraduate research experiences" and assess the quality of research on various types of these research experiences. If possible and based on the strength of the literature, the committee will compare the effectiveness of different mechanisms and programs for providing undergraduate research experiences and provide best-practice examples of successful strategies for involving undergraduates in research experiences. The committee will review the empirical evidence of benefits across a range of outcomes associated with the multitude of educational, student, and institutional goals. It will critically assess the associated costs involved in providing authentic research experiences within the context of undergraduate STEM education across all types of post-secondary institutions of higher learning, and provide recommendations for research and practice. The committee will also discuss the needs of faculty and departmental administrators in order to successfully implement or improve and expand undergraduate research opportunities. The committee will develop a conceptual framework for designing and evaluating undergraduate research opportunities and create a research and development agenda to clarify what additional research is needed to robustly assess the quality and outcomes of undergraduate research experiences. The committee will balance the potential value added of making research or practice experiences more "authentic" with the potential additional investment of time, institutional capacity and financial support needed, and suggest strategies for implementing undergraduate research experiences for various goals and outcomes, and for a variety of institutions with different types and levels of resources at their disposal.

could not determine a way to systematically examine the program evaluations that have been prepared. The National Science Foundation and other funders require grant recipients to submit evaluation data in their annual reports, but that information is not currently aggregated and published.[4]

Over the course of this study, members of the committee benefited from discussion and presentations by the many individuals who participated in our three fact-finding meetings. At the first meeting, Jo Handelsman (Office of Science and Technology Policy), David Asai (Howard Hughes Medical Institute), and Beth Ambos (CUR) described different perspectives on UREs, existing work to build upon, sources to evaluate, and the changing land-

---

[4]Personal knowledge of Janet Branchaw, member of the Committee on Strengthening Research Experiences for Undergraduate STEM Students.

scape. During the second meeting, the committee heard expert testimony on institutional-level data gathering and analysis from Bethany Usher (George Mason University), Stephany Hazel (George Mason University), and Marco Molinaro (University of California, Davis). Mitch Malachowski (University of San Diego) and Paul Hernandez (West Virginia University) provided information on institutional change. Erin Dolan (The University of Texas at Austin) and Tuajuanda Jordan (St. Mary's College of Maryland) provided a commentary on the presentations and helped provide additional perspectives on the day's topics.

The third meeting involved some panel discussions. The first panel included Michael Wolf (Rice University), Suzanne Weekes (Worcester Polytechnic University), and Michael Dorff (Brigham Young University), who discussed UREs in mathematical sciences. The second panel on faculty perspectives on undergraduate research was presented by Sandra Laursen (University of Colorado Boulder), Tracy Johnson (University of California, Los Angeles), and Ariel Anbar (Arizona State University). The third panel involved Lisa Benson (Clemson University) and Ann Saterbak (Rice University), who discussed engineering perspectives on undergraduate research.

The committee commissioned three papers to provide in-depth input on specific topics. Erin Dolan (The University of Texas at Austin) authored an analysis of CUREs. Christine Pfund (University of Wisconsin–Madison) wrote a summary of current thinking about mentorship and how it relates to UREs. Linda Blockus (University of Missouri) prepared a document on issues related to co-curricular research experiences. In addition, the committee built upon the information and experience of the Convocation on *Integrating Discovery-based Research into the Undergraduate Curriculum*, described above.

Discussions about the evidence engaged the full committee, and members shared their expertise in designing and running URE programs; training other faculty to run URE programs and to mentor students; evaluating URE programs; and designing and conducting research on learning, STEM education, higher education, and learning in UREs. The committee's discussions frequently grappled with contrasts between the large body of positive descriptive evidence, the lack of extensive causal evidence, the impassioned calls for expansion of UREs, and the numerous creative UREs that have already been established. We worked to reconcile the perspectives in order to provide guidance to the field. This report synthesizes the committee's findings based on the evidence reviewed and the expertise of its members.

Request to Define Authentic Research

The committee's charge (see Box 1-1) includes providing a definition for authentic undergraduate research experiences. While discussing which

characteristics were appropriate and necessary to include in a definition of
UREs, the committee grappled with the inclusion of the term "authentic"
in their charge. The committee sought out examples in which others had
used the term "authentic" to inform their discussion. The term "authentic"
in the context of STEM education is used in the PCAST report *Engage to
Excel* and in multiple other documents. "Authentic" has also been used by
researchers, notably in previous work on education in STEM fields (e.g.,
Spell et al., 2014) and on education generally (Newmann, 1996). In addition, a framework is forthcoming from the federal government that defines
and explains an authentic STEM experience. In this framework, a URE
would be one example of an authentic STEM experience, but the federal
approach encompasses more than undergraduates and more than research.
Its definition states that "an Authentic STEM Experience is an experience inside or outside of school designed to engage learners directly or
indirectly with practitioners and in developmentally-appropriate practices
from the STEM disciplines that promote real world understanding."[5] It lists
the characteristics of an "Authentic STEM Experience" as an active-doing,
collaborative, meet learners where they are, appropriate learning approach/
practice, leading to real-world understanding.

With these precedents in mind, the committee again discussed the wide
variety of UREs and which features of UREs are essential to a definition.
The committee found that an attempt to sort them into binary categories
of "authentic" or "unauthentic" would not help to achieve a useful construct. The committee's definition of UREs is detailed in Chapter 2, which
provides a discussion of the characteristics that make up a URE. Many of
these characteristics are similar to the activities identified by Auchincloss
and colleagues (2014) and by Brownell and Kloser (2015) in their work
on CUREs. In this report the committee considers a URE to mean that the
student is doing the type of work that STEM researchers would typically
do; that is, the student is engaging in discovery and innovation, iteration,
and collaboration as the student learns STEM disciplinary knowledge and
practices while working on a topic that has relevance beyond the course. A
URE is structured and guided by a mentor; the students are intellectually
engaged and assume increasing ownership of some aspects of the project
over time. The extent and focus on each particular activity will vary across
different types and examples of UREs. Students can engage in STEM-based
undergraduate research in many different ways, across a variety of settings,
and along a continuum that extends from and expands upon learning opportunities in other educational settings. UREs therefore include many

---

[5] Personal communication from Susan Camarena, National Science Foundation, to the Committee on Strengthening Research Experiences for Undergraduate STEM Students, Novem-
ber 10, 2016.

different types of research. For example, undergraduates may participate in wet bench research (such as characterizing human genetic diversity in Pacific Island populations), non–wet bench research (such as exploration and analysis of a genome), hypothesis-driven research (such as hypothesizing that the depths of aftershocks from the 2011 Tohoku earthquake, which was a magnitude 9.0, will be deeper to the west due to the direction of plate subduction), or nonhypothesis-driven research (such as case comparisons done to analyze the geological record).

HOW LEARNING SCIENCE INFORMS THE DISCUSSION

One of the major claims about UREs is that they can motivate students to persist in STEM by providing a window into the creation of knowledge, by strengthening student identity as a member of the STEM community, and by showcasing career options. Claims are also made that research experiences promote the development of robust, integrated, conceptual knowledge by engaging participants in STEM practices (Brownell and Kloser, 2015; Litzinger et al., 2011). Though there is a lack of strong causal and mechanistic evidence to support these claims, research from the learning sciences provides some very strong principles that are relevant to UREs and from which URE designers and researchers can benefit in their efforts to create and study UREs. To develop hypotheses about how UREs might promote the outcomes described above, it is important to draw both on research in the learning sciences broadly (National Academy of Sciences, National Academy of Engineering, Institute of Medicine, 2005; National Research Council, 1999) and on research that specifically examines STEM learning (National Research Council, 2006, 2009, 2012a).

Research from the learning sciences provides a way of thinking about how students engage with their education (Johri and Olds, 2011). This research indicates that prior knowledge and experiences shape learning: in other words, the learners' existing understanding, skills, and beliefs significantly influence how they remember, reason, solve problems, and acquire new knowledge. Therefore, providing students with the opportunity to engage in the work of a STEM professional—focusing on the requisite research and disciplinary skills—through a URE can encourage deeper learning (Auchincloss et al., 2014; Brownell and Kloser, 2015; Johri and Olds, 2011; Litzinger et al., 2011). It is important to remember that when students have misconceptions—ideas, beliefs, and understandings that differ from accepted STEM-specific explanations—they may have difficulty integrating new knowledge with their inaccurate notions. This is because learning is a process of actively constructing knowledge via the process of conceptual reorganization. Individuals actively seek to make sense of new knowledge by connecting it with prior knowledge and experience (diSessa,

1996; Linn, 1995; Linn and Eylon, 2011). The act of discovery can allow students to work through ambiguous results and use evidence-based reasoning (Auchincloss et al., 2014).

The role of metacognition—the mind's ability to monitor and control its own activities—in this process is important. Students who are encouraged to reflect on their learning have a better chance of constructing deeper, more robust knowledge (Litzinger et al., 2011). They monitor their comprehension as they learn—for example, by asking themselves if they truly understand when they encounter a new concept or by pausing to consider whether their strategy is working when they tackle a problem (National Research Council, 2012b).

Students often have difficulty applying their knowledge in a new context. For students to be able to use what they have learned, they need to understand the core concepts and use them as a structure for organizing their knowledge. Spending a lot of time studying material and practicing in rote ways is not sufficient to promote transfer of knowledge; what matters is *how* this time is spent. The goal is to spend time on activities that promote deeper learning, such as engaging in the work of a STEM professional, as this can develop the necessary expertise to know how the research fits within the landscape of the discipline (Litzinger et al., 2011). Evidence suggests that collaborative activities can enhance the effectiveness of student-centered learning over traditional instruction and improve retention of content knowledge (see, for example, Cortright et al., 2003; Johnson et al., 1998, 2007; National Research Council, 2015). When students work together on well-designed learning activities, they sometimes establish a community of learners, which provides cognitive and social support.

As discussed in Chapter 4, researchers have examined many questions about UREs. For instance, does the opportunity to participate in a sustained research experience where the student takes on increasing ownership foster the development of a sense of agency and efficacy (a belief that one's actions can lead to improved understanding)? In typical STEM courses, students often find that they are following a set procedure and have little choice or opportunity for creativity. Does following a procedure that involves STEM practices help students develop a personal belief that they can learn disciplinary content and use the knowledge to solve relevant problems? Do research experiences promote agency by giving students choices in managing their experiment, recognizing and addressing problems, refining the research design, and exploring alternative explanations? Do students develop a sense of belonging, acceptance, and identity as a STEM professional when they feel they are participating in a community that is solving novel problems, have choices to make, and have the opportunity to provide creative input?

A well-designed URE builds on the evidence generated by researchers seeking to answer these types of questions. It builds on evidence-based principles and seeks to provide an inclusive culture in which students from diverse backgrounds feel welcome in the program and are able to generate deeper learning that is relevant to their interests and perhaps values (Johri and Olds, 2011). By its very nature, a research experience requires that students do more than "know" something; it requires that they use their knowledge to "do" something. At various stages, across the various forms of UREs, students may design and carry out experiments or build and test new products or applications. They may analyze and interpret data, using the evidence that they have generated to make arguments; they may design solutions to problems, and almost always, they will need to communicate their work to other audiences. Their knowledge is not generated solely for academic purposes but rather to use in a research setting, and the latter objective enables more robust, deeper learning and integration to occur, tied into current practice within the STEM profession. For some students, the URE also provides a place to explore how the goals of the relevant STEM discipline relate to their personal and perhaps cultural values, which may or may not be reflected in the dominant culture. Furthermore, the setting of most UREs provides an experience that offers the potential for collaboration—engaging others from diverse backgrounds—as well as opportunities for these undergraduate researchers to think about, reflect on, and consolidate what they are doing and learning, which can potentially connect to what is meaningful to the student. In short, the experience provides opportunities both for metacognitive reflection and for integration of their personal and budding professional identities.

STANDARDS OF EVIDENCE

This committee was charged in part with the task of reviewing "the empirical evidence of benefits across a range of outcomes associated with the multitude of educational, student, and institutional goals." In approaching this task, we found it useful to build on an earlier report, *Scientific Research in Education* (National Research Council, 2002). The committee that authored that report distinguished among three types of research questions: descriptive, causal, and mechanistic. *Descriptive* questions simply ask what is happening without making claims as to why it is happening. In the present context, one might ask how students experience undergraduate research and the degree to which their understanding of key concepts or procedures, or their beliefs in their capacity as a scientist or researcher, changes over the course of their research. Note that this description makes no claims as to whether the research experience caused these changes, only that these changes occurred over the same period of time during which students were engaged in undergraduate research. *Causal* questions seek to discover whether a specific intervention leads to a specific response; whether, for example, a summer URE reduced the chances that students would subsequently switch out of STEM fields to pursue degrees in other majors. Finally, questions of *mechanism* or of process seek to understand *why* a cause leads to an effect. Perhaps the URE enhances a student's confidence in her ability to succeed in her chosen field or deepens her commitment to the field by exposing her to the joys of research, and through these pathways it enhances the likelihood that she will persist in STEM.

Approaches to answering descriptive, causal, and mechanistic questions require a combination of theory, method, and measurement. In plain terms, you need to know the question you want to test (theory), know how to look for the outcome of that test (method), and be able to measure that outcome. The committee views the question of URE benefits to be one of cause: did the URE support the student in the career path she was on? Did it provide insights into the nature of STEM and a STEM career that the student would not have gained absent the experience? Did the student acquire new knowledge regarding the STEM discipline to which she was exposed?

Implicit in the causal claim is what social science researchers call a counterfactual: an alternative outcome an individual would have experienced in the presence of a different cause, or absent the cause under investigation. Examining differences between comparable students allows for causal claims. For example, a claim that UREs increase persistence in STEM fields is equivalent to the counterfactual claim that persistence rates in STEM would be lower in the absence of UREs. What is the warrant for such claims? One can never know for sure what would happen to a given individual subject to two different treatments—say a course with a strong, classroom-based research component and one that consists of lectures only. The student takes one class or the other. One could, however, make claims about *average* differences across groups of students experiencing these different approaches to instruction if one believes the groups are, on average, more or less identical prior to enrolling in these disparate courses. The design of the study, and fidelity to that design, forms the foundation of the belief that the groups of students subject to these different experiences are truly comparable.

In evaluating the research on the benefits of UREs, the committee looked for designs that would support not only descriptive but also causal and mechanistic claims. The latter designs would have (1) a clearly identified treatment, (2) a treatment group and at least one comparison group, and (3) an approach to assignment to treatment, or retrospective matching, that would lead one to have some confidence that groups in the two (or more) conditions were likely the same on average, prior to treatment. We were able to find very few such studies. However, some studies used plausible strategies for supporting the claim that the groups on average were equivalent prior to the URE. These studies offered evidence suggestive of various benefits of UREs, in particular in retention of students in STEM programs (e.g., Rodenbusch et al., 2016). For example, Lopatto (National Academies of Sciences, Engineering, and Medicine, 2015; Appendix B) showed the effectiveness of quasi-experimental designs to study UREs.

Finally, many of the studies we reviewed lacked a control or comparison group. The committee considers studies of this sort to be descriptive but not causal or mechanistic. They offer a good foundation for developing hypotheses about causes, and they may be informative regarding potential mechanisms. Descriptive studies may provide a warrant for looking for causal relationships (benefits), but individually they do not offer hard evidence about those benefits. Many of the studies in this category relied either on student self-reports of their increased knowledge of the research process, confidence in their ability to participate, development of their research identity, or some other attribute, with student responses collected either retrospectively or at the beginning and end of the URE being studied.

REPORT ORGANIZATION

This report examines the types of UREs available and considers the roles of students, faculty, administrators, funders, and others involved with UREs.

Variations in types of UREs are examined in Chapter 2, including their structure, location, and the ways they reward students. This chapter also provides examples of the many creative approaches to UREs that can be found at institutions around the country.

Chapter 3 provides a framework for looking at the interacting actors and the situational components influencing UREs. The forces operating on students, faculty, nonfaculty mentors, academic departments, and institutions are complex and multilayered. This chapter also discusses the claims that are made about the benefits of UREs within the context of what is known about learning and learning science.

Chapter 4 examines the evidence for impact of UREs on students by analyzing the available research literature. Many of the most robust studies focus on historically underrepresented groups of students. There are many unanswered questions and opportunities for further research into the role of UREs in student learning and the mechanisms through which UREs have an impact on retention.

Faculty and mentoring are the topics of Chapters 5 and 6. URE programs are not always run by faculty; undergraduates are frequently mentored by nonfaculty instructors, postdoctoral fellows, graduate students, and even fellow undergraduates. Mentoring is a key aspect of the research experience for undergraduates and is therefore discussed in detail here. Mentoring has been studied extensively in many different settings, and there is much to be learned from the literature on this topic. The faculty role in URES is much larger than the opportunity to serve as a mentor. Faculty incentives and rewards for engaging in URES vary across departments and institutions. The opportunity for faculty or staff to engage in relevant professional development also varies. Little research has been done on these aspects of faculty roles.

Chapter 7 presents a research agenda that describes topic areas where further studies could greatly improve understanding of how URES work. Potential questions to be answered, as well as potential methodologies for pursuing the answers, are included in the agenda. Although the chapter advocates for a broad range of research, it stresses the importance of conducting research on the causal effects of URES. It also discusses the different kinds of evidence and the importance of designing good studies that can provide insight into cause and mechanism.

Chapter 8 presents considerations in designing and implementing URES. Although the committee advocates for further studies to better understand URES and identify optimal approaches, we also recognize that many campuses are currently expanding the URES available to their students. Therefore, this chapter aims to provide guidance based on the currently available information for institutions, campus leaders, and URE designers and implementers. It looks at the current policy context and considers campus culture as well as the perspectives of students and faculty. There is a section on the importance of considering equity and access. In addition, big-picture issues and practical questions are presented, as well as topics to consider in the design, implementation, evaluation, and improvement of URES. While the committee was not able to find the information that would be necessary to do a cost-benefit analysis of URES, this chapter does address the topic of financial, human, information, space, and equipment resources.

The final chapter lays out the committee's conclusions about URES and the recommendations for future actions involving the implementation and analysis of URES.

REFERENCES

American Association for the Advancement of Science. (2011). *Vision and Change in Undergraduate Biology Education: A Call to Action.* C. Brewer and D. Smith (Eds.). Washington, DC: American Association for the Advancement of Science.

Association of American Colleges and Universities. (2007). *College Learning for the New Global Century.* Washington, DC: Association of American Colleges and Universities. Available: https://www.aacu.org/sites/default/files/files/LEAP/GlobalCentury_final.pdf [November 2016].

Association of American Colleges and Universities. (2008). *High Impact Educational Practices: What They Are, Who Has Access to Them and Why They Matter.* Washington, DC: Association of American Colleges and Universities. Available: http://provost.tufts. edu/celt/files/High-Impact-Ed-Practices1.pdf [November 2016].

Association of American Colleges and Universities. (2011). *The LEAP Vision for Learning: Outcomes, Practices, Impact, and Employers' Views.* Washington, DC: Association of American Colleges and Universities. Available: https://www.aacu.org/sites/default/files/ files/LEAP/leap_vision_summary.pdf [November 2016].

Auchincloss, L.C., Laursen, S.L., Branchaw, J.L., Eagan, K., Graham, M., Hanauer, D.I., Lawrie, G., McLinn, C.M., Pelaez, N., Rowland, S., Towns, M., Trautmann, N.M.,Varma-Nelson, P., Weston, T.J., and Dolan, E.L. (2014). Assessment of course-based undergraduate research experiences: A meeting report. *CBE–Life Sciences Education, 13*(1), 29-40.

Bangera, G., and Brownell, S.E. (2014). Course-based undergraduate research experiences can make scientific research more inclusive. *CBE–Life Sciences Education, 13*(4), 602-606.

Bennett, N. (2015). *Overview of the NSF REU Program and Proposal Review.* Presentation at the GRC Funding Competitiveness Conference [February 18-21, 2015], Arlington, VA: National Science Foundation.

Brownell, S.E., and Kloser, M.J. (2015). Toward a conceptual framework for measuring the effectiveness of course-based undergraduate research experiences in undergraduate biology. *Studies in Higher Education, 40*(3), 525-544.

Brownell, S.E., Hekmat-Scafe, D.S., Singla, V., Seawell, P.C., Conklin-Imam, J.F., Eddy, S.L., Stearns, T., and Cyert, M.S. (2015). A high enrollment course-based undergraduate research experience improves student conceptions of scientific thinking and ability to interpret data. *CBE–Life Sciences Education, 14*(2), ar21. Available: https://www.ncbi. nlm.nih.gov/pmc/articles/PMC4477737/pdf/ar21.pdf [January 2017].

Clancy, K.B.H., Nelson, R.G., Rutherford, J.N., and Hinde, K. (2014). Survey of academic field experiences (SAFE): Trainees report harassment and assault. *PLOS ONE, 9*(7), e102172. Available: http://dx. Doi.org/10.1371/journal.pone.0102172 [January 2017].

Cortright, R.N., Collins, H.L., Rodenbaugh, D.W., and DiCarlo, S.E. (2003). Student retention of course content is improved by collaborative-group testing. *Advances in Physiology Education, 27,* 102-108.

diSessa, A.A. (1996). Faculty opponent review: On mole and amount of substance: A study of the dynamics of concept formation and concept attainment. *Pedagogisk Forskning i Sverige, 1*(4), 233-243.

Eagan, M.K., Hurtado, S., Chang, M.J., Garcia, G.A., Herrera, F.A., and Garibay, J.C. (2013). Making a difference in science education: The impact of undergraduate research programs. *American Educational Research Journal, 50*(4), 683-713.

Eagan, K., Hurtado, S., Figueroa, T., and Hughes, B. (2014). *Examining STEM Pathways among Students Who Begin College at Four-Year Institutions.* Paper prepared for the Committee on Barriers and Opportunities in Completing 2- and 4-Year STEM Degrees. Washington, DC. Available: http://sites.nationalacademies.org/cs/groups/dbassesite/ documents/webpage/dbasse_088834.pdf [November 2016].

Eddy, S.L., and Brownell, S.E. (2016). Beneath the numbers: A review of gender disparities in undergraduate education across science, technology, engineering, and math disciplines. *Physical Review Physics Education Research, 12*(2). Available: http://journals.aps.org/ prper/pdf/10.1103/PhysRevPhysEducRes.12.020106 [January 2017].

Estrada, M., Burnett, M., Campbell, A.G., Campbell, P.B., Denetclaw, W.F., Gutierrez, C.G., Hurtado, S., John, G.H., Matsui, J., McGee, R., Okpodu, C.M., Robinson, T.J., Summers, M.F., Werner-Washrune, M., and Zavala, M. (2016). Improving underrepresented minority student persistence in STEM. *Cell Biology Education, 15*(3), es5. Available: http:// www.lifescied.org/content/15/3/es5.full [November 2016].

Harsh, J.A., Maltese, A.V., and Tai, R.H. (2011). Undergraduate research experiences from a longitudinal perspective. *Journal of College Science Teaching, 41*(1), 84-91.

Hurtado, S., Eagan, M.K., and Hughes, B. (2012). *Priming the Pump or the Sieve: Institutional Contexts and URM STEM Degree Attainments.* Paper presented at the annual forum of the Association for Institutional Research [June 2-6, 2012], New Orleans, LA. Available: http://www.heri.ucla.edu/nih/downloads/AIR2012HurtadoPrimingthePump.pdf [November 2016].

Johnson, D.W., Johnson, R.T., and Smith, K.A. (1998). Cooperative learning returns to college: What evidence is there that it works? *Change, 30,* 26-35.

Johnson, D.W., Johnson, R.T., and Smith, K.A. (2007). The state of cooperative learning in postsecondary and professional settings. *Educational Psychology Review, 19*(1), 15-29.

Johri, A., and Olds, B.M. (2011). Situated engineering learning: Bridging engineering education research and the learning sciences. *Journal of Engineering Education, 100*(1), 151-185.

Kinkead, J. (2012). What's in a name? A brief history of undergraduate research. *CUR on the Web, 33*(1). Available: http://www.cur.org/assets/1/7/331Fall12KinkeadWeb.pdf [August 2016].

Linn, M.C. (1995). Designing computer learning environments for engineering and computer science: The Scaffolded Knowledge Integration framework. *Journal of Science Education and Technology, 4*(2), 103-126.

Linn, M.C., and Eylon, B.S. (2011). *Science Learning and Instruction: Taking Advantage of Technology to Promote Knowledge Integration.* New York: Routledge.

Litzinger, T.A., Lattuca, L.R., Hadgraft, R.G., and Newstetter, W.C. (2011). Engineering education and the development of expertise. *Journal of Engineering Education, 100*(1), 123-150.

Miller, R.E. (2013). *The Almost Experts: Capstone Students and the Research Process.* Paper presented at the Association of College & Research Libraries, Indianapolis, IN. Available: http://www.ala.org/acrl/sites/ala.org.acrl/files/content/conferences/confsandpreconfs/2013/papers/Miller_Almost.pdf [January 2017].

Moss-Racusin, C.A., Dovidio, J.F., Brescoll, V.L., Graham, M.J., and Handelsman, J. (2012). Science faculty's subtle gender biases favor male students. *Proceedings of the National Academy of Sciences, 109*(41), 16474-16479.

National Academies of Sciences, Engineering, and Medicine. (2015). *Integrating Discovery-Based Research into the Undergraduate Curriculum: Report of a Convocation.* Committee for Convocation on Integrating Discovery-Based Research into the Undergraduate Curriculum. Division on Earth and Life Studies. Division of Behavioral and Social Sciences and Education. Washington, DC: The National Academies Press.

National Academies of Sciences, Engineering, and Medicine. (2016). *Barriers and Opportunities for 2-Year and 4-Year STEM Degrees: Systemic Change to Support Students' Diverse Pathways.* S. Malcom and M. Feder (Eds.). Committee on Barriers and Opportunities in Two- and Four-Year STEM Degrees. Board on Science Education, Division of Behavioral and Social Sciences and Education. Board on Higher Education and the Workforce. Policy and Global Affairs. Washington, DC: The National Academies Press.

National Academy of Sciences, National Academy of Engineering, and Institute of Medicine. (2005). *Facilitating Interdisciplinary Research.* Committee on Facilitating Interdisciplinary Research. Committee on Science, Engineering, and Public Policy. Washington, DC: The National Academies Press.

National Research Council. (1999). *How People Learn: Brain, Mind, Experience, and School.* Washington, DC: National Academy Press.

National Research Council. (2002). *Scientific Research in Education*. R. Shavelson and L. Towne (Eds.). Committee on Scientific Principles for Education Research. Center for Education. Division of Behavioral and Social Sciences and Education. Washington, DC: National Academy Press.

National Research Council. (2006). *America's Lab Report: Investigations in High School Science*. S. Singer, M. Hilton, and H. Schweingruber (Eds.). Committee on High School Science Laboratories: Role and Vision. Board on Science Education, Center for Education, Division of Behavioral and Social Sciences and Education. Washington, DC: The National Academies Press.

National Research Council. (2009). *Learning Science in Informal Environments: People, Places, and Pursuits*. P. Bell, B. Lewenstein, A. Shouse, and M. Feder (Eds.). Committee on Learning Science in Informal Environments. Board on Science Education, Center for Education, Division of Behavioral and Social Sciences and Education. Washington, DC: The National Academies Press.

National Research Council. (2011). *Expanding Underrepresented Minority Participation: America's Science and Technology Talent at the Crossroads*. Committee on Underrepresented Groups and the Expansion of the Science and Engineering Workforce Pipeline. Committee on Science, Engineering, and Public Policy. Policy and Global Affairs. Washington, DC: The National Academies Press.

National Research Council. (2012a). *Community Colleges in the Evolving STEM Educational Landscape: Summary of a Summit*. S. Olon and J. Labov (Rapporteurs). Committee on Evolving Relationships and Dynamics Between Two- and Four-Year Colleges and Universities. Board on Higher Education and Workforce. Policy and Global Affairs. Board on Life Sciences. Division on Earth and Life Studies. Board on Science Education; Teacher Advisory Council. Division of Behavioral and Social Sciences and Education. Washington, DC: The National Academies Press.

National Research Council. (2012b). *Discipline-Based Education Research: Understanding and Improving Learning in Undergraduate Science and Engineering*. Committee on the Status, Contributions, and Future Directions of Discipline-Based Education Research. S. Singer, N. Nielsen, and H. Schweingruber (Eds). Board on Science Education, Division of Behavioral and Social Sciences and Education. Washington, DC: The National Academies Press.

National Research Council (2015). *Reaching Students: What Research Says about Effective Instruction in Undergraduate Science and Engineering*. N. Kober (author). Board on Science Education. Division of Behavioral and Social Sciences and Education. Washington, DC: The National Academies Press.

National Science Foundation. (2014). *Science and Engineering Indicators 2014*. Arlington, VA: National Science Board.

Newmann, F. (1996). *Authentic Achievement: Restructuring Schools for Intellectual Quality*. San Francisco: Jossey-Bass.

President's Council of Advisors on Science and Technology. (2012). *Engage to Excel: Producing One Million Additional College Graduates with Degrees in STEM*. Washington, DC: Executive Office of the President. Available: http://files.eric.ed.gov/fulltext/ED541511.pdf [February 2017].

Rodenbusch, S.E., Hernandez, P.R., Simmons, S.L., and Dolan, E.L. (2016). Early engagement in course-based research increases graduation rates and completion of science, engineering, and mathematics degrees. *CBE–Life Sciences Education, 15*(2), ar20. Available: http://www.lifescied.org/content/15/2/ar20 [February 2017].

Rowles, C.J., Koch, D.C., Hundley, S.P., and Hamilton, S.J. (2004). Toward a model for capstone experiences: Mountaintops, magnets, and mandates. *Assessment Update, 16*(1), 1-2, 13-15.

Spell, R.M., Guinan, J.A., Miller, K.R., and Beck, C.W. (2014). Redefining authentic research experiences in introductory biology laboratories and barriers to their implementation. *CBE–Life Sciences Education, 13*, 102-110.

Van Noy, M., and Zeidenberg, M. (2014). *Hidden STEM Knowledge Producers: Community Colleges' Multiple Contributions to STEM Education and Workforce Development.* Paper prepared for the Committee on Barriers and Opportunities in Completing 2- and 4-Year STEM Degrees. Available: http://sites.nationalacademies.org/cs/groups/dbassesite/documents/webpage/dbasse_088831.pdf [November 2016].

Weaver, G., Wink, D., Varma-Nelson, P., Lytle, F., Morris, R., Fornes, W., Russell, C., and Boone, W. (2006). Developing a new model to provide first and second-year undergraduates with chemistry research experience: Early findings of the center for authentic science practice in education (CASPIE). *Chemical Educator, 11*, 125-129.

Zupanc, G.K. (2012). Undergraduate research and inquiry-based learning: The revitalization of the Humboldtian ideals. *Bioscience Education, 19*(1), 1-11.

2

Heterogeneity of Undergraduate Research Experiences: Characterizing the Variability

Students can engage in undergraduate research experiences (UREs) in science, technology, engineering, and mathematics (STEM) in many different ways, to varying degrees, and across a variety of settings.[1] UREs themselves are heterogeneous and vary in leadership, mentoring, format, and duration. They vary in expectations for students, value for career trajectory, goals and outcome measures, and population served. Institutional support, disciplinary and multidisciplinary expectations, and faculty motivation and rewards also differ. As a result, UREs vary widely even within the same institution.

Outcomes that students gain from UREs are shaped by how the experiences are constructed by faculty and supported by the academic department(s) and institution, by professional organizations in some disciplines, and by external policy and funding structures at the state and national level. Student characteristics may affect the design of the program or the outcomes for the students themselves. A broad goal beyond simply student persistence in STEM would be for students to develop not only conceptual understanding of relevant disciplinary and/or multidisciplinary knowledge, but also the abilities to conduct an investigation and develop STEM literacy. For some UREs, the goal might be to have students persist in a STEM discipline, but for other UREs the goal may be to have students become an informed citizen

---

[1] This chapter includes content from papers commissioned by the committee titled *Strengthening Research Experiences for Undergraduate STEM Students: The Co-Curricular Model of the Research Experience* by Linda Blockus (Blockus, 2016) and *Course-based Undergraduate Research Experiences: Current Knowledge and Future Directions* by Erin Dolan (Dolan, 2016).

and a savvy consumer of STEM information, in order to know how to make informed decisions based on the strength of evidence.

In developing a definition for UREs, the committee considered the diverse types of programs available and synthesized descriptions from reports throughout the literature to arrive at a way to describe UREs. The Council on Undergraduate Research defines undergraduate research as "an inquiry or investigation conducted by an undergraduate student that makes an original intellectual or creative contribution to the discipline."[2] Faculty associated with the group CUREnet proposed a definition of a course-based undergraduate research experience (CURE) that requires the integration of five dimensions: use of scientific practices, discovery, broadly relevant or important work, collaboration, and iteration (Auchincloss et al., 2014). Building on the work of that group, the committee included those five dimensions in our definition of a URE (the first five bullets below). Four additional characteristics are also included in the committee's definition in order to broaden the scope to include UREs that are not CUREs and to be inclusive of all STEM disciplines.

In preparing this list, the committee considered which aspects of an experience would allow a URE to more closely align with the work of research professionals, while keeping in mind that this work varies across the many STEM disciplines. Due to the variation in the types of UREs, not all experiences will include all of the following characteristics in the same way; experiences vary in how much a particular characteristic is emphasized. The committee includes the following characteristics in our definition of a URE:

- *They engage students in research practices including the ability to argue from evidence.*
- *They aim to generate novel information with an emphasis on discovery and innovation or to determine whether recent preliminary results can be replicated.*
- *They focus on significant, relevant problems of interest to STEM researchers and, in some cases, a broader community (e.g., civic engagement).*
- *They emphasize and expect collaboration and teamwork.*
- *They involve iterative refinement of experimental design, experimental questions, or data obtained.*
- *They allow students to master specific research techniques.*
- *They help students engage in reflection about the problems being investigated and the work being undertaken to address those problems.*
- *They require communication of results, either through publication or presentations in various STEM venues.*

---

[2] See http://www.cur.org/about_cur/frequently_asked_questions_ [November 2016].

- *They are structured and guided by a mentor, with students assuming increasing ownership of some aspects of the project over time.*

Auchincloss and colleagues (2014) pointed out that many of the individual characteristics listed can be found in courses that are not UREs, but it is the integration of these characteristics that makes the experience a URE. For example, a course focused on reviewing published articles may expose students to the way that research is performed and communicated, but not engage them in doing research themselves. A research methods course may teach the details of specific procedures without engaging the students in an actual research project. A course may contain a component for which undergraduates perform experiments in the laboratory, but these tasks may be done in a predetermined step-wise manner, sometimes called a "cookbook laboratory" (Brownell and Kloser, 2015), that requires little problem solving or analysis on the part of the student.

UREs can be designed to meet the needs of undergraduate students at various career stages and from various backgrounds; some of the characteristics listed above may be more crucial for certain learning objectives or for specific populations of students. The degree to which the characteristics are emphasized for an individual URE varies depending on many factors (e.g., discipline, goals for students, time, resources) and the emphasis on a particular characteristic may also change over time within a single URE. For example, developing technical skills and knowledge is often a focus in early research learning experiences, while opportunities to learn how to deal with failure and develop resiliency tend to emerge as students get more deeply involved in a research project. Ideally, formative assessment by research mentors, program directors, and instructors can be used to monitor student development and achievement throughout the experience and to make appropriate adjustments along the way.

Many different names have been used to describe types of UREs. These names vary across disciplines and are not used consistently in practice or in the literature. To help demonstrate the wide variety of experiences that have developed, this chapter groups UREs into the following types:

- Individual faculty research group (apprentice-style);
- Capstone experiences and senior theses;
- Internships and co-ops;
- CUREs;
- Wrap-around experiences;
- Bridge programs;
- Consortium/project-based programs; and
- Community-based research programs.

ATTRIBUTES OF URES

There are several attributes—duration, costs, research topic, mentoring, student expectations—of UREs that can have significant impact on the quality of and access to the URE. These attributes have been identified in several recent reports (e.g., American Association for the Advancement of Science, 2011; National Research Council, 2006, 2007, 2012; Next Generation Science Standards Lead States, 2013) and are summarized in Table 2-1, where they are presented as a series of questions with possible answers to be considered when designing UREs. A more nuanced discussion on many of these questions and their answers follow the table.

Mentor

An important component of the URE is the research mentor and the role the mentor plays. In UREs, students often work in groups under the supervision of a mentor. Positive mentoring relationships can expose students to the culture of STEM, and mentorship is one of the aspects of UREs that may promote students' identities as STEM professionals. Mentorship refers to a relationship between a seasoned, experienced person—the mentor—and a less experienced person—the protégé (Rhodes, 2005). Within the context of

TABLE 2-1 Questions About the Attributes of UREs

Question	Possible Answers
Who is the research mentor?	• Faculty member • Postdoctoral scholar • Industry researcher • Laboratory manager • Graduate student • Peer • Combination of the above
What roles might the mentor(s) play?	• Guide students and acclimate them to the social and cultural norms of the research environment (e.g., identity, self-efficacy, self-confidence, specific experiences around gender and race in STEM) • Guide students in learning about and exploring future educational or career pathways • Construct research experience appropriate to students' skills and understanding of disciplinary material • Introduce relevant concepts, ways of thinking, and skills • Assign research tasks • Encourage lab participation • Monitor progress of students

TABLE 2-1 Continued

Question	Possible Answers
For how many students is each mentor responsible?	• Smaller ratios are typical in co-curricular research experiences (assistantships, interns, or as part of programs); one mentor responsible for 1-10 students • Medium ratios of 12 to 25 students per faculty member are typical in long-term project-based research experiences • Larger ratios are likely in classroom research experiences; may have 1 faculty member mentoring 40 or more students. Larger ratios are typically offset by graduate teaching assistants or postdoctoral scholars/lecturers as instructors
How long is the research experience?	• Short course or portion of a quarter/semester (1 to several weeks) • Quarter or semester course (10-16 weeks; ~4-5 hours per week) • Summer research experiences (8-10 weeks; ~40 hours per week) • Academic year research placement (30 or more weeks) • Multiple academic years of experience as part of a research team
Is the student compensated and if so how?	• Uncompensated • Academic credit • Hourly wage • Stipend
How are students recruited to participate?	• Home institution students versus national recruitment • Recruitment of specific targeted populations • Enroll in a course (may need to satisfy prerequisites)
What costs are associated with offering UREs, and who pays them?	• Students pay tuition for academic credit • Students receive wages or stipends • Mentor salaries • Lab space and materials • Travel to and housing at the research site • Travel to conferences for student presentations
How is the research topic selected?	• Assigned by faculty/instructor • Assigned with options decided by the student • Choice of student (within material relevant to the course or research area) • Open-ended with resources limited to those available
What, if any, presentation requirements for students are there?	• Final reports • Posters • Oral presentations • Peer-reviewed published research papers
What other factors impact UREs?	• Accreditation requirements (capstone experiences) • Culture of the discipline or department • Integration of UREs (especially CUREs) as part of the normal introductory and/or upper-level curriculum • Cultural background of the participating students and faculty

this relationship, there is an expectation that the protégé will develop professionally under the guidance of the mentor (Eby et al., 2007). Substantial variability exists not only for who serves as the mentor but also with respect to the number of mentors a given student might have, as well as the contributions that the mentors provide throughout the research experience. For example, the research question might be designed with the principal investigator for the project; however, many of the daily mentoring functions may be carried out by a postdoctoral fellow, graduate student, or lab manager with oversight by the principal investigator (Russell et al., 2009). Mentors provide *instrumental support* by providing resources and opportunity to the protégé to engage in goal attainment (Kram, 1985) and *psychosocial support* when a mentor enhances "an individual's sense of competence, identity, and effectiveness in a professional role" (Kram, 1985, p. 32). *Relationship quality* has been shown to be related to positive mentorship outcomes. Issues related to mentorship are discussed in more detail in Chapter 5.

Costs

Students can be compensated for their participation through primarily two different mechanisms: stipend (salary or hourly wage), academic credit, or both. Stipends are typically provided for summer research experiences and academic-year extensions of those experiences. When the experience is part of the curriculum, the student is more likely to receive academic credit than a stipend. The need for student compensation is intimately connected to program costs and sustainability. Student stipends are often provided by external funding, providing an opportunity for faculty grant leadership but also introducing a threat to the sustainability of the program. Credit-based courses may be easier to sustain but also impose costs on the student, faculty, and institution. Additional costs may include faculty and staff salaries, lab space and materials, travel to and housing at the research site, and travel to conferences for students' presentations.

Research Focus

The focus of research in a URE can be driven by faculty preferences, departmental or institutional constraints, or student interest; it may also be influenced by the direction of research in the disciplinary field. In apprentice-style UREs and some long-term CUREs, the topic of research is typically aligned with the faculty member's or instructor's program of research and is often supported on some level by the faculty member's grants. Advanced undergraduate research students may progress to develop their own research questions but would typically remain in the same general area of research as their advisor. CUREs of one- or two-semester duration are also frequently related to the faculty member's area of research, but they are more likely to differ, particularly when a faculty member's research topic is not optimal for undergraduates due to a lack of facilities or the students' limited background knowledge. Divergence from the mentor's area of research can also occur when CUREs build on pre-existing examples developed on another campus. In some cases these CUREs become part of a network that provides resources, or even training, for faculty on the approach and subject. A student's research topic can also be influenced by a need to meet requirements of the student's major or program—for example, a capstone course required by the accreditation requirements in an engineering department.

Presentation of Research

Many experiences replicate the dissemination mechanisms of STEM researchers by offering the opportunity, or requiring students, to make presentations and prepare publications. As addressed in Chapter 4, being able to describe not only the methods one uses but also the importance of the research question situated within the field has been linked with improved learning outcomes and with development of the student's identity as a STEM professional. Many forms of UREs, including both independent UREs and CUREs (described in the next section), typically embed delivery of posters and/or presentations within the experience, often as a culminating event that involves presenting to the program's faculty, staff, and participants. For example, many institutions hold annual on-campus research conferences to celebrate student research. These conferences may be scheduled to maximize attention to the undergraduate research on campus (e.g., a conference held on alumni weekends, during visits by prospective students, or even during trustee meetings). In some cases, students are encouraged to present at a professional society conference, exposing them to the broader STEM enterprise and to peers and graduate students from other institutions. Many professional societies have a funding mechanism to which undergraduate students can apply and which will subsidize their travel expenses. Moreover, students also may develop manuscripts for submission or may be included in publications as a coauthor with others, depending on the research group's policies.

Institution Type

As characterized in Chapter 3, the type of institution can have a substantial impact on the types of UREs offered. Some institutions might have UREs as a prominent feature of undergraduate education for all students, whereas for other institutions only a select few may have the opportunity to participate in a URE. Moreover, there could be differences in the availability of resources (e.g., space, equipment, libraries, journal access) across different institutions. Relying upon national networks, including disciplinary and educational societies, could help facilitate a "community of practice" enabling institutions with limited resources to develop and refine existing practices.

Department and Academic Program

The access to and attributes of UREs may also differ across departments on a single campus, as discussed in Chapter 3. Some departments have a disciplinary history or local tradition of offering or requiring undergraduates to do research or requiring students to do a senior capstone project that includes research and/or design as part of accreditation (e.g., engineering departments accredited by the Accreditation Board for Engineering and Technology [ABET]).

Departmental decisions not only have an impact on faculty expectations and course assignments (discussed in greater detail in Chapter 6), but also can impact undergraduates' access to research experiences. Departments that encourage faculty to take actions that embed research experiences into the curriculum through the use of independent studies, credit-bearing summer research programs, academic year seminars, and CUREs may increase the number of students who participate in UREs (Free et al., 2015). Many scholars have reported on models for integrating research experience into the curriculum (Gates et al., 1999; Hakim, 2000; Kierniesky, 2005; Kortz and van der Hoeven Kraft, 2016; Lopatto et al., 2014; Merkel, 2001; Pukkila et al., 2007; Reinen et al., 2007; Rueckert, 2007; Temple et al., 2010).

Students who participate in research experiences should be aware of the importance of ethics and responsible conduct, and some UREs provide students with this type of training. In some instances, this training can be embedded within the research experience, whereas other programs might require this training before participation in the URE can begin. The literature has suggested that although ethics training may be a requirement for students to engage in research, it can have the added benefit of helping students to better understand the importance of ethical awareness. For example, Hirsch and colleagues (2005) reported on a summer URE that was part of a National Science Foundation (NSF)-supported Engineering Research Center in Bioengineering. The objective of the study was to examine the results of core competency instruction in ethics and communications as they were integrated in students' research experiences outside of formal courses. Students were presented with case studies, and the results showed that they developed greater ethical awareness of key concepts, such as respect for persons (informed consent), beneficence, justice, and integrity.

THE VARIETY OF URE PROGRAMS

UREs do not fit neatly into discrete categories. As stated above, they contain the definitional characteristics the committee described above to some degree. That is, some UREs might place a higher premium on collaborative teamwork, whereas others place less of an emphasis on this characteristic and instead devote significant time to improving presentation skills (Russell et al., 2009). Moreover, students may participate in multiple UREs during their undergraduate education, but there is not a consensus around a clear progression of the types of experiences a student should have. Given this variability, it can be challenging to organize and catalogue the different programs and systematically collect data on the students who participate in UREs. This lack of data collection can be observed not only at a national level but also at an institutional level. Box 2-1 summarizes the challenges encountered by one university official in his efforts to determine how many students participated in UREs at the University of California, Davis.

BOX 2-1
Efforts to Document the Number of
Undergraduate Researchers

Professor Marco Molinaro, Assistant Vice Provost for Undergraduate Education at the University of California, Davis, recently summarized many of the most important challenges and opportunities in this area. He indicated that the diversity of types of experiences makes it difficult to document participation, activities, and outcomes and also hinders accountability. Difficulty in documenting participation means that institutions also probably do not know the number of women, historically underrepresented minorities, first generation college students, students with disabilities, etc., who are participating in the UREs. When examining course catalogs or transcripts, it is often difficult to determine from a course's name whether it is a CURE. The variety of different types of course names for CUREs, as well as the variety of formats and goals, makes it difficult to document the content of the course and the research-based aspects of the course. The lack of clear paths for students to become involved in research and the lack of centralized tracking systems for research participation means that UREs will not all be documented on a student transcript. Prof. Molinaro pointed out that creating a transcript notation to document student participation in any type of research activity would provide a permanent record of their research participation, which students could use when applying for graduate school and as a credential with future employers.

SOURCE: Presentation to the committee by Marco Molinaro, University of California, Davis; September 16, 2015.

Moreover, UREs can vary on other dimensions, such as the size of the research group or the timing of when the research project might take place. For example, individual or small group experiences typically fall under the purview of apprentice-style research projects, with a few students working with an individual faculty member, as compared to group-oriented UREs in which undergraduates are organized into teams of moderate to significant size to enable more students to benefit from participation in research. Whether the design of the URE is more apprentice-style (one or several students who work mainly as individuals) or more group-based, these experiences can be offered during the academic year or outside of the academic year, with many programs spanning this particular dimension.

Summer bridge programs, like other summer URE programs, are offered outside of the academic year but are shorter than a full year. However, summer bridge programs are more likely to be group-based, whereas summer URE programs cover a wide variety of program styles ranging from group-based efforts to students working independently within a research environment (e.g., a faculty member's lab or field opportunity, an industry setting). CUREs are more likely to be offered within the academic year (or even over multiple academic years, depending on the nature of the research question and project) and range in size from classes that have smaller groups to larger programs. Finally, internships are more likely to involve independent work in an industrial or corporate setting.

What we present next are brief descriptions of several of the more commonly used types of UREs, with examples of each type from actual URE programs. This discussion is meant not as an exhaustive list but as an illustration of the variability of programs, depending on the intended goals of the experience and its other attributes. The examples provided for each program type were chosen to cover the range of different settings and disciplines. Appendix B contains additional examples of UREs.

Individual Faculty Research Group

A common pathway to research is for students to begin working on a part-time basis in a faculty research lab or team and to work for a semester or more to "learn the ropes" before taking ownership of advanced responsibilities. Faculty may pair inexperienced students with an intermediary supervisor, such as a graduate student or lab technician, for day-to-day training. Although some students develop their research skills and independence over an extended period of time, other students (visiting summer interns, for example) may enter a research environment with previous experience and have a shorter and steeper learning curve. This approach to situational and observational learning in the context of a URE is sometimes labeled an "apprentice model."

During the academic year, generally 10-15 hours per week is the standard expectation for the student to participate in the lab; however, full-time immersive summer programs are also pervasive and last between 8-12 weeks, during which the student typically works full-time on research. Students may earn credit, experience (voluntary basis), or receive monetary compensation (although some institutions have policies against students earning money and credit simultaneously). Moreover, students are expected to be engaged in the research process, including the dissemination of results whether by presenting at a national conference or publishing within a peer-reviewed journal.

Summer programs in this category are more typically funded by an extramural funding agency or by a host institution. These programs can be more formally structured and include a professional development program designed to support students as they progress through their research experience. For example, NSF supports a wide range of projects across the STEM subdisciplines through the Research Experiences for Undergraduates (REU) programs.[3] Students typically apply for REUs through a competitive process so that they can spend the summer in a laboratory or at a field site (domestic or international) conducting research in their desired discipline. Box 2-2 describes a summer apprentice-style program in mathematics developed by Willamette University in Oregon.

Collaborations with industry and other government agencies can also be forged to develop and fund projects on a topic of mutual interest. For example, Box 2-3 highlights a URE program that is jointly funded by NSF and the Department of Defense to provide undergraduates with an opportunity to learn more about, and conduct research on, particular issues associated with unmanned aerial vehicles (UAVs).

Capstone Experiences and Senior Theses

Capstone experiences not only can be a requirement for graduation but also are part of the accreditation of particular programs—for example, ABET accreditation for engineering programs.[4] These experiences have been defined as "a culminating experience in which students are expected to integrate special studies with the major and extend, critique, and apply knowledge gained in their major" (Wagenaar, 1993, p. 209). Many of these programs occur during the senior year, with variability in administration: the course may be a single semester, a full academic year, or even interleaved

---

[3]For more information on NSF's REU initiative, see https://www.nsf.gov/funding/pgm_summ.jsp?pims_id=5517 [November 2016].

[4]The website for the ABET accreditation is at http://www.abet.org/accreditation/ [November 2016].

BOX 2-2
Summer Apprentice-Style Program:
Willamette Mathematics Consortium REU

The summer immersive URE offered by the Willamette University Mathematics Consortium and funded by NSF was designed to provide students with an intensive 8-week research experience. The goal of the URE is to recruit students from underrepresented populations or those with limited access to research opportunities, in order to promote a more diverse research community within mathematics. Each summer, three teams are formed, consisting of three undergraduate students with one faculty mentor, which develop a research question centered on a common theme (e.g., ring and matrix theory, statistics and random processes, graph theory and combinatorics). In addition to exposure to research and the potential to create new mathematics, the program activities include career development workshops and training, as well as opportunities to present at regional and national conferences. Students receive a $4,000 stipend, $400 for travel costs to present their work at conferences, travel support to and from the URE, and shared on-campus housing.

SOURCE: Committee developed from the consortium website at http://www.willamette.edu/cla/math/reu [November 2016].

BOX 2-3
Summer Apprentice-Style Program:
Auburn University REU on Smart UAVs

NSF, in collaboration with the Department of Defense, has provided funds for a program that brings together faculty from computer science and aerospace engineering to work with 9 to 12 undergraduate students over the course of 8 weeks during a summer. The goals of the program are to develop research skills and promote an interest in UAVs. Students are expected to work at least 36 hours per week, which includes attending weekly seminars and programs. All students are required to submit a written report, give an oral presentation of the work performed, and design a web page that describes their project and experience. The program provides students with up to $8,000 in compensation including housing.

SOURCE: Committee developed from the website for the Smart UAV REU at http://www.pathwaystoscience.org/programhub.aspx?sort=SUM-AuburnU-UAVs [November 2016].

BOX 2-4
Capstone Experiences:
Olin College of Engineering

Olin College of Engineering provides students with the opportunity to work with an industry sponsor on a capstone experience that is intended to address and provide a novel solution to a real-world problem of importance to the sponsoring company. For example, students worked with Facebook to investigate how to improve Facebook's application on Android systems. Students explored different technologies to better understand how to reduce the amount of data consumed by the application and created technologies within the Facebook application to improve its usability. Other students have worked with imaging technology, such as computed tomography scans, to help create nontraditional lesion detection methods for patients with lung cancer, to ensure that biopsied tissue was from the cancerous lesion and not from surrounding healthy tissue. This detection technique can be used in the early detection and diagnosis of cancer, with the ultimate goal of improving survival rates.

SOURCE: Committee developed from the website at http://www.olin.edu/projects-research/capstone-culminating [November 2016].

---

with cooperative education (co-op) or internship experiences (discussed next) in industry (Saad, 2007). In 2014, the Council on Undergraduate Research devoted an issue to capstone experiences to illustrate the classic role that these experiences play in undergraduate research.[5] Moreover, there are several programs published in the literature that have found promising practices spanning topics such as chemistry (Kovac, 1991), electrical and computer engineering (Saad, 2007), civil engineering (Gnanapragasam, 2008; Hanna and Sullivan, 2005), and statistics (Spurrier, 2001). Box 2-4 highlights a few research topics from Olin College of Engineering that can serve as a capstone experience and illustrate the impact these experiences can have on real-world problems.

Internships and Co-ops

Internships and co-ops are professional experiences that often involve doing research, typically take place in the private sector, and are paid positions (usually at a rate commensurate with the student's experience and the disciplinary field). The internship or co-op experience can be for a summer, a semester, or an academic year. Examples include positions working with

---

[5]The issue can be found at http://www.cur.org/download.aspx?id=3035 [November 2016].

BOX 2-5
Cooperative Education Program at Northeastern University

Founded a century ago, this co-op program is one of the largest globally. In this URE, students alternate academic instruction with full-time employment in positions related to their chosen field. Northeastern uses a practice-oriented education model that blends liberal arts and science curriculum with a focus on practical skills in the classroom, practice, and application. Physics majors have opportunities ranging from engineering jobs at New York Power Authority and Raytheon to assistantships in Northeastern's physics labs, hospitals, and more. The concept behind these experiences is to add depth to the classroom studies, provide exposure to different career paths and options, and encourage students to delve deeper and pursue greater academic challenges.

Through three phases of the co-op (preparation, activity, reflection), students are able to earn experiential education credit after completion of each step. For the first phase (preparation), students actively participate in structured group and individual projects with the Physics Cooperative Education Faculty Coordinator. This stage helps students with job readiness, including resume and cover letter development, interview skills, and business behavior and conduct. In the second phase (activity), the faculty coordinator provides guidance and oversight to student job searches. The third phase (reflection) involves the faculty coordinator guiding students to identify activities and experiences they participated in and to reflect on what they accomplished, how those accomplishments connect to their studies, and how those experiences added to their intellectual growth. This phase ends with students interacting at faculty conferences, discussing their employer's performance evaluation, debriefing with the faculty coordinator, and delivering an oral presentation.

SOURCE: Committee developed from the website at http://www.northeastern.edu/physics-coop [November 2016].

---

researchers in industry, at government agencies such as the National Institutes of Health (NIH), or at Federally Funded Research and Development Centers such as Lawrence Livermore National Laboratory or the Jet Propulsion Laboratory. Although these experiences typically occur off campus, there are on-campus opportunities as well. These experiences may even be repeated—the same students with the same researcher—for a number of semesters or summers. UREs of this type are especially prevalent in engineering and technology fields. An institutional office frequently facilitates placement into the internship or co-op, and professional staff members in the office oversee evaluation of the learning experience.

Co-op programs are primarily based on partnerships between academic universities and private-sector companies. Students who participate in a co-op program or internship often alternate between academic theory-based classroom learning and off-campus hands-on research experiences. Students apply classroom knowledge to work situations, gain knowledge, and develop skills that further clarify their academic focus and career interests. See Box 2-5 for an example of a cooperative education program developed at Northeastern University.

Co-ops and internships can be a bit more complicated than other types of UREs, as these opportunities are typically located off campus. That is, students need to be able to get to the research site and they need to fit the URE around their traditional courses or take a semester to focus exclusively on the co-op or internship. Moreover, there needs to be a mutual interest that is based on both the researchers' interest in working with undergraduates and the possibility for the students to make at least modest contributions to the overall research effort. These experiences are also highly individualized, with the mentoring skills of the researchers involved playing an important role in the depth of the experience and the level of outcomes.

The primary costs of this type of URE are (1) the researchers' time in mentoring the student or small team of students; (2) the cost of space and equipment needed to support the research experience of the student or small team of students; (3) the cost of a stipend for each student that is paid to participate, if payment for participation is an option; and (4) the administrative costs of matching students with researchers. Box 2-6 highlights the components in costs and mentoring at Drexel University for co-op experiences offered there.

Course-Based Undergraduate Research Experiences

In CUREs, students investigate novel research questions and therefore contribute new knowledge to the field. These courses can provide students with opportunities to engage in research in a more controlled fashion and are designed for cohorts of students, allowing faculty to engage large numbers of students in research projects at one time. They can also be scaled and adapted to fit the needs and resources across a variety of institutions. For example, the Genomics Education Partnership, sponsored by Washington University in St. Louis, St. Louis, Missouri, and funded by the Howard Hughes Medical Institute (HHMI) and NSF, organizes research projects and provides training/collaboration workshops for faculty from multiple institutions on an established curriculum in which students annotate sections of the Drosophila fruit fly genome.[6]

---

[6]For more information, see the Genome Education Partnership website at https://gep.wustl. edu [November 2016].

BOX 2-6
Cooperative Education Program at Drexel University

At Drexel University, the Provost office provides a small number of opportunities for students and faculty to engage in undergraduate research during a 6-month full-time period that coincides with students' participation in a co-op. In this initiative, 50 percent of the student's co-op salary is funded by the university and the other 50 percent comes from the faculty member's grant-funded research program. The salary levels of these positions are equivalent to private-sector employment. Students often also work with research faculty during the academic year for minimal or no remuneration but may receive course credits.

In the case of full-time research during the co-op period, if the faculty member has a lapse in research grant support, the department leadership has the challenge of providing the resources needed to maintain continuity for both the student and the research initiative itself. Continuity is important to the student to enable continuous engagement with the topic of research throughout the student's undergraduate tenure. A quality involvement, whether in full-time opportunities or more traditional part-time work with a faculty member, requires faculty time dedicated to mentoring of the undergraduate, as well as teaching the specific scientific or technical aspects related to the research. For the student, this opens a horizon to relate classroom work to real research problems, but without continuity in the research component, the student may lose interest. From the institution's perspective, involvement in this initiative enhances the student retention objective.

Drexel also tracks students' cooperative education experiences, identified through specific employer position descriptions. During any 6-month period, approximately 500 students are doing research as part of a co-op with a private-

CUREs can be a required course in a discipline or a core elective. These experiences can be multidisciplinary as well, such as a course developed by Miller and Watson (2010) in mathematical biology to bridge the gap between mathematics and the life sciences. Because these experiences might be a standard part of the curriculum, this type of URE is automatically accessible to students of almost all skill levels and backgrounds. That is, there is no screening of students other than that they have had the required prerequisite course and/or they meet a given minimum standard of academic accomplishment, such as a grade point average above a probationary level.

In a CURE, the research projects investigated by the class are typically, though not always, linked to a faculty member's research program. Students earn academic credit for participating in the CURE, which may replace required traditional course labs in some cases. Some CUREs offer the opportunity to continue research in the summer. Given the short period of time available for a CURE, the depth of the experience provided may vary

sector or government employer. In this instance, in contrast with the student having a research position with a Drexel faculty member, the responsibilities for supplying adequate facilities and supplies to enable a quality research experience rest with the employer.

In 2012-2013, approximately 1,000 students and employers were surveyed on the co-op experience. Students answered questions that focused on rating their opportunities during their research experience to demonstrate their own initiative, develop leadership skills, network and engage in professional development, and have progressive responsibilities. The survey found that the fraction of students who rated their experience as meeting or exceeding their expectations was 92 percent for opportunities to demonstrate own initiative, 84 percent for development of leadership skills, 89 percent for networking and professional development, and 92 percent for opportunities for progressive responsibilities. The employers were surveyed on the students' overall performance and on their ability to contribute original ideas, to critically analyze and solve complex problems, and to make well-reasoned arguments based on the evidence. Approximately 83 percent of employers reported that they would hire the students who participated in the program, with a comparable percentage rating the students' overall performance as good or exemplary. Moreover, approximately 73 percent of employers rated the students' ability to make a novel contribution to the work as exemplary or good. Students also received high ratings (good or exemplary) for complex problem solving (69 percent) and making well-reasoned arguments (78 percent).

SOURCES: Committee developed from the Drexel websites on co-op experiences, http://drexel.edu/difference/co-op and http://drexel.edu/scdc, and from personal communication from Stephanie Sullivan, Assistant Director, Program Assessment & Operations, Steinbright Career Development Center, Drexel University, to the committee, September 8. 2015.

significantly, based on the design of the CURE, the nature of the discipline, and the cost of research efforts in the area covered by the CURE. Some CUREs are a single semester, others last for two semesters (see Box 2-7 on the SEA-Phages program and Box 2-8 on the Binghamton University Lyme and Other Tick-Borne Disease Project), whereas others can last three or more semesters (see Box 2-9 on the Freshman Research Initiative at The University of Texas at Austin).

Wrap-Around Experiences

UREs have been integrated into programs that span multiple semesters or multiple academic years and include academic support services such as tutoring. See Box 2-10 for a program designed to build a community through a residential program. These comprehensive programs frequently target students who enter college less well prepared and students who are

---

BOX 2-7
Science Education Alliance-Phage Hunters CURE

The Science Education Alliance-Phage Hunters (SEA-Phages), spearheaded by Graham Hatfull (University of Pittsburgh) with funding from HHMI, involves thousands of introductory biology students at diverse institutions in identifying and characterizing soil bacteriophage with the collective aim of studying their genetic diversity and evolutionary mechanisms (Hatfull et al., 2006). The course begins the first semester with students digging in the soil to find viruses; by the end of the second semester students are using a variety of bioinformatics techniques to annotate genomes. Jordan and colleagues (2014) provided additional information about the program and associated outcomes.

SOURCE: Committee developed from the website on the SEA-Phages CURE, see http://seaphages.org/ and http://phagesdb.org/phagehunters [November 2016].

---

members of underrepresented groups in the discipline and may be more likely to face challenges as they navigate the majority culture of their discipline. For example, the psychology department at CUNY Baruch College uses funding from an NSF REU grant to fund an academic year–long research experience with the purpose of enhancing graduate school enrollment of individuals from underrepresented groups.[7] Trainee activities include a minimum of 10 hours per week working with a faculty-led research team and contributing to ongoing research through collecting and analyzing data during the fall and spring semesters. In addition, students enroll in a year-long preparation course for graduate school and receive financial compensation for their research in the lab.

A program sponsored by NIH, Maximizing Access to Research Careers (MARC), is a national-level program that provides financial support to historically underrepresented minority students for a 24-month period to improve their preparation for high-caliber graduate training at the doctoral level.[8] MARC institutions select the trainees, typically students in the last 2 years of undergraduate study who have expressed interest in pursuing an advanced degree. MARC institutions are encouraged to design programs that address their unique mission, strengths, and demographics; however, a cornerstone of the funding is that each program must provide students with

---

[7] For more information on this program, see http://www.baruch.cuny.edu/wsas/academics/psychology/NSFUndergraduateResearchExperience.htm [November 2016].

[8] See https://www.nigms.nih.gov/Training/MARC/Pages/USTARAwards.aspx [November 2016] for details about this program.

BOX 2-8
A Cross-Disciplinary CURE:
Binghamton University Lyme and
Other Tick-Borne Disease Project

The Binghamton University Lyme and Other Tick-Borne Disease Project combines field and laboratory research experience as part of a two-course sequence. Students conduct original research as part of five cross-disciplinary research teams (field ecology, reservoir and vector trapping, behavioral and demographic analysis, molecular pathogen identification, and mathematical modeling). The project includes faculty from the disciplines of anthropology, biological sciences, and biomedical engineering and system science. The overall goal of the program is to understand the human risk of Lyme disease and other tick-borne diseases in built environments: those areas where humans live, work, and recreate on a daily basis. All participating students are required to conduct research 10 hours per week in the field and laboratory. Students must join at least two teams, a field team and either the laboratory team or modeling team, to obtain an appropriate cross-disciplinary perspective on the project.

Students who wish to receive credit for their research must take the two-course sequence, with once-weekly lectures on research design and the ethical conduct of research, in addition to their 10 hours per week in the field and laboratory. Students in the first course in the sequence work as a group throughout the semester to develop a research project and present their work at the end of the semester as a team PowerPoint presentation. They must also individually develop an annotated bibliography and a research paper on a related topic by the end of the semester. The second-semester course is an extension of the first but with a primary focus on the development of an independent research project while the student still attends lectures once every 3 weeks. Faculty and graduate students act as mentors to assist students with their individual project proposals. Students in the second course of the two-course sequence are required to present their individual research projects using a PowerPoint briefing in lieu of an annotated bibliography and paper.

SOURCE: Committee developed from the website on the Binghamton University Lyme and Other Tick-Borne Disease Project, see https://www.binghamton.edu/undergraduate-research/hhmi/current-projects.html#five [November 2016].

---

a summer research experience at a research-intensive institution outside of the MARC institution. During the academic year, institutions may also provide research training/experience opportunities as appropriate.

Bridge Programs

Bridge programs are usually UREs incorporated into an extended orientation program that serves to support student transitions. The targeted

BOX 2-9
CURE: Freshman Research Initiative Program

The Freshman Research Initiative at The University of Texas at Austin is a program in which students are able to participate in natural science research from the beginning of their college career. The program integrates laboratory and classroom experiences, and students enrolled in the program earn three credit hours for each semester they participate. Throughout the program students participate in experiences that lead to publications in peer-reviewed journals and presentations at national conferences.

All entering freshman are enrolled in a research methods course or another preparatory course for their major. Then students enter a "research stream" where they are able to earn credit for spring, summer, and fall research courses. To provide varying experience opportunities, professors shape each research stream according to their own research. Each research stream includes 6-12 hours of guided inquiries, techniques ranging from basic to advanced, and results ranging from known to unknown, based on the skill level of the student. Responsibility is delegated to a research educator (either a long-term Ph.D.-level educator or a postdoctoral fellow), who works under a faculty member and manages a research team that includes graduate and undergraduate students (approximately 15-35 students per stream). Professors oversee the research goals on a broad scale and conduct classes, while the day-to-day operations of lab teaching and research are conducted by the research educators. The program has grown from 40 students in 2005-2006 to roughly 900 freshmen enrolled each year in 2016, which is just more than 40 percent of the entering class. Over the course of 10 years, the program has involved more than 6,200 freshmen; built bridges between industry, philanthropy, and academia; and led to more than 170 scientific papers with student co-authors.

SOURCE: Committee developed from the Freshman Research Initiative website at https://cns.utexas.edu/fri [November 2016].

transition can be at the start of college—students transitioning from high school or transferring from another institution—or at the transition from undergraduate to graduate school. The latter programs are typically referred to as postbaccalaureate programs. Bridge programs can serve to introduce research early in a student's career, when they not only provide the opportunity to begin making connections between classroom and learning within the research environment, but also can provide access to research faculty with whom undergraduate students would not otherwise interact until they took more advanced courses. Box 2-11 illustrates two examples of partnerships with community colleges that serve to bridge the transition from two-year to four-year institutions.

BOX 2-10
Wrap-Around Experiences:
Living/Learning Residence Hall UREs

The Michigan Research Community was developed more than 15 years ago as an add-on residential option for freshmen participating in the University of Michigan's undergraduate research opportunity program (UROP) for underclassmen. Current residents in the community include 113 first-year students and 35 returning students. The community is not limited to STEM majors; however, 40 percent of the residents are in engineering and greater than 50 percent of residents are enrolled in the College of Literature, Science and the Arts. The Michigan Research Community residents hold their own research symposium in addition to attending the larger UROP symposium.

Based on the success at Michigan, the L.E.A.R.N. (Learning Environment and Academic Research Network) at the University of Central Florida was established in 2011 with funding from NSF. L.E.A.R.N. participants receive a scholarship, enroll in a two-semester "introduction to research" course, and participate in a 12-week research apprentice experience. The program is limited to fewer than 30 first-year students but is open to all STEM disciplines. The program seeks to build pathways for students to apply for upperclass research programs such as McNair or the Louis Stokes Alliances for Minority Participation.

The programs at both University of Michigan and University of Central Florida were developed by leadership from the institutions' undergraduate research offices. The concept of a residential community for undergraduate researchers is currently being adopted at Florida Atlantic University[a] and Western Carolina University.[b] More detailed information can be found in Schneider and Bickel (2015) and Schneider and colleagues (2015).

---

[a]See http://www.fau.edu/class/learning-community [November 2016] for more information
[b]For more information, see http://www.wcu.edu/learn/academic-success/learning-communities [November 2016].

SOURCES: Committee developed from the University of Michigan's UROP website at http://www.lsa.umich.edu/mrc [November 2016] and the University of Central Florida's L.E.A.R.N. website at htt;P//www.our.ucf.edu/learn/freshman.php [November 2016].

Bridge programs are also offered for incoming graduate students, for whom they provide an opportunity to begin research group rotations before their formal graduate training program begins. Generally lasting 1-2 years, these postbaccalaureate programs provide intensive research experiences and academic preparation for students who have completed their undergraduate degrees but would benefit from additional experience and preparation before beginning a graduate training program. For example, students participating in the NIH-supported (through an R25

BOX 2-11
Undergraduate Bridge Programs:
Partnerships with Community Colleges
and Research Labs (Bay Area)

The NIH-sponsored Bridge to Baccalaureate Program (funded through an NIH R25 grant) provides institutional support to students to make the transition from a two-year institution to a four-year institution, with the aim of increasing the pool of students who pursue research careers in biomedical sciences.[a] Numerous partnerships have been funded across the country, in 21 states. One of these is the partnership between City College of San Francisco, Skyline College, and San Francisco State University. During their first summer in the program, students participate in an academic success and leadership workshop and a research training class. For their second summer, the program matches the community college students with a faculty mentor at San Francisco State University for an independent research project, which typically lasts 8 weeks.

The Bridge to Biotech (B2B) partnership between City College of San Francisco and the University of California, San Francisco, is funded by an NSF Advanced Technology Education grant. It supports community college biotechnology students as they gain an introduction to biosciences and strengthen their skills in math and communication through learning communities, problem-based learning, and hands-on training in research and industry laboratories. B2B focuses on supporting economically disadvantaged and historically underrepresented students in sciences (participants are 76 percent African American, Asian, or Hispanic), and most participants are adults with prior work experience who want to transition to the biotechnology workforce. A unique aspect of this program is that mentors at the university, who are often senior graduate students or postdoctoral fellows, complete a multiday workshop on becoming effective mentors, led by the career development office staff and B2B faculty. Following completion of a semester of training in math, science, and lab skills at the community college, the participating students complete an unpaid 4-month, part-time (10-20 hours per week) internship, at the laboratory assistant level, in Bay Area labs and biotech companies. B2B students can then go on to complete a certificate or AS degree in biotechnology.

---

[a]For additional information on NIH's Bridges to Baccalaureate Program (R25) see https://www.nigms.nih.gov/Research/Mechanisms/Pages/BridgesBaccalaureate.aspx [November 2016].

SOURCES: Committee developed from the Bridge to Baccalaureate Program website at http://biology.sfsu.edu/faculty-pages/bridges_main [November 2016] and the Bridge to Biotech website at https://www.ccsf.edu/Departments/Biotech_Training/bridge.htm [November 2016].

BOX 2-12
Keck Geology Consortium

This consortium began in 1987 as a collaboration of faculty at private liberal arts colleges who were interested in pooling resources and opportunities for field and lab research in the geological sciences. The consortium now has 18 member institutions and has been successful in securing funding from Exxon and NSF. Undergraduate students apply to participate in summer research teams of five to eight students and two or more collaborating faculty. In addition to field sites in North America, many teams travel abroad, gaining both geology research experience and exposure to other cultures. Funding from NSF has enabled a greater diversity of student participants from underrepresented backgrounds and nonmember institutions, as well as underclassmen. In a typical summer, there are six projects, two of which are earmarked for underclassmen. A key feature of the program is the annual Keck Symposium, hosted each April by a different member institution. Students present posters and attend workshops, while faculty mentors have opportunities to sustain their research collaborations and discuss best practices. Over the past 2.5 decades, more than 1,400 students have participated in the Keck program.

SOURCE: Committee developed from the Keck Geology Consortium website at http://www.keckgeology.org [November 2016].

grant) Post-Baccalaureate Research Education Program are paired for their research experience with a faculty mentor and work in the mentor's lab at one of the graduate-level institutions.[9] In addition, students also receive supplemental training in scientific writing, literature evaluation, and interaction with the academic community. Many of these postbaccalaureate bridge programs are funded by extramural sources. Students earn academic credit for the courses they complete and a stipend for the research they do. Upon program completion, students are better positioned for admission to top-tier graduate programs, often the program at the institution where they participated in the postbaccalaureate program.

Consortium/Project-Based Programs

Consortiums allow for collaboration with faculty and students from different colleges and universities, which serves to create a multidisciplinary context for the work. The scale of the research and the questions that can be addressed are beyond what could be accomplished through more tradi-

---

[9] See https://www.training.nih.gov/programs/postbac_irta [November 2016].

tional apprentice-style models because teams of researchers (faculty and students) can work on specific themes of research. Consortiums can provide opportunities for a pooling of resources across institutions to allow more students an opportunity to participate in research. Box 2-12 provides an example of this approach developed by the Keck Geology Consortium.

Moreover, these programs span across multiple semesters, including the summer, and may be a larger commitment on the part of the student than some other forms of UREs. Box 2-13 provides an example of a program—the Vertically Integrated Projects Program—that highlights an innovative process for engaging teams of undergraduate students over multiple years in research and for sustaining the functionality of the team for many years, even decades.

Consortiums also allow for more creative ways to increase undergraduate research, such as by providing opportunities for faculty to develop skills, through workshops, that they can use throughout the academic year. Box 2-14 provides an example of this type of approach for mathematics. Moreover, these programs have encouraged diversity in research by specifically supporting programs geared toward students from groups historically underrepresented in STEM. Box 2-15 highlights two such programs, one at the undergraduate level (HHMI Exceptional Research Opportunities Program) and the other geared specifically toward getting students into graduate programs (Leadership Alliance).

Community-Based Research Programs

Often linked to service-learning courses, community-based research experiences are a unique type of URE that includes service to the community as an outcome of the research. They may take the form of a CURE or an individual faculty research group URE as described above, but they also have a component in that in addition to a research mentor, students interact with a community partner who contributes to the design of the research project and provides the venue in which the research takes place. Ultimately, the goal of this type of research is to provide results and understanding that advance the work of the community partner in using evidence-based approaches. For example, public health is a priority for many of the participating organizations, with research examining a variety of topics from environmental health to infectious diseases. Box 2-16 illustrates the range of these topics through three programs. The first two use different approaches to address environmental health, whereas the third is a program geared toward infectious disease.

BOX 2-13
The Vertically Integrated Projects Program and Consortium

The Vertically Integrated Projects (VIP) Program supports long-term, large-scale, multidisciplinary teams of undergraduates that are embedded in the research efforts of faculty and other researchers on or near campus (Coyle et al., 2006, 2016). Each team is vertically integrated, which means it is composed of sophomores, juniors, seniors, graduate students, and the faculty.

A VIP team is typically launched with 6 to 10 undergraduates from different years and from all disciplines needed for the success of the research effort. Over time, a team grows to a size that best suits its mission. The average size of a mature team is 16 students, but teams with as many as 35 undergraduates each semester exist. A team size of 12 or more undergraduates essentially guarantees that a sufficient number of students return from one semester to the next for the team to grow and pass on its knowledge and skills over many semesters or years. The longest functioning teams are now 16 years old; they started when the VIP Program started.

Each undergraduate student on a VIP team can register for academic credit for up to six semesters, receiving a letter grade each semester. When seniors graduate, everyone else on the team moves up in responsibility and new sophomores and juniors are added. The students who return to the team run the process that introduces new students to the team and helps them acquire the knowledge and skills to become productive team members. This peer mentoring process saves the faculty and graduate students considerable time and effort and helps the new undergraduates fit quickly into the team.

Each team has a primary adviser and may have one or two co-advisers who are faculty, research staff, or members of off-campus organizations that are partners in the project. Teams have been started at the request of faculty from the STEM disciplines of computing, engineering, and science and by faculty from architecture, liberal arts, and public policy. The VIP Program is thus broadly multidisciplinary. In fact, every team is multidisciplinary.

During the first year a team is in operation, the task of educating the team falls primarily on the faculty advisers and their graduate students. By the second year, returning students take over this process and the faculty and graduate students oversee the process. Thus, from year 2 onward, the students on the team are producing benefits for a faculty members' research, receiving significant educational benefits from the experience, and receiving credit toward their degrees.

As of 2016, 22 four-year universities, 17 of which are within the United States, had joined the VIP Program. They represent a variety of institutions: large, small, public, private, universities classified as R1 through R3, historically Black colleges and universities, Hispanic-serving institutions, etc. These institutions, with the assistance of a grant from the Helmsley Charitable Trust, have formed the VIP Consortium. Its purpose is to facilitate the growth and dissemination of the VIP Program, to share tools and processes between VIP sites, and to conduct evaluation of the impact of the program on students, faculty, and institutions.

SOURCE: Committee developed from the VIP Program website at http://www.vip.gatech.edu [November 2016].

BOX 2-14
Center for Undergraduate Research in Mathematics

The Center for Undergraduate Research in Mathematics (CURM) provides an interesting model for expanding the practice of undergraduate research in the mathematical sciences. Each summer, approximately 16 mathematics faculty gather for a 3-day professional workshop to prepare to mentor teams of 2-5 undergraduates during the academic year at their home institution (approximately 45 students per year). Funding is provided by CURM to the faculty/home institution to reduce the teaching load of the mentor, and students receive a $3,000 stipend. All participants gather at an annual CURM meeting, and students and faculty are encouraged to attend other regional and national professional conferences. According to the CURM website, approximately 350 students (27 percent minority, 52 percent female) and more than 100 faculty have participated in the program. The major source of funding for CURM is NSF. CURM was recognized by the American Mathematical Society in 2015 for its impact on efforts to promote the study of mathematics to underrepresented students.

SOURCE: Committee developed from the CURM website at http://curm.byu.edu [November 2016].

BOX 2-15
Two Programs for Increasing Diversity in STEM Research

The HHMI Exceptional Research Opportunities Program was established by HHMI to diversify the next generation of scientists. It brings together outstanding undergraduates (nominated by HHMI-funded educational program directors, HHMI research professors, or from a Science Education Alliance school) and pairs the selected students with HHMI research professors across the country for a summer research experience. Student applications and matching with HHMI professors are coordinated by HHMI staff. Local arrangements and educational programming occur as appropriate for the HHMI mentor's institution. Although not a true consortium, the commonalities are a target audience of outstanding underrepresented students from institutions with some connection to existing HHMI funding and high-profile HHMI professors serving as mentors. Approximately 70 students each year are selected. They participate in a student conference at HHMI facilities in May before their experience and return a year later for a follow-up meeting. The professional development and networking at the May conference is a purposeful component of the program. HHMI has recently begun offering a second summer of funding for qualified students from the program to continue their research at an

---

BOX 2-15 Continued

accelerated pace in the same HHMI lab. According to the HHMI website, approximately 45 percent of program alumni enter graduate programs.

The Leadership Alliance was begun in 1992 with 23 member institutions. The current 35 institutional members include research institutions (including all of the Ivy League universities, University of Chicago, Stanford University, University of Virginia, and New York University), historically Black college and universities (such as Howard University, Xavier University, and Spelman College), and institutions with substantial numbers of underrepresented students in STEM disciplines (including University of Maryland, Baltimore County; North Carolina A&T State University; University of Puerto Rico). The goal of the alliance is to increase the number of underrepresented students in graduate programs and to develop these students for leadership positions in academia, industry, and the public sector. Although there is a heavy STEM focus, opportunities are available for students in the humanities and social sciences. The signature program of the Leadership Alliance is the Summer Research Early Identification Program, which provides access to undergraduate research internships for almost 300 students per year at 22 Alliance institutions. Students from any institution can apply for a position at up to three institutions through a common application. Each institution coordinates and funds its own program. A national symposium is held at the end of the summer for more than 600 undergraduate interns, faculty from the Alliance member institutions, and program alumni (either still in graduate school or having finished advanced degrees). The Leadership Alliance reports that more than 700 program alumni have completed terminal degrees. The Doctoral Scholars program and a newly established alumni organization are essential to the networking mission of the Alliance. A newly established First Year Research Experience initiative aims to encourage best practices among Leadership Alliance institutions. Additional information, including demographic data, can be found on the Leadership Alliance website.

SOURCES: Committee developed from the programs' websites at http://www.hhmi.org/programs/exceptional-research-opportunities-program [November 2016] and http://www.theleadershipalliance.org [November 2016].

BOX 2-16
Community-Based Research Programs

The Great Lakes Innovative Stewardship through Education Network (GLISTEN) is "a collaborative effort by local colleges, universities and environmental community partners to engage students in direct-action efforts to preserve and restore the environmental health of the Lake Michigan watershed." The program was established in 2010 through a grant to the National Center for Science

continued

BOX 2-16 Continued

and Civic Engagement at Harrisburg University from the Learn and Serve America Higher Education Program of the Corporation for National and Community Service. GLISTEN not only provides undergraduate students with an opportunity to conduct research during the summer, but also has developed courses that contextualize the project and learning experiences.

The National Center for Earth-Surface Dynamics 2 at the University of Minnesota received funding from the NSF Science and Technology Center to develop a program that introduces undergraduate students to research with a focus on community-based participatory research and diverse disciplinary teams. Students work on one of three teams on projects that integrate Earth-surface dynamics, geology, ecology, and other disciplines using quantitative and predictive methods. The research teams, in addition to ongoing projects at the University of Minnesota, are hosted on two Native American reservations, with projects developed in collaboration with the tribes' resource management divisions.

To develop more than just the technical research skills, the program is designed to increase intellectual understanding of the project and the participants' self-confidence working as a STEM professional. These objectives are accomplished through weekly writings and blog posts, a research paper of 15-plus pages, posters, and conference presentations. Emphases of this NSF REU program are to increase participation in STEM of nontraditional students and those from underrepresented groups, potentially help them develop an identity as a STEM professional, and encourage STEM persistence.

The Biomedical Anthropology program at Binghamton University has collaborated with the Ministry of Health of the 83-island nation of Vanuatu (68 of which are inhabited), which is going through a health transition as a result of modernization, market integration, tourism, and inter-island migration. Binghamton University and the government of Vanuatu have established a memorandum of understanding to facilitate an inter-island, community-based research program on the health transition. The overall goal of this community-based research program is to improve the health of the people of Vanuatu and to gain a better understanding of the factors involved in the development and impact of chronic diseases such as overweight, obesity, diabetes, and hypertension on transitioning Vanuatu communities. Students at both undergraduate and graduate levels participate in the research during 1-to 3-month summer experiences, working on chronic and infectious diseases. Students' research can be taken for academic credit or as part of a formal internship and usually results in students presenting their research at regional and national scientific conferences, becoming authors or co-authors on peer-reviewed research publications, or both.

SOURCES: Committee developed from the following websites: Quoted passage and other details about GLISTEN are from the program's website at http://www.iun.edu/glisten [November 2016]. For the National Center for Earth-Surface Dynamics 2, see http://www.nced.umn.edu/research-experience-undergraduates [November 2016]. For the Binghamton University–Vanatu project, see https://www.binghamton.edu/anthropology/about-us/biological-anthropology/research/health-transitions.html [November 2016].

PREPARATORY COURSES AND EXTENSIONS OF URE PROGRAMS

In addition to the variety of UREs discussed above, there are a few different types of approaches that could prepare students for or serve as extensions of UREs. These approaches include more preparatory classes, like an introductory methods course, or are extensions such as bridge programs to prepare students for future graduate work. The format for these experiences exhibit the same variability as has been discussed throughout this chapter.

Introductory Course on Reviewing Scientific Literature

An important skill to have when conducting research is the ability to think critically about research and the existing literature. Gottesman and Hoskins (2012) developed a course at the City University of New York that uses a strategy called *CREATE*: Consider, Read, Elucidate hypotheses, Analyze and interpret data, and Think of the next Experiment. Freshmen students were enrolled in this introductory, one-semester course that used targeted readings to develop these analytical skills. Through this course, students self-reported gains in their ability to think critically and understand primary STEM literature.

A different program has been created to teach first- and second-year students at the University of California, Los Angeles, about research. In that program students hear a full seminar by an invited biologist and then spend 5 weeks deconstructing the speaker's research, reading his or her papers, and learning about the speaker's motivations, decisions, and methods. The speaker then returns for the students to ask questions based on their new found knowledge (Clark et al., 2009).

Introductory Courses on Research Methods

Inquiry-based activities—namely, activities that do not have simple "right or wrong" answers but instead generate results that are "messy" and open to interpretation—can be integrated into traditional laboratory (or field-based) courses. These types of learning experiences would not necessarily meet the committee's definition of a URE, as they do not typically generate new knowledge, but they could lay the groundwork for students to participate in a later URE or could occur alongside a student's first URE to give the student a structured introduction to the relevant approaches and topics. These introductory experiences with open-ended inquiry might be in the form of a research methods class that allows students to perform many aspects of the research experience—formulating, executing, and presenting the results of a research project—with the goal of developing the skills, motivation, and confidence to engage further as a STEM professional.

Courses that follow instructional approaches such as Modeling Instruction[10] or Investigative Science Learning Environment,[11] as well as some Process-Oriented Guided Inquiry Learning courses,[12] engage students in discovery-based experiences in which the content is not novel but well established. The activities are designed for students to discover the laws of nature by carrying out experiments, making rules or models, and iterating and refining their models after additional experimentation or discovery. The curricula and pedagogy facilitate a discovery-as-if-new experience, build collaboration skills, and support development of science/engineering identity.

For example, selected geology undergraduate students at Hope College completed two international field expeditions to Sweden in the past 10 years.[13] Goals of the program included reinforcing how research questions are formulated and answered with field observations. Students gained field mapping experience, and the research project highlighted the international collaborative process with fellow Swedish scientists. Project funding was assembled from a faculty development grant, supplemental departmental funding, and student research grants from the Geological Society of America.

Graduate Bridge Programs

Similar to undergraduate bridge programs, graduate-level bridge programs support a student's transition from a master's program to a doctoral program. For example, there is an NSF-sponsored program at Fisk University in collaboration with Vanderbilt University in Nashville, Tennessee, developed to improve demographic diversity within STEM disciplines. Through this program, students earn a master's degree at Fisk University in physics, biology, or chemistry with full funding support. Students are then recommended to specific departments by the Fisk-Vanderbilt committee and the Dean of the College of Arts and Sciences at Vanderbilt. Students then take various courses depending on their undergraduate preparation and specific area of studies. They also receive research experience with faculty, connection with Vanderbilt professors, and support in the application to Vanderbilt's Ph.D. program. The program provides full instructional opportunities to undertake Ph.D. coursework completion at both Fisk and Vanderbilt.

---

[10] For more information on the Modeling Instruction approach, see http://perg.fiu.edu/resources/modeling-instruction/ and http://modelinginstruction.org [November 2016].

[11] See http://paer.rutgers.edu [November 2016].

[12] See https://pogil.org [November 2016].

[13] See http://www.hope.edu/pr/nfhc/current/nfhc1214pg14-15.pdf [November 2016].

Pre-Research

- Minimal intellectual engagement in research
- Learn about research outside the research setting
- Develop basic technical skills in the research setting by supporting a research team through assigned tasks (e.g., washing dishes, preparing solutions)

Research Project

- Moderate intellectual engagement in research
- Join a research team and assume responsibility for part of an ongoing research project under the guidance of a mentor
- Develop technical research skills
- Learn data management practices and analysis skills
- Construct explanations or develop arguments based on evidence

Research Experience

- Extensive intellectual engagement in research
- Participate in a research team's community of practice by attending team meetings, journal clubs, etc.
- Assume responsibility for a novel independent research project from beginning to end
- Review, evaluate, and integrate findings from the primary literature to design and interpret the results of the project
- Conduct research under the guidance of a mentor and make decisions to adjust or change the direction of the project when necessary
- Analyze data, draw conclusions, and communicate research findings verbally or in writing to the research team
- Define directions for future studies based on research results

Research Program

- Extensive intellectual engagement in research and professional development
- Develop contextual understanding through peer review by communicating research findings beyond the immediate research community of practice
- Build a research professional network by socializing into the culture of research beyond the immediate research community of practice
- Explore research careers
- Develop research identity through guided reflection and self-evaluation

FIGURE 2-1 Model for student research engagement.
SOURCE: Committee adapted from Blockus (2016) commissioned paper.

STAGES OF RESEARCH ENGAGEMENT

The extent to which each type of URE includes each of the various characteristics and attributes discussed at the beginning of this chapter differs, but a continuum of experiences reflecting student development from observer to independent researcher can be articulated (see Figure 2-1). That is, students may first be exposed to the research environment primarily as observers, so that they can become physically involved in the business of research while acclimating themselves to the culture and community of practice. The expectation of intellectual engagement at this stage may be minimal, as it is merely intended to provide students with opportunities to develop basic research skills appropriate to their discipline. As students participate in more and different experiences, the level of engagement may increase as the student becomes more fluent with the practices of research, which may lead to greater independence in the work they undertake.

In addition to increasing intellectual engagement, students increasingly develop technical research skills (i.e., using instrumentation and appropriate methods) and begin to explore and understand the data that are being collected. Students involved in a research project may conduct minimal analysis, as this is the first stage at which students begin to develop the ability to think through the research questions to conduct proper analyses. As students are engaged in a research experience or research program, they not only can articulate how the data were collected and analyzed, but also can draw conclusions and communicate the findings to a broader audience. Lastly, as students transition to becoming a STEM researcher, they have extensive engagement with research, developing their own research identity. This includes critically reading and actively reflecting upon primary STEM literature.

This trend in engagement can be articulated as a continuum that reflects different stages and levels of engagement in a research experience. Although these stages are additive in nature, a student need not progress through each stage sequentially; that is, a student can immediately participate at the highest level of engagement (termed the "Research Program" in Figure 2-1). An important point is that students can realize the benefits of research at any stage.

SUMMARY

As highlighted throughout this chapter, there is substantial variability in programs of undergraduate research. That is, students can engage in UREs in STEM in many different ways, to varying degrees, and across a variety of different settings. Given the heterogeneity of UREs, it is difficult to draw conclusions that apply generally to all types of UREs. Moreover, the lack of systematic data collection makes it difficult to know how many students participate in UREs, where UREs are offered, and if there are gaps in access to UREs across different institutional types, disciplines, or groups of students. Although learning objectives differ across the various types of UREs, there are some crosscutting characteristics that all UREs exhibit and that form the basis for the committee's definition of UREs. UREs engage the students in the type of work that STEM researchers do, including discovery, iteration, and collaboration as the students learn STEM disciplinary knowledge and practices while working on a topic that has relevance beyond the course. UREs are structured and guided by a mentor, and they intellectually engage students with the goal that students assume increasing ownership of some aspects of the project over time. The frequency and intensity of approaches varies among UREs due to choices made by faculty, program directors, and others in response to their goals, constraints, and preferences. Information about which attributes of UREs are most significant for their effects on students outcomes would be helpful to those planning and implementing UREs; the currently available research on this topic will be discussed in Chapter 4.

REFERENCES

American Association for the Advancement of Science (2011). *Vision and Change in Undergraduate Biology Education: A Call to Action.* C. Brewer and D. Smith (Eds.). Washington, DC: American Association for the Advancement of Science.

Auchincloss, L.C., Laursen, S.L., Branchaw, J.L., Eagan, K., Graham, M., Hanauer, D.I., Lawrie, G., McLinn, C.M., Pelaez, N., Rowland, S., Towns, M., Trautmann, N.M., Varma-Nelson, P., Weston, T.J., and Dolan, E.L. (2014). Assessment of course-based undergraduate research experiences: A meeting report. *CBE–Life Sciences Education, 13*(1), 29-40.

Blockus, L. (2016). *Strengthening Research Experiences for Undergraduate STEM Students: The Co-Curricular Model of the Research Experience.* Paper commissioned for the Committee on Strengthening Research Experiences for Undergraduate STEM Students. Board on Science Education, Division of Behavioral and Social Sciences and Education. Board on Life Sciences, Division of Earth and Life Studies. National Academies of Sciences, Engineering, and Medicine.

Brownell, S.E., and Kloser, M.J. (2015). Toward a conceptual framework for measuring the effectiveness of course-based undergraduate research experiences in undergraduate biology. *Studies in Higher Education, 40*(3), 525-544.

Clark, I.E., Romero-Calderon, R., Olson, J.M., Jaworski, L., Lopatto, D., and Banerjee, U. (2009). Deconstructing scientific research: A practical and scalable pedagogical tool to provide evidence-bases science instruction. *PLoS Biology, 7*(12), e1000264. Available: http://journals.plos.org/plosbiology/article?id=10.1371/journal.pbio.1000264 [December 2016].

Coyle, E.J., Allebach, J.P., and Garton Krueger, J. (June 2006). *The Vertically Integrated Projects (VIP) Program in ECE at Purdue: Fully integrating undergraduate education and graduate research.* Paper presented at the Proceedings of the 2006 ASEE Annual Conference and Exposition, Chicago, IL. Pp. 11.1336.1-11.1336.16. Available: https://peer.asee.org/1421 [November 2016].

Coyle, E.J., Krogmeier, J.V., Abler, R.T., Johnson, A., Marshall, S., and Gilchrist, B.E. (2016). The Vertically Integrated Projects (VIP) Program: Leveraging faculty research interests to transform undergraduate STEM education. Pp. 223-234 in G.C. Weaver, W.D. Burgess, A.L. Childress, and L. Slakey (Eds.), *Transforming Institutions: Undergraduate STEM Education for the 21st Century.* West Lafayette, IN: Purdue University Press.

Dolan, E. (2016). *Course-Based Undergraduate Research Experiences: Current Knowledge and Future Directions.* Paper commissioned for the Committee on Strengthening Research Experiences for Undergraduate STEM Students. Board on Science Education, Division of Behavioral and Social Sciences and Education. Board on Life Sciences, Division of Earth and Life Studies. National Academies of Sciences, Engineering, and Medicine.

Eby, L.T., Rhodes, J.E., and Allen, T.D. (2007). Definition and evolution of mentoring. Pp. 1-20 In T.D. Allen and L.T. Eby (Eds), *Blackwell Handbook of Mentoring.* Oxford: Blackwell Publishing.

Free, R., Griffith, S., and Spellman, B. (2015). Faculty workload issues connected to undergraduate research. *New Directions for Higher Education, 2015(169),* 51-60.

Gates, A.Q., Teller, P.J., Bernat, A., Delgado, N., and Della-Piana, C.K. (1999). Expanding participation in undergraduate research using the Affinity Group model. *Journal of Engineering Education, 88(4),* 409-414.

Gnanapragasam, N. (2008). Industrially sponsored senior capstone experience: Program implementation and assessment. *Journal of Professional Issues in Engineering Education and Practice, 134(3),* 257-262.

Gottesman, A.J., and Hoskin, S.G. (2012). CREATE cornerstone: Introduction to scientific thinking, a new course for STEM-interested freshmen, demystifies scientific thinking through analysis of scientific literature. *CBE–Life Sciences Education, 12(1),* 59-72.

Hakim, T.M. (2000). *How to Develop and Administer Institutional Undergraduate Research Programs.* Washington, DC: Council on Undergraduate Research.

Hanna, A.S., and Sullivan, K.T. (2005). Bridging the gap between academics and practice: A capstone design experience. *Journal of Professional Issues in Engineering Education and Practice, 131(1),* 59-62.

Hatfull, G.F., Pedulla, M.L., Jacobs-Sera, D., Cichon, P.M., Foley, A., Ford, M.E. Gonda, R.M., Houtz, J.M., Hryckowian, A.M., Kelchner, V.A., Namburi, S., Pajcini, K.V., Popovish, M.G., Schleicher, D.T., Simanek, B.Z., Smith, A.L., Zdanowicz, G.M., Kumar, V., Peebles, C.L., Jacobs Jr., W.R., Lawrence, J.G., and Hendrix, R. (2006). Exploring the mycobacteriophage metaproteome: Phage genomics as an educational platform. *PLoS Genetics, 2(6),* e92. Available: http://journals.plos.org/plosgenetics/article?id=10.1371/journal.pgen.0020092 [February 2017].

Hirsch, L.S., Kimmel, H., Rockland, R., and Bloom, J. (2005). Implementing pre-engineering curricula in high school science and mathematics. *Frontiers in Education Conference, 35(3),* S2F21-S2F26.

Jordan, T.C., Burnett, S.H., Carson, S., Caruso, S.M., Clase, K., DeJong, R.J., Dennehy, J.J., Denver, D.R., Dunbar, D., Elgin, S.C.R., Findley, A.M., Gissendanner, C.R., Golebiewska, U.P., Guild, N., Hartzog, G.A., Grillo, W.H., Hollowell, G.P., Hughes, L.E., Johnson, A., King, R.A., Lewis, L.O., Li, W., Vazquez, E., Ware, V.C., Barker, L.P., Bradley, K.W., Jacobs-Sera, D., Pope, W.H., Russell, D.A., Cresawn, S.G., Lopatto, D., Bailey, C.P., and Hatfull, G.F. (2014). A broadly implementable research course in phage discovery and genomics for first-year undergraduate students. *MBio, 5(1),* e01051-13. Available: http://mbio.asm.org/content/5/1/e01051-13.full.pdf [February 2017].

Kierniesky, N.C. (2005). Undergraduate research in small psychology departments: Two decades later. *Teaching of Psychology, 32*(2), 84-90.

Kortz, K.M., and van der Hoeven Kraft, K.J. (2016). Geoscience Education Research Project: Student benefits and effective design of a course-based undergraduate research experience. *Journal of Geoscience Education, 64*(1), 24-36.

Kovac, J. (1991). A capstone experience in chemistry. *Journal of Chemical Education, 68*(11), 907-910.

Kram, K.E. (1985). *Mentoring at Work: Developmental Relationships in Organizational Life.* Glenview, IL: Scott, Foresman.

Lopatto, D., Hauser, C., Jones, C.J., Paetkau, D., Chandrasekaran, V., Dunbar, D., MacKinnon, C., Stamm, J., Alvarez, C., and Barnard, D. (2014). A central support system can facilitate implementation and sustainability of a classroom-based undergraduate research experience (CURE) in genomics. *CBE–Life Sciences Education, 13*, 711-723.

Merkel, C.A. (2001). *Undergraduate research at six research universities: A Pilot Study for the Association of American Universities.* Pasadena, CA: California Institute of Technology. Available: http://www.aau.edu/workarea/downloadasset.aspx?id=1900 [February 2017].

Miller, J.E., and Walston, T. (2010). Interdisciplinary training in mathematical biology through team-based undergraduate research and courses. *CBE–Life Sciences Education, 9*, 284-289.

National Research Council. (2006). *America's Lab Report: Investigations in High School Science.* S.R. Singer, M.L. Hilton, and H.A. Schweingruber (Eds.). Committee on High School Science Laboratories: Role and Vision. Board on Science Education, Division of Behavioral and Social Sciences and Education. Washington, DC: The National Academies Press.

National Research Council. (2007). *Rising Above the Gathering Storm: Energizing and Employing America for a Brighter Economic Future.* Committee on Prospering in the Global Economy of the 21st Century: An Agenda for American Science and Technology. Committee on Science, Engineering, and Public Policy. Washington, DC: The National Academies Press.

National Research Council. (2012). *A Framework for K-12 Science Education: Practices, Crosscutting Concepts, and Core Ideas.* Committee on a Conceptual Framework for New K-12 Science Education Standards. Board on Science Education, Division of Behavioral and Social Sciences and Education. Washington, DC: The National Academies Press.

Next Generation Science Standards Lead States. (2013). *Next Generation Science Standards: For States, by States.* Available: http://www.nextgenscience.org [February 2017].

Pukkila, P., DeCosmo, J., Swick, D.C., and Arnold, M.S. (2007). How to engage in collaborative curriculum design to foster undergraduate inquiry and research in all disciplines. Pp. 341-357 in K.K. Karukstis and T.E. Elgren (Eds.), *Developing and Sustaining a Research-supportive Curriculum: A Compendium of Successful Practices.* Washington, DC: Council on Undergraduate Research.

Reinen, L., Grasfils, E., Gaines, R., and Hazlett, R. (2007). Integrating research into a small geology department's curriculum. Pp. 331-339 in K.K. Karukstis and T.E. Elgren (Eds.), *Developing and Sustaining a Research-supportive Curriculum: A Compendium of Successful Practices.* Washington, DC: Council on Undergraduate Research.

Rhodes, J.E. (2005). A theoretical model of youth mentoring. Pp. 30-43 in D.L. DuBois and M.J. Karcher (Eds.), *Handbook of Youth Mentoring.* Thousand Oakes, CA: Sage Press.

Rueckert, L. (2007). Flexible curricular structures to provide time for research within the classroom. Pp. 285-294 in K.K. Karukstis and T.E. Elgren (Eds.), *Developing and Sustaining a Research-supportive Curriculum: A Compendium of Successful Practices.*Washington, DC: Council on Undergraduate Research.

Russell, C.B., Bentley, A.K., Wink, D.J., and Weaver. G.C. (2009). Materials development for a research-based undergraduate laboratory curriculum. *The Chemical Educator, 14*, 55-60.

Saad, A. (March 2007). *Senior Capstone Design Experiences for ABET Accredited Undergraduate Electrical and Computer Engineering Education.* Paper presented at the Proceedings of the 2007 IEEE Southeast Conference, pp. 294-299. Available: http://ieeexplore.ieee.org/abstract/document/4147435/ [February 2017].

Schneider, K.R., and Bickel, A. (2015). Modeling undergraduate research: Matching graduate students with first-year mentees. *CUR Quarterly, 36*(1), 25-31.

Schneider, K.R., Bickel, A., and Morrison-Shetlar, A. (2015). Planning and implementing a comprehensive student-centered research program for first-year STEM undergraduates. *Journal of College Science Teaching, 44*(3), 37-43.

Spurrier, J.D. (2001). A capstone course for undergraduate statistics majors. *Journal of Statistics Education, 9*(1). Available: http://ww2.amstat.org/publications/jse/v9n1/spurrier.html [December 2016].

Temple, L., Sibley, T., and Orr, A.J. (2010). *How to Mentor Undergraduate Research.* Washington, DC: Council on Undergraduate Research.

Wagenaar, T.C. (1993). The capstone course. *Teaching Sociology, 21*(3), 209-214.

3

Undergraduate Research Experiences in the Larger System of Higher Education: A Conceptual Framework

National reform efforts have begun to look at undergraduate research experiences (UREs) as a potential mechanism to encourage interest and retention within science, technology, engineering, and mathematics (STEM) fields. This interest has resulted in an overall increase in the funding and implementation of URE-oriented programs over the past decade. From the committee's review of the extant literature on UREs, it is clear that there is a substantial range in the type and design of URE programs. The committee has developed the conceptual framework presented here to help designers, researchers, and evaluators organize their thinking about UREs. The committee sought to create a framework that would take into account two different components that contribute to the design, implementation, and evaluation of UREs. The first part of the framework articulates the goals for students participating in UREs and how these goals are related to different features of UREs, giving rise to a set of design principles. The second part characterizes the multiple systemic factors of the higher education landscape and how UREs are situated within that context.

The chapter begins with a review of the goals for student outcomes that have been associated with UREs. This review is followed by a discussion on the design of UREs that reflect the varied goals for students. The chapter concludes with a review of the relevant systemic factors (institutional, departmental, disciplinary, and financial), as well as policy issues impacting undergraduate research.

GOALS FOR STUDENTS PARTICIPATING IN
UNDERGRADUATE RESEARCH

Reviewing the extant literature on programs of undergraduate research, the committee found several different themes for the goals that have informed the design and evaluation of UREs. As described in Chapter 1, programs of undergraduate research arose from national calls that encouraged institutions to provide high-impact practices that would allow students to better face the challenges of the 21st century (Boyer Commission on Education of Undergraduates in the Research University, 1998). The focus of these reports was to find opportunities that helped to keep students in STEM programs to support workforce needs (Auchincloss et al., 2014; Brownell et al., 2015; Litzinger et al., 2011). Therefore, retention and persistence in STEM fields was a primary motivating factor.

As more programs developed, the emphasis of the research on UREs began to shift away from simply trying to determine whether UREs led to retention in STEM (majors and graduation) and toward understanding why these programs had an effect. Evaluation of the programs began to look at student outcomes, such as content learning, and affective outcomes, such as whether URE students like doing research more than non-URE peers. Framing the questions in this way has begun to set the stage for uncovering answers about the importance of UREs not only for the purposes of keeping students in STEM majors or developing the STEM workforce, but also for their potential to have broader impacts on the citizenry.

Synthesizing across the literature and based upon the committee's experience, we identified the primary goals for UREs to include developing and supporting students' identities as researchers, increasing student knowledge of STEM content, increasing feelings of belonging in STEM, improving the understanding of the research enterprise, promoting greater ability to engage with STEM issues they will face as citizens, developing academic skills and strategies, increasing student persistence in STEM fields, and guiding student decisions about STEM courses and careers (Blockus, 2016; Dolan, 2016; Pfund, 2016). The outcomes students gain from UREs are shaped by how the experiences are constructed by faculty and supported by the department; institution; professional organizations; and external policy, accreditation, and funding structures at the state and national levels (Blockus, 2016; Dolan, 2016). As discussed in later sections of this chapter, these external factors influence which of the potential goals are prioritized by URE designers and implementers and also the details of how, when, and where UREs are implemented.

We discuss the goals for students participating in UREs under three major categories: (1) increasing retention and persistence of students in STEM, (2) promoting STEM disciplinary knowledge and practices, and

(3) integrating students into STEM culture (see Figure 3-1). These categories were determined by organizing the literature into themes that captured the primary motivations discussed above, whether it be participation/retention (category 1), cognitive outcomes (category 2), or affective outcomes (category 3). As discussed in Chapter 2, URE designers make choices about which goals to emphasize depending on their situation (e.g., how the URE fits into the curriculum, background of the students) and the types of

---

INCREASE PARTICIPATION & RETENTION OF STEM STUDENTS

Participation in STEM courses (for nonmajors)
Retention in STEM major
Continued enrollment and/or graduation/degree completion
Enrollment in graduate education
Confirmation/clarification of career path
Develop STEM literacy

PROMOTE STEM DISCIPLINARY KNOWLEDGE & PRACTICES

Learn content information
Develop skills/techniques
Understand concepts/research questions
Know importance of iteration
Appreciate value of teamwork
Reflect on one's work

Utilize disciplinary research practices:
- Ask questions and define problems
- Develop and use models
- Plan and carry out investigations
- Analyze and interpret data
- Use mathematics and computational thinking
- Construct explanations and design solutions
- Engage in argumentation from evidence
- Obtain, evaluate, and communicate information

INTEGRATE STUDENTS INTO STEM CULTURE

Increase interest in STEM field
Promote agency and develop STEM identity
Increase ownership of project
Become enculturated or socialized into STEM community
Commit to the discipline
Act professionally
Perform work as collaborative member of team
Develop a sense of belonging/inclusion
Recognize and overcome stereotype threat

FIGURE 3-1 Goals for students participating in UREs.

students participating in the URE. They select methods for implementing these goals based on their beliefs about how students learn.

For example, an overarching goal of student participation in UREs, as part of an undergraduate's overall STEM learning experience, could include increasing conceptual understanding of relevant disciplinary knowledge, to learn to conduct an investigation, and to develop "literacy" for STEM. That is, the goal might not always be to persist in a STEM discipline but to be an informed citizen and a savvy consumer of scientific information in order to know how to make reasonable conclusions and arguments based on the strength of evidence. Any single URE may be designed to emphasize some goals and not others. For example, for students making decisions about STEM courses and careers, STEM majors might be inspired by their URE to continue to graduate school or get a job in a STEM field because of a love of research, whereas others may decide against these paths because they do not enjoy research; nonmajors may make progress toward becoming more STEM literate.

Overall, the goals presented here for students participating in UREs could be viewed through the lens of research on learning and instruction as it provides a way of thinking about the mechanisms that lead to outcomes (National Academy of Sciences, National Academy of Engineering, Institute of Medicine, 2005; National Research Council, 2000a, 2000b, 2006, 2009, 2012). This research provides a context for considering how learners' and designers' existing understanding and beliefs influence how UREs impact remembering, reasoning, solving problems, and acquiring new knowledge. Each of the primary goals are described in more detail below.

Increase Retention and Persistence of Students in STEM

A primary goal of UREs, driven by national-level calls for reform, is to improve STEM education in an effort to strengthen the STEM workforce. Research has suggested that participation in UREs could improve student outcomes such as higher grade point averages and increased retention in STEM majors, as well as an associated increase in college completion. (Chapter 4 provides a more nuanced discussion of these outcomes.) In this context, UREs are seen as a potential way to increase retention of students in STEM majors through graduation. Many argue that since UREs allow students to engage in the work of a STEM researcher, this experience can provide confirmation/clarification of their intended career paths (Auchincloss et al., 2014; Corwin et al., 2015). These paths might include pursuing opportunities outside of STEM by becoming a more literate citizen. Alternatively, the student may matriculate into a graduate program and/or enter into the STEM workforce.

Promote STEM Disciplinary Knowledge and Practices

To persist in a field, one must acquire knowledge about it. UREs seek to help students to better understand what it means to do research and what the process entails. This understanding consists of (at least) three parts: (1) understanding the disciplinary knowledge related to the topic under investigation and how the research questions fit within the landscape of the discipline, (2) development of the requisite research skills, and (3) understanding of the research enterprise and how disciplinary knowledge is built. Understanding the research enterprise includes being able to use disciplinary research practices (see Figure 3-1 for a list of these practices), understanding the importance of interaction, and appreciating the value of teamwork.

For students to develop a conceptual understanding of how a research question fits within the landscape of the discipline, they must also develop the relevant content knowledge associated with the field. That is, students need to understand the nature of the research discipline, be it science, engineering, or math. As discussed in *How People Learn* (National Research Council, 2000b) and *Discipline-Based Education Research* (National Research Council, 2012), learning is not only the accrual of information but also a process of conceptual reorganization. This has been explained as a process in which individuals actively seek to make sense of new knowledge by connecting it with prior knowledge and experience (National Research Council, 2015).

To develop coherent and robust understanding of a URE's research question and related content knowledge, students need to sort out their existing ideas along with the new ideas they encounter as part of that URE. Often, new ideas have a fleeting trajectory, and the pre-existing ideas students bring to research experiences (and STEM courses) have been used and refined over multiple experiences. Therefore, a goal for UREs is to encourage students to engage in a process of distinguishing among ideas so that their understanding of the research topic grows, based on the evidence and their experience (diSessa, 1996; Johri and Olds, 2011; Linn, 1995; Linn and Eylon, 2011; Litzinger et al., 2011). Meaningful collaborative experiences can also facilitate student learning about STEM content as students engage in research (Cortright et al., 2003; Johnson et al., 1998, 2007).

Research suggests that students can enhance their understanding when opportunities for reflection are embedded within the learning experience (Weinstein et al., 2000), despite few students reporting the spontaneous use of such strategies (Karpicke et al., 2009; National Research Council, 2015). For example, in engineering education, Svinicki and McKeachie (2011) reported that incorporating reflection steps and self-explanation prompts into instruction led to improvements in students' problem solving. In this way, UREs can promote the goal of developing STEM disciplinary knowledge by providing students with the opportunity to engage in reflection.

Moreover, to capture the nature of actual STEM research in UREs, instructors and mentors can broaden student understanding by noting and explicating their own frustrations when things do not go as planned, thereby highlighting the importance of iteration and refinement. For example, when instructors make their own thinking visible, they can reveal the wrong paths and complexities of software design (Clancy et al., 2003), the struggles involved in mathematical thinking (Schoenfeld, 2010), and the challenges of scientific reasoning (Clement, 2009). Used this way, UREs can promote an understanding of the research process in a way that lectures and explanations in traditional STEM course delivery cannot, as these approaches often articulate the outcome rather than the process that led to the insights from a line of research. Although in a traditional lecture course, faculty *can* emphasize the process and not just the outcomes, it is possible that this type of understanding can be solidified when students are active participants in the process. Situating students within a URE can allow students to get a sense of the process of conjecture, refinement, redesign, and reconceptualization involved in the research enterprise, while developing the requisite research skills (Johri and Olds, 2011; Koretsky et al., 2011; Litzinger et al., 2011).

Integrate Students into STEM Culture

In addition to promoting STEM disciplinary knowledge and practices, research experiences are intended to promote a sense of agency and identity as a STEM research professional by engaging students in the work and situating them in the disciplinary context. Several studies show that students can develop a sense of identity as a STEM professional by engaging in well-designed activities typical of STEM professionals. Activities that can promote a sense of agency include being involved in designing their own studies, choosing experimental methods, and collecting data that are of intrinsic interest; all these activities encourage autonomy and allow for a greater sense of project ownership (Corwin et al., 2015). As Corwin and colleagues noted, providing students with the opportunity to gain a sense of ownership may increase the students' motivation to complete projects even when faced with challenges, which can further develop their sense of scientific self-efficacy.

Related to the development of agency and STEM identity, providing opportunities for students to be integrated into the STEM culture or providing them with a STEM experience that is sensitive to the students' cultural background may be an additional aspect of this goal. As alluded to previously, students may have an ill-formed idea of what it means to do research and therefore may not know what it means to be a STEM researcher. Academic enculturation—situating students in the social and environmental context of the research so that they can learn/acquire the values of the discipline—through UREs may help to shape not only student's learning but also their identity as a STEM researcher (Mendoza et al., 2015; Prior and Bilbro, 2012).

Alternatively, dominant STEM culture may be uninviting to students from nondominant cultures. UREs allow students to "experience" research, sometimes in a new context, and might help them better understand and appreciate the work that is involved (Litzinger et al., 2011). For example, Visintainer and Linn (2015) found that individuals from nondominant cultures gained a sense of identity by participating in programs led by mentors who came from similar cultural backgrounds and imparted respect for engaging in STEM-based practices such as collecting data, analyzing data, and presenting their findings to high status individuals. That is, UREs could make STEM accessible by making the discipline-specific topics understandable and relevant to the learner and by providing a culturally aware environment (National Research Council, 2012). Designing an environment that communicates these understandings requires a culturally aware design team.

Substantial research illustrates that students often feel that the STEM disciplinary topics they encounter in classes are inaccessible and irrelevant to their lives (Barr et al., 2010). This is especially true for students from nondominant cultures who may have met fewer scientists than those from dominant cultures and who hold different value systems (Hurtado et al., 2010; Ong et al., 2011). Students have reported through surveys or interviews that mentors helped them learn how to pursue research problems and develop resilience to inevitable failures (Adedokun et al., 2012; Hernandez et al. 2013; Schwarz, 2012). When students embark on personally selected problems with uncertain outcomes and feel that their work is respected, they have the potential to learn a great deal about the nature of research and about their own identity as an investigator, which can create a sense of belonging to the STEM community of researchers (e.g., Johri and Olds, 2011; Pryor et al., 2007) and lead to persistence (Estrada et al., 2011).

Another important component associated with the goal of integrating students into the STEM culture is collaboration and teamwork. To address complex, systemic problems such as climate change, disease vectors, and the motility of organisms, multiple perspectives are needed. For such reasons, many programs of research are multidisciplinary, capitalizing on the multiple forms of experiences that can lead to innovative methods for solving complex problems. Learning from others with different experiences who can give hints and encouragement rather than providing immediate solutions is a hallmark of complex research programs (Johnson and Johnson,

1998; Linn and Hsi, 2000; Vygotsky, 1978). Although working in groups can be beneficial, groups often find communicating and collaborating difficult due to different cultural or methodological practices. To help better prepare students for working in multidisciplinary and diverse groups, one goal for UREs is to provide opportunities for collaboration. Hurtado and colleagues (2008) identified competencies for a multicultural world as including the abilities to interact with individuals from different social identity groups and to negotiate ethical decisions in situations characterized by inequality and conflict.

DESIGN PRINCIPLES FOR URES

There has been a growing emphasis on engaging students in research and inquiry and how to make curricular changes that will best support this high-impact practice (Brew, 2013; Koretsky et al., 2011). The learning sciences provide a grounding for considering the instructional practices that allow for effective learning experiences (Brew, 2013; Johri and Olds, 2011; Litzinger et al., 2011). Many STEM disciplines have been using the ideas developed by learning sciences to ensure that the experiences undergraduate students receive while conducting research are optimally designed (Brownell and Kloser, 2015; Litzinger et al., 2011). However, it is not always clear to what degree existing UREs have been designed using the extent literature on pedagogy and the learning sciences. To follow up on our discussion of goals for students in the previous section (increasing retention and persistence in STEM, promoting STEM disciplinary knowledge and practices, and integrating students into STEM culture), the committee drew on the robust research base on how to support students' learning in STEM and mapped these goals to the common elements of UREs. This exercise allowed us to articulate a set of design principles for UREs.

The design, implementation, and evaluation of UREs depend on the interactions among designers, instructors, researchers, evaluators, students, and instructional resources. The design team negotiates the goals for the URE, taking into consideration the systemic factors in the higher education setting (such as available resources, reward structure for faculty, and disciplinary certification programs). To gain some traction on how to think about the design and evaluation of UREs, the committee identified characteristics that typify UREs (see Chapter 2 for an in-depth discussion) and might distinguish them from other courses and experiences. These principles for design are listed in Figure 3-2 and grouped into four categories: (1) make STEM research accessible and relevant; (2) support students to learn from each other; (3) make thinking visible; and (4) promote autonomy. URE leaders need to assist undergraduates to integrate the experiences, activities, mentoring, and assignments they encounter as

Make STEM research accessible and relevant

- Focus on significant, relevant problems of interest to STEM professionals, and in some cases a broader community from which students come (e.g., civic engagement).
- Allow students to master specific research techniques.
- Understand the process of research and design by generating novel information and using iterative refinement.

Promote autonomy

- While providing structured guidance from a mentor, also provide opportunities for student decisions, promoting student ownership over time.
- Engage students in research practices including the ability to argue from evidence.

Learn from each other

- Emphasize and expect collaboration and teamwork.
- Require communication of results, either through publication or presentations in various STEM venues.

Make thinking visible

- Help students engage in reflection about their knowledge of problems being investigated and the work being undertaken to address those problems.

FIGURE 3-2 Characteristics of UREs organized around the committee's design principles.

they participate in UREs and to connect these experiences with their prior experiences and education. Consideration also needs to be given to how students will be assessed. Preliminary work by Brownell and Kloser (2015) has begun to explore this issue for course-based UREs (CUREs). This section explores how thinking about the four categories of characteristics can assist in URE design and how to foster knowledge integration for each learner.

Make STEM Research Accessible and Relevant

UREs can help students recognize the relevance of their STEM courses by situating the investigation in the context of a personally relevant, contemporary problem such as climate change, global health, human genetics, or earthquake safety (e.g., Jordan et al., 2014). UREs can make STEM accessible by illustrating the role of knowledge, culture, and identity in STEM and policy decision making (Barton, 1998; Keller, 2016; Lemke, 1990). Relevant topics motivate students to continue to explore the topic even after the course is completed (Wigfield et al., 2007). Designing UREs so students can explore a topic that is relevant to their lives can promote identity in STEM (Johri and Olds, 2011).

Understanding the underlying theories and concepts in a research project is essential for students to make sense of and engage in STEM practices (Thiry et al., 2012). Students may not have taken courses that support the concepts, topics, or ideas that underlie their URE projects. These students, therefore, may not recognize the importance of the research question or its relevance for their lives. Some students only begin to feel capable of understanding the work of the URE by the third semester of their URE placement (Feldman et al., 2013). An important role for instructors and mentors is to design the URE so the rationale for the research questions is accessible. This may involve activities to help students connect the research design and potential contributions of the URE project to their prior knowledge. It will also include explicitly clarifying for students what role *they* will play in moving the research project forward and how their contribution will fit in to the big picture of the research project.

UREs can make STEM disciplinary knowledge accessible by helping students build on their existing ideas. It is not sufficient for URE instructors or mentors to articulate accurate ideas and expect students to incorporate them into their understanding of the field. Instead, students benefit from making predictions to identify their prior knowledge. UREs can allow students to distinguish among their own diverse ideas as well as the new ideas by using evidence from experiments, observations, or other sources that they obtain during the URE. Research has identified promising ways to guide students to distinguish among ideas (e.g., Quintana et al., 2004).

To succeed in STEM, students need opportunities to organize often contradictory, fragmented, and disconnected ideas along with the new ideas they encounter. Knowledge that is organized and coherent is easier to remember because there are multiple links between items that can aid in recall. Organizing knowledge involves noticing patterns, relationships, and discrepancies among ideas (Reif and St. John, 1979). Moreover, when students develop integrated, organized understanding, they have knowledge that can be used to solve new problems.

Students often have difficulty applying their knowledge in a new context. One way to create the potential for transferring ideas about the process skills or competencies that are most important for UREs is to help students develop an understanding of the core concepts and patterns, in addition to the requisite skills, that can serve as a structure for organizing knowledge (Bransford and Schwartz, 2009). Spending a lot of time studying material and practicing its application is not sufficient to promote transfer of knowledge and skills; what matters is *how* this time is spent (Bjork and Bjork, 2011). The goal is to spend time on activities that promote deeper learning. To start, students need complex, realistic problems that encourage extracting relevant information and analyzing it against prior knowledge. They need to apply the research process to new situations (Shaffer, 2012).

One way that designers can determine whether they have succeeded in making the topics of the URE accessible is by assessing the products that students prepare such as posters, journals, research reports, and presentations. Other forms of student success will require different assessments that measure understanding of the research process or of the nature of STEM. Students are more likely to produce products that feature integrated ideas and identify patterns in results or data when the problems they study are accessible and illustrate the process of linking and connecting ideas (Linn and Eylon, 2011).

Promote Autonomy

A salient aspect of UREs is that they have the potential to promote autonomy. In a STEM research context, autonomy may be characterized as the ability to initiate research activities and carry them to completion by taking advantage of multiple resources including peers, experts, technologies, and media. This concept of autonomy is consistent with Hurtado and colleagues (2012, p. 50), who called for developing "habits of mind [that] involve the way students integrate different sources of knowledge." UREs can promote autonomy by giving students the opportunity to make decisions about the problem to be studied, the research design, and the appropriate methodology to use (Bjork et al., 2013). Designers of UREs can carefully design tasks and opportunities for students to gradually develop skills that are necessary to promote autonomy (Brew, 2013).

As part of promoting autonomy, instructors can take advantage of reflection. By building a practice of reflecting on their evidence and identifying consistencies and open questions, students may develop autonomy. This is essential for achieving durable research understanding.

Linn's (2006) *knowledge integration framework* calls for engaging students in distinguishing between their existing ideas and new ideas. In this process, students use many of the reasoning strategies desired in STEM fields, such as drawing on evidence and forming arguments to reach conclusions. Activities that require students to generate their own explanations of concepts or explain a concept to another person are thought of as revealing an element of reflection. Studies indicate that these "self-explanation" strategies can enhance learning more than just having students read a passage or examine the diagrams in a textbook (National Research Council, 2012). To assess student ability to investigate research dilemmas autonomously, designers can examine the progress students make in UREs as reflected in the products they create, such as research reports or posters for meetings. Another approach is to build online miniprojects that could reveal student progress in developing these skills; some such assessments employ automated scoring, an advantage when increasing the size of a program (e.g., Liu et al., 2016; Quellmalz et al. 2012).

Learn from Each Other

Research increasingly involves collaboration and learning from others as problems become more and more complex (e.g., Cook-Deegan, 1994). Many argue that students learn more effectively when they collaborate (Brown and Campione, 1994; Linn and Hsi, 2000; Vygotsky, 1978). Yet collaboration is not universally efficient or effective for learning (Kollar et al., 2007; Webb, 1997). To benefit from collaboration, students often need to learn how to learn from each other. When students work together on well-designed learning activities, they establish a community of learners that provides cognitive and social support for the efforts of the community's individual members. In such a community, students share the responsibility for thinking and doing. They can help each other solve problems by building on each other's knowledge, asking each other questions, and suggesting ideas that an individual working alone might not have considered (Brown and Campione, 1994; Okita and Schwartz, 2013). By challenging each other's thoughts and beliefs, they can compel the members of the group to be explicit about what they mean and to negotiate any conflicts that arise, which in turn fosters metacognition. Social interactions may also have a positive effect on motivation by making individuals feel they are contributing something to others (Schwartz, 1999). Facilitating interactions among various cultural groups could help improve student's communication skills while also integrating students into the research enterprise (Hurtado et al., 2008). Supporting and promoting collaboration has potential for UREs (Brownell et al., 2015). However, orchestrating collaboration is difficult. Students must be able to respect the ideas of their peers, negotiate meaning, and guide peers who are less able.

Make Thinking Visible

Individual students come to UREs with a complex set of ideas stemming from their own cultural identity, previous academic experiences, and personal reflection. Students might have specific ideas about STEM-related topics, but they might also have "knowledge in pieces." That is, the ideas might be fragmented and contradictory (diSessa, 2000). As noted above, students may need to distinguish new ideas and prior knowledge.

An important step in helping students learn and gain a better understanding of the research enterprise is to ask them to make their ideas visible. When students are asked to articulate their existing ideas, they reveal to themselves and their mentors/instructors the current understanding that they have developed about a topic. Previous research has shown that student's knowledge can be assessed by asking them to make predictions about phenomena. Students develop better conceptual understanding when they make predictions than when they do not (Linn and Songer, 1991; Mayer et al., 2003; White and Gunstone, 1992). In addition, the process of reflecting and explaining their reasoning often helps students recognize flaws in their own reasoning (Collins and Brown, 1988).

Encouraging students to make their thinking visible both when they generate explanations and when they revise them can promote knowledge integration. These activities can set in motion a process of revisiting STEM-specific issues when they arise in new contexts, such as news articles or public lectures. Autonomous learners sort out their existing ideas and integrate them with new ideas in order to continue to build coherent understanding. By practicing reflection regularly, students can develop the ability to monitor their own progress and to recognize new connections as they arise.

Reflection is common when STEM professionals maintain notebooks where they record results and identify trends. Instructors and mentors can encourage students to maintain notebooks and use them to make their thinking visible. They can ask students to include discussions of their struggles to conduct their project and the limitations of their work. In CUREs, instructors can include essay examinations rather than relying on multiple-choice questions to instill a practice of reflection. This approach has the advantage of being both part of the instruction and a source of insights into student progress (Lee et al., 2011).

SYSTEMIC FACTORS IMPACTING URES

Programs of undergraduate research are nested within multiple contexts. There are systemic factors—national and state policy, institutions, and departments and disciplines—that can have a top-down influence by promoting opportunities or placing constraints on UREs through reforms and funding. There are also more-local factors involved in the implementation of UREs—that is, designers (including faculty, mentors, and evaluators) and students.

As described in Chapter 2, UREs are heterogeneous, which is not surprising given the variation in systemic factors and the diverse views of student learning held by the key actors. They vary on multiple dimensions. Programs of undergraduate research can differ in terms of leadership (i.e., who is responsible for the program), design, and duration. UREs also can vary in expectations or goals for students, mentoring provided, value for career trajectory (e.g., strengthen likelihood of graduate school admissions or industry employment, preparation as an informed citizen), and measured outcomes, as well as the population(s) served (e.g., STEM majors, non-majors, historically underrepresented students, first generation students). Moreover, UREs can vary in how they are funded and how they are situated within the university. Given this variability, it can be challenging to cleanly categorize UREs and even more difficult to identify how many programs of any given type are being offered. (Chapter 2 provides a more in-depth discussion of program types.) In fact, data on the number of students who participate in UREs nationally is not systematically collected, although some funders do collect data on programs they sponsor.

Systemic factors include variation in institutional support (e.g., rare in community college, common in small liberal arts colleges), extramural funding, disciplinary expectations (e.g., common in chemistry and engineering, less common in mathematics, and rare in computer science), faculty motivation (e.g., improve instruction, make the laboratory experience more relevant and meaningful, meet funding requirement), and faculty rewards (e.g., no reward, release from course-teaching requirement, enhancement of research capability, value for promotion). In short, the substantial heterogeneity of UREs across multiple dimensions is due in part to the nature of the higher education system. These systemic factors interact with each other as shown in Figure 3-3. That is, national and state-level policies interact with institutional and/or departmental policies to shape opportunities and place constraints on UREs. A discussion of each of these three systemic factors and their impacts on UREs follows.

National and State Policy

As highlighted in Chapter 1, there have been many calls for reform focused on making undergraduate STEM education "more practical, relevant, engaging, and grounded in research on how people learn" (Laursen et al., 2010, p. 7). One of the major catalysts for this national-level reform was the Boyer Commission (Boyer Commission on Education of Undergraduates in the Research University, 1998), which issued a report calling for research-based learning to become the standard in undergraduate education, particularly at research universities. Moreover, national bodies have called for increasing opportunities that are student-centered and inquiry-based in STEM disciplines (Kuh, 2008; National Research Council, 1999; National Science Foundation, 1996).

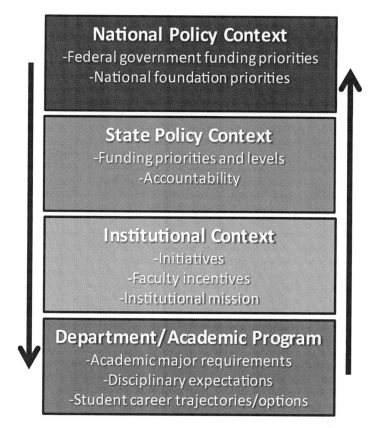

FIGURE 3-3 Connections among systemic factors. The arrows along the side indicate that the interaction among these factors occurs in both a top-down and bottom-up direction.

Although these national-level calls for reform can encourage funding for undergraduate research, new initiatives can also shift research priorities and the types of projects that are funded, which can have substantial impacts on broader opportunities for students to engage in research. Several organizations, such as the National Science Foundation (NSF), the Howard Hughes Medical Institute (HHMI), and the National Institutes of Health, have developed funding initiatives specifically targeted at increasing access to UREs for more diverse students. An external review conducted by Russell and colleagues (2007) of NSF's funding for undergraduate research suggested that engaging students in undergraduate research was associated with positive outcomes, such as increasing the undergraduates understanding, confidence, and awareness of the importance of research.

For example, the National Institutes of Health has developed two initiatives geared toward increasing the participation of historically underrepresented groups in the biomedical sciences by providing them with access to resources and preparation for graduate-level work. The Maximizing Access to Research Careers/Undergraduate Student Training in Academic Research initiative[1] provides support to undergraduate, honors-level, junior and senior students. In contrast, the Research Initiative for Scientific Enhancement (RISE) program aims to reduce the gap between underrepresented and non-underrepresented students in Ph.D. degree completions by providing support to institutions. This RISE funding can be used to pay salaries to undergraduates participating in research.[2]

HHMI provides funding through multiple mechanisms and encourages colleges and universities to build "capacity to effectively engage all students in science," which includes transfer students from community colleges, first generation students, and historically underrepresented students.[3] For example, HHMI has funded the development, implementation, and expansion of the Freshman Research Initiative at The University of Texas at Austin. Thousands of freshmen students have participated in this initiative since 2006 (Rodenbusch et al., 2016). Students in this program (40 percent of the incoming freshman class) join a "research stream" in which they engage in progressively more intense research experiences over time. For more information on this initiative, see Box 2-9 in Chapter 2.

NSF also has a portfolio dedicated to supporting UREs, called Research Experiences for Undergraduates (REU) that provides funding for programs and projects that encourage active research participation by undergraduate students.[4] Over the years, REU has experienced increases in both the number of awards granted each year and the amount of money being awarded. For this report, the committee used the DIA2 tool[5] to extract the number of awards and the award amount per year for REU grants from 1995 to 2015. Figure 3-4 depicts this gradual increase from 1995 through 2015 in number of awards (left side) and total award amount (right side); there is a relative plateau beginning around 2007 for both measures of funding level.

Although external funding provides essential resources, it also imposes

---

[1] See https://www.nigms.nih.gov/Training/MARC/Pages/USTARAwards.aspx [February 2017].

[2] See https://www.nigms.nih.gov/training/RISE/Pages/default.aspx [February 2017].

[3] See http://www.hhmi.org/programs/undergraduate-science-education-grants [February 2017].

[4] See http://www.nsf.gov/funding/pgm_summ.jsp?pims_id=5517&from=fund [February 2017].

[5] The DIA2 tool is a public search tool that was developed with NSF funding to Purdue University. The tool currently accesses a database of more than 200,000 grants awarded by NSF from 1995 to present.

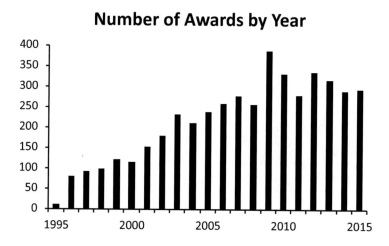

FIGURE 3-4 Overview of NSF REU award numbers and total amount of awards, 1995-2015. The award amount by year is the total amount allocated for the year, not the average award amount. Data obtained from http://ci4ene04.ecn.purdue.edu/ DIA2/pages [May 2016].

some constraints. Federal and state policy, including the length of time that individual grants for UREs are awarded, and the funding priorities of major foundations affect the kinds of undergraduate research that are offered at colleges and universities nationally. A large problem is nonrenewable funding that is available to launch and start UREs. To see sustained impacts, there must be enough time elapsed that cohorts can progress through their college career, which takes a good deal of time after the initial funding is available, especially if there is a ramp-up/development stage that prevents the first cohorts from happening in the first 2 years of the grant award. This can make it difficult to show the impacts and secure additional funding.

In addition to the availability and kinds of funding for UREs (e.g., individual initiatives versus supplements to existing faculty grants), education priorities are established through national and state policy making, as well as through other policy priorities of the government that can affect the breadth and scope of such programs. For example, it is possible that recent emphasis on having students complete their degrees as quickly as possible could discourage institutions from supporting longer-term (e.g., multiple semesters) projects if they do not allow students to obtain credit toward graduation and if the time required to be engaged with them results in students taking fewer credits per semester. Policies that emphasize keeping tuition and fees as low as possible could discourage development of CUREs, which sometimes may be funded in part by an increase in student lab fees or by additional costs for enrolling in STEM courses compared with those in other disciplines. When a project is funded with external support, funding agencies determine the amount of resources given to support research and evaluation of programs or they might request periodic reports and dictate what type of information to be tracked and measured to demonstrate a programs' success. Access to program evaluations may not be widely available unless published in peer-reviewed journals or disciplinary society publications.

Institutional Context

Institutional initiatives, mission, and culture can impact the degree to which there is financial and logistical support for the development of UREs and how those activities may be structured. These institutional priorities, in turn, are influenced by national and state education policies and priorities. A study that examined the relationship between campus missions and the five benchmarks for effective educational practice (measured by the National Survey of Student Engagement) showed that certain programs, policies, and approaches may work better depending on the institution's mission (Kezar and Kinzie, 2006). Other research on this topic shows that if institutions align policies and practices that support student success, then students are more likely to persist (Berger, 2001-2002; Kuh, 2001-2002).

Opportunities to participate in UREs may be limited at certain campuses due to those institutions' mission, priorities, or funding sources. Institutional support for UREs may be less common in community colleges than at small liberal arts colleges and research-intensive universities. Universities with more research funding often have more research opportunities for undergraduates (Kezar and Kinzie, 2006); however, for large institutions that have more students, this might not translate into an increase in the number of opportunities for an individual student.

Institutions also provide the infrastructure and resources to support undergraduate research more generally. This may include providing space and assisting in procuring the requisite laboratory and field equipment, which might be shared among multiple departments and/or faculty. At a broader level, it might include the creation of an office of undergraduate research to facilitate the promotion and implementation of such programs. Moreover, the institution might sponsor campus-wide initiatives that support UREs by providing supplemental funds to students engaging in research (i.e., funds to help acquire necessary equipment or supplies) or in the dissemination of research at national disciplinary meetings or through a campus-sponsored event.

However, institutions can broaden or impede student participation in UREs through their faculty promotion and reward structures. In some institutions, involving students in URE programs might take away faculty time from other activities that are expected by the university's promotion and reward system (i.e., publishable funded research). In other institutions, supporting undergraduates in research is an expected activity.

When individual institutions decide to expand participation in undergraduate research, they may do so through a variety of approaches. For example, some colleges or universities may make participation in at least one URE mandatory rather than optional for the student. This could be achieved by supporting the development of more course-based experiences to involve more undergraduates per mentor. It could also be achieved through partnering with other institutions of higher education, local or regional research organizations, or industries that conduct research and development. Decades-long partnerships between predominantly white institutions and historically black colleges and universities through undergraduate research programs are one example of such partnerships (Louis et al., 2015). Similarly, community colleges sometimes partner with baccalaureate-granting institutions to provide their students with access to faculty and facilities (Russell et al., 2007). Additional opportunities may exist through study abroad programs or with local, national, or international consortia.

Departments and Disciplinary Context

Academic departments play an important role in shaping the type of experiences that are available to the students in their program and the requirements for participating in UREs, especially as schools are moving toward a "culture of undergraduate research" (Merkel, 2001). The requirements for degree completion in terms of the types of courses one needs to take can have an impact on students' options for research. Making a URE a graduation requirement increases participation, whereas numerous other requirements could likely decrease participation in research. An evaluation of the existing curriculum might spur departments to adapt or add courses to increase accessibility to UREs for their majors, and potentially also for nonmajors.

Each department's decisions are influenced by its particular disciplinary culture and context. The likelihood of participating in UREs is dependent upon the specific area of STEM considered. For example, one national study sent out a web-based survey to all recipients of eight NSF-funded grants that included an undergraduate research component. Almost 15,000 students responded to the survey. Approximately 72 percent of students that majored in chemistry and 74 percent that majored in environmental science stated that they had participated in UREs, whereas 34 percent of students in mathematics and computer science stated they had such opportunities (Russell et al., 2007). These disciplinary differences may be driven in part by the various STEM disciplines promoting different kinds of knowledge, skill sets, and approaches. For example, some fields have different expectations for learning specific content because these fields prepare students for specific professional careers and/or require certification (e.g., engineering, business, computer science, and information science). For other fields, such as mathematics, the learning of content is not specifically tied to an occupation. For fields such as engineering, where the curriculum may lead to a career path in certain industries, participating in UREs that focus on the relevant knowledge may be important.

Faculty participation in UREs may be motivated by a desire to improve instruction, enrich the students' experience in an existing lab/research experience, boost research productivity, or satisfy requirements necessary to receive funding. Success of UREs may depend upon administrators and institutional policies to support interested faculty, along with the resources and professional development to encourage/compensate faculty. Furthermore, facilities and time to allow faculty to properly engage undergraduate students in research are important (Shortlidge et al., 2016).

Disciplinary societies, professional societies, and national networks also play an important role in the national policy discussion and shape the context that supports UREs. Societies of STEM research professionals traditionally have served as a platform for leaders and members from their respective STEM fields and subspecialties to present their research and to discuss challenges and opportunities in their field. These meetings provide opportunities for professional development and provide networking opportunities among members at regional and national levels. Some also have sessions or entire conferences focused on education, in addition to those that invite undergraduate researchers to present their research during poster sessions and/or talks. For example, the National Conferences on Undergraduate Research are meetings completely devoted to undergraduates sharing their own research.

Systemic Influences and the Dynamic Interplay

Institutions, departments, and individual faculty each impact the precise nature of UREs in multiple ways and at multiple levels. The physical resources available, including laboratories, field stations, engineering design studios, and testing facilities, can influence the design of the research question as well as the ability to access resources in the surrounding community (including other parts of the campus). Institutions with an explicit mission to promote undergraduate research may provide more time, resources (e.g., financial, support personnel, space, equipment), and recognition and rewards to URE-engaged departments and faculty than those institutions with another focus. The culture of the institution with respect to innovation in pedagogy and support for faculty development can impact the extent to which UREs are introduced or improved.

Departmental and institutional differences affect students' access to undergraduate research (Katkin, 2003). Many reform efforts that begin in a single department are not broadly adopted across programs, in other departments, or across colleges/universities in the STEM disciplines. "Student advising, faculty professional development, student research mentoring, academic support programs, clear STEM-focused institutional articulation agreements, external partnerships with business and industry related to internships and other research experiences, and many other critical programs and areas that have been identified as central to student success are often overlooked within reform efforts" (Elrod and Kezar, 2015, p. 67). These conditions suggest that UREs may need support from the institutional level in order to become sustainable and widespread in an institution.

SUMMARY

The goals for students participating in UREs are to increase retention/participation in STEM, promote STEM disciplinary knowledge and practices, and integrate students into STEM culture. These goals, coupled with the design principles—make STEM research accessible, help students learn from each other, make thinking visible, and promote autonomy—can set the stage for a robust experience that can help students generate deeper learning. This process begins by engaging students in research experiences that require students to do more than "know" something. Many research experiences are intended to empower students to appreciate their potential as creative contributors to their chosen discipline. The degree to which UREs are designed using the existing educational literature on pedagogy and how people learn is not clear.

The heterogeneity of UREs as described in Chapter 2 stems from variability associated with the multiple systemic factors, goals, and design principles described in this chapter. National calls for reform efforts and opportunities for funding shape UREs on campus. However, institutions, departments, and faculty play a big role in creating the context that surrounds the URE. Local policies and culture can provide a supportive environment that promotes undergraduate research as a "normal" part of STEM undergraduate education. When there is alignment between the policies and culture, there may be an increase in the likelihood of sustaining a URE.

REFERENCES

Adedokun, O.A., Zhang, D., Parker, L.C., Bessenbacher, A., Childress, A., Burgess, W.D., and Adedokun, B.O.A. (2012). Understanding how undergraduate research experiences influence student aspirations for research careers and graduate education. *Journal of College Science Teaching*, 42(1), 82-90.

Auchincloss, L.C., Laursen, S.L., Branchaw, J.L., Eagan, K., Graham, M., Hanauer, D.I., Lawrie, G., McLinn, C.M., Pelaez, N., Rowland, S., Towns, M., Trautmann, N.M., Varma-Nelson, P., Weston, T.J., and Dolan, E.L. (2014). Assessment of course-based undergraduate research experiences: A meeting report. *CBE–Life Sciences Education*, 13(1), 29-40.

Barr, D.A., Matsui, J., Wanat, S.F., and Gonzalez, M.E. (2010). Chemistry courses as the turning point for premedical students. *Advances in Health Sciences Education*, 15(1), 45-54.

Barton, A.C. (1998). Reframing "science for all" through the politics of poverty. *Educational Policy*, 12(5), 525-541.

Berger, J.B. (2001-2002). Understanding the organizational nature of student persistence: Empirically-based recommendations for practice. *Journal of College Student Retention*, 3(1), 3-21.

Bjork, E.L., and Bjork, R. (2011). Making things hard on yourself, but in a good way: Creating desirable difficulties to enhance learning. Pp. 56-64 in M.A. Gernsbacher, R.W. Pew, L.M. Hough, and J.R. Pomerantz (Eds.), *Psychology and the Real World: Essays Illustrating Fundamental Contributions to Society*. New York: Worth Publishers.

Bjork, R.A., Dunlosky, J., and Kornell, N. (2013). Self-regulated learning: Beliefs, techniques, and illusions. *Annual Review of Psychology*, 64, 417-444.

Blockus, L. (2016). *Strengthening Research Experiences for Undergraduate STEM Students: The Co-Curricular Model of the Research Experience*. Paper commissioned for the Committee on Strengthening Research Experiences for Undergraduate STEM Students. Board on Science Education, Division of Behavioral and Social Sciences and Education. Board on Life Sciences, Division of Earth and Life Studies. National Academies of Sciences, Engineering, and Medicine. Available: http://nas.edu/STEM_Undergraduate_Research_Apprentice.

Boyer Commission on Education of Undergraduates in the Research University. (1998). *Reinventing Undergraduate Education: A Blueprint for America's Research Universities*. Stony Brook, NY: State University of New York at Stony Brook for the Carnegie Foundation for the Advancement of Teaching.

Bransford, J.D., and Schwartz, D.L. (2009). It takes expertise to make expertise: Some thoughts about why and how. Pp. 748-774 in K.A. Ericsson (Ed.), *Development of Professional Expertise: Toward Measurement of Expert Performance and Design of Optimal Learning Environments.* Cambridge, UK: Cambridge University Press.

Brew, A. (2013). Understanding the scope of undergraduate research: A framework for curricular and pedagogical decision-making. *Higher Education, 66,* 603-618.

Brown, A.L., and Campione, J.C. (1994). *Guided Discovery in a Community of Learners.* Cambridge, MA: The MIT Press.

Brownell, S.E., and Kloser, M.J. (2015). Toward a conceptual framework for measuring the effectiveness of course-based undergraduate research experiences in undergraduate biology. *Studies in Higher Education, 40*(3), 525-544.

Brownell, S.E., Hekmat-Scafe, D.S., Singla, V., Seawell, P.C., Conklin-Imam, J.F., Eddy, S.L., Stearns, T., and Cyert, M.S. (2015). A high enrollment course-based undergraduate research experience improves student conceptions of scientific thinking and ability to interpret data. *CBE–Life Sciences Education, 14*(2), ar21. Available: https://www.ncbi.nlm.nih.gov/pmc/articles/PMC4477737/pdf/ar21.pdf [January 2017].

Clancy, M., Titterton, N., Ryan, C., Slotta, J., and Linn, M. (2003). New roles for students, instructors, and computers in a lab-based introductory programming course. *ACM SIGCSE Bulletin, 35*(1), 132-136.

Clement, N. (2009). Perspectives from research and practice in values education. Pp. 13-25 in T. Lovat and R. Toomey (Eds.), *Values Education and Quality Teaching.* Dordrecht, Netherlands: Springer.

Collins, A., and Brown, J.S. (1988). The computer as a tool for learning through reflection. Pp. 1-18 in M.M Sebrechts, G. Fisher, and P.M. Fisher (Eds.), *Learning Issues for Intelligent Tutoring Systems.* New York: Springer US.

Cook-Deegan, R.M. (1994). *The Gene Wars: Science, Politics, and the Human Genome.* New York: Norton.

Cortright, R.N., Collins, H.L., Rodenbaugh, D.W., and DiCarlo, S.E. (2003). Student retention of course content is improved by collaborative-group testing. *Advances in Psychology Education, 27,* 102-108.

Corwin, L.A., Graham, M.J., and Dolan, E.L. (2015). Modeling course-based undergraduate research experiences: An agenda for future research and evaluation. *CBE–Life Sciences Education, 14,* es1. Available: http://www.lifescied.org/content/14/1/es1.full.pdf+html [January 2017].

diSessa, A.A. (1996). Faculty opponent review: On mole and amount of substance: A study of the dynamics of concept formation and concept attainment. *Pedagogisk Forskning i Sverige, 1*(4), 233-243.

diSessa, A.A. (2000). *ChangingMinds.* Cambridge, MA: MIT Press.

Dolan, E. (2016). *Course-Based Undergraduate Research Experiences: Current Knowledge and Future Directions.* Paper commissioned for the Committee on Strengthening Research Experiences for Undergraduate STEM Students. Board on Science Education, Division of Behavioral and Social Sciences and Education. Board on Life Sciences, Division of Earth and Life Studies. National Academies of Sciences, Engineering, and Medicine. Available: http://nas.edu/STEM_Undergraduate_Research_CURE [February 2017].

Elrod, S., and Kezar, A. (2015). Increasing student success in STEM. *Peer Review, 17*(2). Available: https://www.aacu.org/peerreview/2015/spring/elrod-kezar [February 2017].

Estrada, M., Woodcock, A., Hernandez, P.R., and Schultz, P. (2011). Toward a model of social influence that explains minority student integration into the scientific community. *Journal of Educational Psychology, 103*(1), 206-222.

Feldman, A., Divoll, K.A., and Rogan-Klyve, A. (2013). Becoming researchers: The participation of undergraduate and graduate students in scientific research groups. *Science Education, 97*(2), 218-243.

Hernandez, P.R., Schultz, P., Estrada, M., Woodcock, A., and Chance, R.C. (2013). Sustaining optimal motivation: A longitudinal analysis of interventions to broaden participation of underrepresented students in STEM. *Journal of Educational Psychology, 105*(1). Available: https://www.ncbi.nlm.nih.gov/pmc/articles/PMC3838411/pdf/nihms512414. pdf [February 2017].

Hurtado, S., Eagan, M.K., Cabrera, N.L., Lin, M.H., Park, J., and Lopez, M. (2008). Training future scientists: Predicting first-year minority student participation in health science research. *Research in Higher Education, 49*(2), 126-152.

Hurtado, S., Eagan, K., and Chang, M. (2010). *Degrees of Success: Bachelor's Degree Completion Rates among Initial STEM Majors.* Higher Education Research Institute at UCLA. Available: http://www.heri.ucla.edu/nih/downloads/2010%20-%20Hurtado,%20 Eagan,%20Chang%20-%20Degrees%20of%20Success.pdf [January 2010].

Hurtado, S., Eagan, M.K., and Hughes, B. (2012). *Priming the Pump or the Sieve: Institutional Contexts and URM STEM Degree Attainments.* Paper presented at the annual forum of the Association for Institutional Research Annual Form [June 2-6, 2012], New Orleans, LA. Available: http://www.heri.ucla.edu/nih/downloads/AIR2012HurtadoPrimingthePump. pdf [June 2016].

Johnson, D.W., and Johnson, R. (1998). Cooperative learning and social interdependence theory. In R. Tindale, L. Heath, J. Edwards, E. Posavac, F. Bryant, Y. Suzrez-Balcazar, E. Henderson-King, and J. Myers (Eds.), *Theory and Research on Small Groups (4)*, 9-36. New York: Plenum.

Johnson, D.W., Johnson, R.T., and Smith, K.A. (1998). Cooperative learning returns to college: What evidence is there that it works? *Change, 30,* 26-35.

Johnson, D.W., Johnson, R.T., and Smith, K.A. (2007). The state of cooperative learning in postsecondary and professional settings. *Educational Psychology Review, 19*(1), 15-29.

Johri, A., and Olds, B.M. (2011). Situated engineering learning: Bridging engineering education research and the learning sciences. *Journal of Engineering Education, 100*(1), 151-185.

Jordan, T.C., Burnett, S.H., Carson, S., Caruso, S.M., Clase, K., DeJong, R.J., Dennehy, J.J., Denver, D.R., Dunbar, D., Elgin, S.C.R., Findley, A.M., Gissendanner, C.R., Golebiewska, U.P., Guild, N., Hartzog, G.A., Grillo, W.H., Hollowell, G.P., Hughes, L.E., Johnson, A., King, R.A., Lewis, L.O., Li, W., Rossenzweig, F., Rubin, M.R., Saha, M.S., Sandoz, J., Shaffer, C.D., Taylor, B., Temple, L., Vazquez, E., Ware, V.C., Barker, L.P., Bradley, K.W., Jacobs-Sera, D., Pope, W.H., Russell, D.A., Cresawn, S.G., Lopatto, D., Bailey, C.P. and Hatfull, G.F. (2014). A broadly implementable research course in phage discovery and genomics for first-year undergraduate students. *MBio, 5*(1), e01051-13. Available: http:// mbio.asm.org/content/5/1/e01051-13.full.pdf [February 2017].

Karpicke, J.D., Butler, A.C., and Roediger III, H.L. (2009). Metacognitive strategies in student learning: Do students practise retrieval when they study on their own?. *Memory, 17*(4), 471-479.

Katkin, W. (2003). The Boyer Commission Report and its impact on undergraduate research. *New Directions for Teaching and Learning, 2003*(93), 19-38.

Keller, C. (2016). *Using STEM Case Studies to Prepare Today's Students for Tomorrow's Jobs. An Evaluation of Spark 101 Interactive STEM videos.* Available: http://www.spark101. org/media/user_files/2016-03-07_SparkEvaluation-Final.pdf [February 2017].

Kezar, A.J., and Kinzie, J. (2006). Examining the ways institutions create student engagement: The role of mission. *Journal of College Student Development, 47*(2), 149-172.

Kollar, I., Fisher, F., and Slotta, J.D. (2007). Internal and external scripts in computer supported collaborative inquiry learning. *Learning and Instruction, 17*(6), 708-721.

Koretsky, M., Kelly, C., and Gummer, E. (2011). Student perception of learning in the laboratory: Comparison of industrially situated virtual laboratories to capstone physical laboratories. *Journal of Engineering Education, 100*(3), 540-573.

Kuh, G.D. (2001-2002). Organizational culture and student persistence: Prospects and puzzles. *Journal of College Student Retention, 3*(1), 23-39

Kuh, G.D. (2008). Excerpt from *High-Impact Educational Practices: What They Are, Who Has Access to Them, and Why They Matter*. Available: https://www.aacu.org/leap/hips [April 2015].

Laursen, S., Hunter, A.-B., Seymour, E., Thiry, H., and Melton, G. (2010). *Undergraduate Research in the Sciences: Engaging Students in Real Science*. San Francisco, CA: Jossey-Bass.

Lee, Jr., J.M., Contreras, F., McGuire, K.M., Flores-Ragade, A., Rawls, A., Edwards, K., and Menson, R. (2011). *The College Completion Agenda: 2011 Progress Report*. College Board Advocacy & Policy Center. Available: http://media.collegeboard.com/digitalServices/pdf/advocacy/policycenter/college-completion-agenda-2012-progress-report.pdf [February 2017].

Lemke, J.L. (1990). *Talking Science: Language, Learning, and Values*. Norwood, NJ: Ablex Publishing Corporation.

Linn, M.C. (1995). Designing computer learning environments for engineering and computer science: The Scaffolded Knowledge Integration framework. *Journal of Science Education and Technology, 4*(2), 103-126.

Linn, M.C. (2006). The knowledge integration perspective on learning and instruction. Pp. 243-264 in R.K. Sawyer (Ed.) *The Cambridge Handbook of the Learning Sciences*. New York: Cambridge University Press.

Linn, M.C., and Eylon, B.-S. (2011). *Science Learning and Instruction: Taking Advantage of Technology to Promote Knowledge Integration*. New York: Routledge.

Linn, M.C., and Hsi, S. (2000). *Computers, Teachers, Peers: Science Learning Partners*. New York: Routledge.

Linn, M.C., and Songer, N.B. (1991). Cognitive and conceptual change in adolescence. *American Journal of Education, 99*(4), 379-417.

Litzinger, T.A., Lattuca, L.R., Hadgraft, R.G., and Newstetter, W.C. (2011). Engineering education and the development of expertise. *Journal of Engineering Education, 100*(1), 123-150.

Liu, O.L., Rios, J.A., Heilman, M., Gerard, L., and Linn, M.C. (2016). Validation of automated scoring of science assessments. *Journal of Research in Science Teaching, 53*(2), 215-233.

Louis, D.A., Phillips, L.L., Louis, S.L., and Smith, A.R. (2015). Historically black colleges and universities: Undergraduate research, mentoring and extending the graduate pipeline. *Perspectives on Undergraduate Research & Mentoring, 4*(1). Available: https://works.bepress.com/dave_louis/41/ [February 2017].

Mayer, R.E., Dow, G.T., and Mayer, S. (2003). Multimedia learning in an interactive self-explaining environment: What works in the design of agent-based microworlds? *Journal of Educational Psychology, 95*(4), 806-812.

Mendoza, N., Richard, J., and Dugat Wickliff, T. (2015). Enculturation of diverse students to the engineering sciences through first year engineering college experiences at a southwestern institution: An exploratory work in progress. Paper presented at the 7th First Year Engineering Experience (FYEE) Conference, Roanoke, VA. Available: http://fyee.org/2015/papers/5079.pdf [February 2017].

Merkel, C.A. (2001). *Undergraduate Research at Six Research Universities: A Pilot Study for the Association of American Universities.* California Institute of Technology. Available: https://pdfs.semanticscholar.org/ebeb/1024b664b2ee093daf7e09911fc1aa28959d. pdf [February 2017].

National Academy of Sciences, National Academy of Engineering, and Institute of Medicine. (2005). *Facilitating Interdisciplinary Research.* Committee on Facilitating Interdisciplinary Research. Committee on Science, Engineering, and Public Policy. Washington, DC: The National Academies Press.

National Research Council. (1999). *How People Learn: Bridging Research and Practice.* M. Donovan, J. Bransford, and J. Pellegrino (Eds.). Committee on Learning Research and Educational Practice. Board on Behavioral, Cognitive, and Sensory Sciences, Division of Behavioral and Social Sciences and Education. Washington, DC: National Academy Press.

National Research Council. (2000a). *How People Learn: Brain, Mind, Experience, and School.* Washington, DC: National Academy Press.

National Research Council. (2000b). *How People Learn: Brain, Mind, Experience, and School: Expanded Edition.* Committee on Developments in the Science of Learning. Committee on Learning Research and Educational Practice. Board on Behavioral, Cognitive, and Sensory Sciences, Division of Behavioral and Social Sciences and Education. Washington, DC: National Academy Press.

National Research Council. (2006). *America's Lab Report: Investigations in High School Science.* S.R. Singer, M.L. Hilton, and H.A. Schweingruber (Eds.). Committee on High School Science Laboratories: Role and Vision. Board on Science Education, Division of Behavioral and Social Sciences and Education. Washington, DC: The National Academies Press.

National Research Council. (2009). *Learning Science in Informal Environments: People, Places, and Pursuits.* Committee on Learning Science in Informal Environments, P. Bell, B. Lewenstein, A.W. Shouse, and M.A. Feder (Eds.). Board on Science Education, Center for Education, Division of Behavioral and Social Sciences and Education. Washington, DC: The National Academies Press.

National Research Council. (2012). *Discipline-Based Education Research: Understanding and Improving Learning in Undergraduate Science and Engineering.* S. Singer, N.R. Nielsen, and H.A. Schweingruber (Eds). Committee on the Status, Contributions, and Future Directions of Discipline-Based Education Research. Board on Science Education, Division of Behavioral and Social Sciences and Education. Washington, DC: The National Academies Press.

National Research Council. (2015). *Reaching Students: What Research Says about Effective Instruction in Undergraduate Science and Engineering.* N. Kober (author). Board on Science Education, Division of Behavioral and Social Sciences and Education. Washington, DC: The National Academies Press.

National Science Foundation. (1996). *Shaping the Future: New Expectations for Undergraduate Education in Science, Mathematics, Engineering, and Technology* (NSF 96-139). Washington, DC: National Science Foundation. Available: http://www.nsf.gov/pubs/stis1996/nsf96139/nsf96139.txt [February 2017].

Okita, S.A., and Schwartz, D.L. (2013). Learning by teaching human pupils and teachable agents: The importance of recursive feedback. *Journal of the Learning Sciences, 22*(3), 375-412.

Ong, M., Wright, C., Espinosa, L., and Orfield, G. (2011). Inside the double bind: A synthesis of empirical research on undergraduate and graduate women of color in science, technology, engineering, and mathematics. *Harvard Educational Review, 81*(2), 172-208.

Pfund, C. (2016). *Studying the Role and Impact of Mentoring on Undergraduate Research Experiences.* Paper commissioned for the Committee on Strengthening Research Experiences for Undergraduate STEM Students. Board on Science Education, Division of Behavioral and Social Sciences and Education. Board on Life Science, Division of Earth and Life Studies. National Academies of Sciences, Engineering, and Medicine. Available: http://nas.edu/STEM_Undergraduate_Research_Mentoring.

Prior, P., and Bilbro, R. (2012). Academic enculturation: Developing literate practices and disciplinary identities. Pp. 19-31 in M. Castell and C. Donahue (Eds.), *University Writing: Selves and Texts in Academic Societies.* Bingley, UK: Emerald Group Publishing Limited.

Pryor, J.H., Hurtado, S., Saenz, V.B., Santos, J.L., and Korn, W.S. (2007). *The American Freshman: Forty Year Trends.* Los Angeles: Higher Education Research Institute. Available: https://heri.ucla.edu/PDFs/40TrendsManuscript.pdf [February 2017].

Quellmalz, E.S., Timms, M.J., Silberglitt, M.D., and Buckley, B.C. (2012). Science assessments for all: Integrating science simulations into balanced state science assessment systems. *Journal of Research in Science Teaching, 49*(3), 363-393.

Quintana, C., Reiser, B.J., Davis, E.A., Krajcik, J., Fretz, E., and Golan Duncan, R., Kyza, E., Edelson, D., and Soloway, E. (2004). A scaffolding design framework for software to support science inquiry. *Journal of the Learning Sciences, 13*(3), 337-386.

Reif, F., and St. John, M. (1979). Teaching physicists' thinking skills in the laboratory. *American Journal of Physics, 47*(11), 950-957.

Rodenbusch, S.E., Hernandez, P.R., Simmons, S.L., and Dolan, E.L. (2016). Early engagement in course-based research increases graduation rates and completion of science, engineering, and mathematics degrees. *CBE–Life Sciences Education, 15*(2), ar20. Available: http://www.lifescied.org/content/15/2/ar20 [February 2017].

Russell, S.H., Hancock, M.P., and McCullough, J. (2007). Benefits of undergraduate research experiences. *Science, 316,* 548-549.

Schoenfeld, A.H. (2010). *How We Think: A Theory of Goal-Oriented Decision Making and Its Educational Applications.* New York: Routledge.

Schwartz, D.L. (1999). The productive agency that drives collaborative learning. Pp. 197-218 in P. Dillenbourg (Ed.), *Collaborative Learning: Cognitive and Computational Approaches.* New York: Elsevier Science.

Schwarz, J. (2012). Faculty as undergraduate research mentors for students of color: Taking into account the costs. *Science Education, 96,* 527-542.

Shaffer, D.W. (2012). Models of situated action: Computer games and the problem of transfer. Pp. 403-432 in C. Steinkuehler, K. Squre, and S. Barab (Eds.), *Games, Learning, and Society: Learning and Meaning in the Digital Age.* New York: Cambridge University Press.

Shortlidge, E.E., Bangera, G., and Brownell, S.E. (2016). Faculty perspectives on developing and teaching course-based undergraduate research experiences. *BioScience, 66*(1), 54-62.

Svinicki, M., and McKeachie, W.J. (2011). *McKeachie's Teaching Tips: Strategies, Research, and Theory for College and University Teachers.* Belmont, CA: Wadsworth, Cengage Learning.

Thiry, H., Weston, T.J., Laursen, S.L., and Hunter, A.B. (2012). The benefits of multi-year research experiences: Differences in novice and experienced students' reported gains from undergraduate research. *CBE–Life Sciences Education, 11*(3), 260-272.

Visintainer, T., and Linn, M. (2015). Sixth-grade students' progress in understanding the mechanisms of global climate change. *Journal of Science Education and Technology, 24*(2-3), 287-310.

Vygotsky, L. (1978). Interaction between learning and development. *Readings on the Development of Children, 23*(3), 34-41.

Webb, N.M. (1997). Assessing students in small collaborative groups. *Theory into Practice, 36,* 205-213.

Weinstein, C.E., Husman, J., and Dierking, D.R. (2000). Self-regulation interventions with a focus on learning strategies. Pp. 727-747 in M. Boekaerts, P.R. Pintrich, and M. Zeidner (Eds.), *Handbook of Self-Regulation*. San Diego, CA: Academic Press.

White, R., and Gunstone, R. (1992). Prediction-observation-explanation. Pp. 44-64 in *Probing Understanding*. New York: Routledge.

Wigfield, A., Eccles, J.S., Schiefele, U., Roeser, R.W., and Davis-Kean, P. (2007). Development of achievement motivation. In W. Damon and N. Eisenberg (Eds.), *Handbook of Child Psychology: Social, Emotional, and Personality Development*. New York: John Wiley & Sons, Inc.

4

Research Documenting Student Participation in UREs

This chapter focuses on the studies that have been done on student learning experiences in undergraduate research experiences (UREs), whereas later chapters address the context in which the UREs happen by discussing mentorship, faculty, institutional administration, and policy issues.[1] While there are many opportunities for undergraduates to engage in research, as discussed in the previous chapters, the goals and structures of these experiences vary significantly. The studies on UREs also vary greatly in their content, approach, and perspectives; in gathering information about UREs, the committee was not able to find data on all of the topics we sought. Even so we learned of many interesting and creative programs at various types of institutions around the country.

This chapter examines information from those programs that have been the subject of focused study. Some of the more recent studies have focused on course-based UREs (CUREs) specifically. In examining the evidence that has been gathered to date on the outcomes of UREs, the committee found that much of the published data are for retention in the major and graduation rates. Although this focus may be because many UREs were set up specifically to promote the participation of students in research to support their retention in science, technology, engineering, and mathematics (STEM) fields, it may also be because these data are readily available, as

---

[1] This chapter includes outcomes from participation in course-based undergraduate research experiences (CUREs) from a paper commissioned by the committee titled *Course-Based Undergraduate Research Experiences: Current Knowledge and Future Directions* by Erin Dolan (2016).

they are already collected for other purposes. These data are discussed here in the section on participation and retention. Other studies are discussed in sections on increased understanding of STEM practices (e.g., content, concepts, and research skills) and integration of students into STEM culture (e.g., belonging, teamwork, ownership). Overall, the studies that document outcomes of UREs are relatively new and were developed by researchers and instructors who are early adopters of this high-impact practice; therefore, the motivation and self-selection of students included is not always articulated for each study. When possible, information about the selection of students and student motivation is highlighted for each study and discussed here. This would also include describing the comparison group when possible; the importance of proper comparison group selection and the impact on research design is discussed in detail in Chapter 7.

TOOLS FOR MEASURING OUTCOMES

A wide range of outcomes have been proposed as potential benefits of UREs for students, for faculty, and for the institution as a whole. However, few of these benefits have been well documented. Clearly, with such a wide range of potential outcomes, there are different approaches to gathering evidence, not only for each type of outcome, but also with regard to the evidence of benefit that is being sought.

As discussed in Chapter 1, there are three types of evidence that might be collected to support claims of benefit for these outcomes: (1) evidence that provides a description of outcomes from UREs or suggests ways in which UREs may influence outcomes, (2) evidence that provides a causal explanation for the outcomes of UREs, and (3) evidence that supports improved understanding of the mechanisms by which UREs affect outcomes. Descriptive evidence may come from institutional or national datasets (such as the Cooperative Institutional Research Program Freshman Survey and the National Survey of Student Engagement) that have information about student enrollment and persistence; it can also be obtained from student self-reports, surveys, pre and post testing, and interviews. However, unless a careful experimental or quasi-experimental design is used, gathering this type of descriptive evidence is unlikely to provide causal evidence for any changes that are observed after participation in UREs.

Similarly, studies that attempt to show why participation in a URE might bring about a particular outcome—that is, to provide a mechanism for fostering desired outcomes—must also be carefully designed. Some insight into mechanisms may emerge from phenomenographic studies—which require URE participants to describe their experiences. Table 4-1 outlines reliable measurement tools that have been used to measure student outcomes from UREs.

TABLE 4-1 Measurement Tools for UREs

Instrument Name	Domains Measured	Further Information
Experimental Design Ability Test	Students' understanding of experimental design criteria through open-ended prompt	Differentiates between students' scientific thinking gains in research-based vs. traditional course lab sections. Can be used in pre and post testing format; test is independent of disciplinary content (can be used in a variety of contexts) (Sirum and Humberg, 2011). Has been modified to be more sensitive for students majoring in biology (Expanded-Experimental Design Ability Test; Brownell et al., 2014).
Laboratory Course Assessment Survey	Students' perceptions of 3 design features of CUREs: collaboration, discovery and relevance, and iteration	Self-report survey. The discovery and relevance and iteration scales differ for CUREs versus traditional lab courses (Corwin et al., 2015b).
Networking Survey	Students' personal and professional networks through self-report of degrees of conversation	Self-report survey. Student networking related to project ownership. Survey can differentiate between research experiences with low-networking or high-networking design (Hanauer and Hatfull, 2015).
Project Ownership Survey	Extent of students' project ownership within research experience	Self-report survey. Results support argument that project ownership is one design aspect of UREs that fosters increased retention. Defines five categories of project ownership (Hanaeur and Dolan, 2014).
Rubric for Experimental Design Knowledge and Difficulties	Knowledge of experimental design and ability to diagnose problems in research design	Assessment that can be used in UREs and CUREs in pre and post format. Examines students' difficulties with: identifying variable properties of experimental subject, manipulation of variables, measurement of outcomes, accounting for variability, and recognizing the scope of inferences appropriate for experimental findings (Dasgupta et al., 2014).
Survey of Undergraduate Research Experiences (SURE)	Cognitive (understanding research process, etc.); skills; personal (confidence, temperament)	Self-report survey. Students report gains in all areas. Highest gains are in understanding research process and learning lab techniques. Personal gains rated second highest (Lopatto, 2004).

continued

TABLE 4-1 Continued

Instrument Name	Domains Measured	Further Information
URSSA Survey	Thinking and working like a scientist; personal gains; skills; attitudes and behaviors	A self-report survey. The four domains (survey constructs) are separate but related. Analysis shows that "attitudes and behaviors" items act like satisfaction items and measure similar constructs. Comparison of Likert-scale and open-ended items showed inflation in students rating themselves as more likely to go to graduate school (Weston and Laursen, 2015).

INCREASED PARTICIPATION AND RETENTION OF STEM STUDENTS

Many studies on the outcomes of UREs have focused on outcomes of participation, retention, and persistence. Data on these outcomes are often already gathered by the institution, thereby providing a reasonably accessible entrée for faculty interested in examining the results of UREs. Obtaining information on whether URE participants continue on to graduate school or into STEM careers is more difficult to gather, though the National Student Clearinghouse does track national degree completion, and analysis of existing information could provide important insights into the effects of UREs.[2]

Performance and Continued Enrollment in STEM Major

One prevalent argument for UREs is that participation in a research experience improves students' academic outcomes, such as retention in STEM majors, college completion, and grade point average (GPA) (Graham et al., 2013).

Nagda and colleagues (1998) conducted one of the few studies to randomly select applicants for research experiences, notably before UREs were widely available, to measure outcomes associated with retention. They found that for students who applied and were randomly selected for a URE program, there was a statistically significant decrease in attrition (retention in major) for those students who participated compared to those who did not, although findings varied by racial/ethnic groups. The difference in retention rate was strongest and statistically significant for African Americans. Non-Hispanic white students who had participated in research showed half the STEM attrition rate of the matched group of control

---

[2] See http://www.studentclearinghouse.org [January 2017].

students, though the difference was not statistically significant. Moreover, Hispanic students had a slightly higher, though not statistically significant, retention rate compared with control students.

The remaining studies report outcome data on students who self-selected into UREs, and although they were matched for demographic characteristics with comparison groups who did not participate in a URE, it is not clear that the groups were matched for motivation or other characteristics that may have contributed to their success in college and in continuing in a STEM major. A recent study by Rodenbusch and colleagues (2016) examined GPA, graduation rates, and retention in STEM majors among students who chose to participate in CUREs as part of the Freshman Research Initiative at The University of Texas at Austin, which offers students up to three sequenced courses in which they engage in research at increasing levels of independence.[3] The study used propensity score matching to account for selected student-level differences[4] and concluded that students who participated in the full three-semester sequence were more likely to graduate with a STEM degree and more likely to graduate within 6 years. In contrast to the usual observation of greater minority attrition in STEM majors and STEM degree completion, students from historically underrepresented groups participating in this initiative succeeded at the same rate as other students; that is, they were more likely to stay in the STEM major and graduate with a STEM degree. This study found no difference in GPA between those students participating in the URE compared to those who did not. However, a study comparing research[5] and nonresearch students at another university showed that extended participation in research for more than a semester was associated with an increase in GPA, even after controlling for SAT scores, though this GPA gain was not evident in students with a single semester of research experience (Fechheimer et al., 2011).

UREs may also contribute to subsequent course-taking patterns in STEM. After controlling for background characteristics such as early college coursework, GPA, math SAT scores, gender, and minority status, Junge and colleagues (2010) found that students who chose to participate in the

---

[3] The Freshman Research Initiative is discussed in Chapter 2.

[4] The model included 13 variables that were used to create the comparison group. These variables included: gender, race/ethnicity, parental education levels, parental income level, Pell grant eligibility, SAT total score or ACT equivalent, number of high school science credits earned, number of high school math credits earned, whether students graduated from a Texas or out-of-state high school, enrollment year at UT Austin, first semester enrolled (e.g., Fall), first college students entered at The University of Texas at Austin, and enrollment in the Texas Interdisciplinary Program.

[5] The definition of undergraduate research used "invokes the traditional one-faculty-mentor-to-one-student relationship focused on a directed-research project" (Fechheimer et al., 2011, p. 157). No demographic data were provided for each group (research, nonresearch) beyond gender and SAT scores.

Summer Undergraduate Research at Emory [University] program took significantly more science courses and earned higher grades in those courses than nonparticipants. There is some evidence that student participation in UREs correlates with a shorter time to degree. Based on student transcript data at a single site, 98.5 percent of undergraduates in a summer research program graduated within 5 years, compared to the overall graduate rate of 82 percent (Craney et al., 2011).

Deek and colleagues (2003) conducted a study to examine research experiences as a factor in academic achievement. The study compared 39 students who participated in a one-semester engineering Research Experiences for Undergraduates program with 230 students who did not; the two groups were matched on demographics and academic performance prior to the research semester. Comparisons between the groups on retention, cumulative GPA, and ratio of earned and attempted credit hours showed a statistically significant difference between the groups. Overall, students who participated in research had higher grades, earned more credits relative to attempted credits, and were more likely to persist in the program after completing the URE. Moreover, analysis of survey responses from both faculty and students found that the program increased students' motivation and interest toward research.

Studies Focusing on Historically Underrepresented Students

Other studies have documented the educational and career benefits of apprentice-style UREs for historically underrepresented students in particular. In recent years, a variety of research programs, using quasi-experimental designs and statistical modeling, have started to show consistent evidence that research experience correlates with higher likelihood of degree completion and persistence in interest in STEM careers (Chemers et al., 2011; Jones et al., 2010; Schultz et al., 2011). For example, *TheScienceStudy*[6] tracked a cohort of 1,400 historically underrepresented students who were participating in the Research Initiative for Scientific Enhancement (RISE) program, an initiative funded by the National Institutes of Health to increase the participation of students from underrepresented populations in the biomedical sciences. Schultz and colleagues (2011) found that students with science research experiences (e.g., in classes, working independently with a faculty member, or at a job) who reported no active enrollment in a co-curricular science program retained interest in science careers more strongly than those who did not engage in research but were enrolled in

---

[6] *TheScienceStudy* is a nationwide longitudinal study of the academic and professional experiences of students and professionals. It was sponsored by the National Institutes of Health. See https://ssl1.csusm.edu/thesciencestudy [September 2016].

a science program that did not include any hands-on research experience. All students who were a part of this study had reported high intention to pursue a biomedical career when the study began. Interestingly, participation in the RISE undergraduate research program did not increase the career interest of these already interested students. Rather, it appeared to buffer students from losing interest. The "match" students were not enrolled in any undergraduate research programs but at the beginning of the study shared a similar interest in the biomedical sciences with the RISE students. The study did not report whether the "match" students had similar access to UREs.

Chang and colleagues (2014) found that participation in UREs by students who were from groups historically underrepresented in STEM and who entered college with high grades and aspirations moderated the negative correlation between being an underrepresented minority and persistence. "Five college experiences significantly predicted the likelihood of historically URM students [underrepresented minority students] following through on their freshman intentions to major in STEM. The strongest of these predictors was participation in an undergraduate research program. URM students who participated in programs that exposed them to research were 17.4 percentage points more likely to persist in STEM than those who did not" (Chang et al., 2014, p. 567).

A comprehensive analysis of the transcripts and admissions applications of 7,664 University of California, Davis students who declared biology as a major between 1995 and 1999 found that underrepresented minority students who participated in a research experience, especially during their first 2 years, were more likely to have high academic performance and persist in biology, as well as go on to graduate, than those who did not (Jones et al., 2010). More specifically, for Hispanic and African American students, those students who participated in a URE were more likely to obtain a biology degree than those students who did not participate in research. Similarly, research by Villarejo and colleagues found that participants in the Biology Undergraduate Scholars Program, an undergraduate research enrichment program for underrepresented students in biology, were more likely than other students to persist to graduation with a biology major (Barlow and Villarejo, 2004; Villarejo and Barlow, 2007). Their analyses suggested that research participation contributed to persistence.

Together, these studies were almost all of highly motivated students who do not lose their motivation when they participate in UREs. Although these studies do not describe how to build motivation, they do describe how to sustain it.

The Meyerhoff Scholars program, a long-standing, comprehensive program to provide academic and social support to increase the retention of underrepresented minority STEM students at University of Maryland-

Baltimore County, has collected nearly 20 years of outcomes data on participants.[7] As part of the program, all students are required to participate in on-campus, academic-year research. However, the structure and intensity of that research can vary. For example, some students only participate in a yearly undergraduate research symposium, some students complete research courses for academic credit, and others participate in the Minority Access to Research Careers (MARC)[8] Undergraduate Student Training in Academic Research (U-STAR) program. The MARC U-STAR program is designed for students who intend to pursue a Ph.D. in biomedical research. Carter and colleagues (2009) examined the educational outcomes of 13 cohorts of students in relation to the structure (annual symposium, course, or MARC U-STAR program) and the intensity (symposium, two semesters, or more than two semesters) of the students' on-campus, academic-year research experiences. They found that those students who participated in the more structured and/or intense experiences (i.e., participation in MARC U-STAR, more than three semesters of research courses, or both) were significantly more likely to enroll in a STEM Ph.D. program after graduation than students who did not participate in such research experiences. As noted by Carter and colleagues, participants in this program are from a highly select group and thus the findings may not be generalizable.

Graduate School and Future Career Choice

As detailed below, URE alumni have reported that the experience allowed them to test their fit with the profession; develop a close relationship with a faculty member; and gain insight into the social, cultural, and intellectual processes of science. Socialization into the professional STEM community might also help to shape students' future interests and goals (Corwin et al., 2015a; Litzinger et al., 2011). A few researchers have explored the processes by which UREs may shape students' career or educational decisions; some of these studies are described below.

Mastery of research skills might have a predictive effect on students' efficacy beliefs, which in turn can be predictive of their graduate school aspirations (Adedokun et al., 2013). Particular student characteristics or aptitudes, such as curiosity about the unknown, a desire for autonomy and independence, and openness to the unknown in their career path, may be predictive of research students' pursuit of a Ph.D. (McGee and Keller, 2007), although these same traits may be what motivates some students to seek out UREs. Experiences that take place during UREs, such as developing a close relationship with a faculty member, have helped students to

---

[7]See http://meyerhoff.umbc.edu/about/results [January 2017].

[8]The MARC program, which like RISE is sponsored by the National Institutes of Health, is discussed in Chapters 2 and 3.

confirm that graduate school was the correct path and have clarified their field of interest for their graduate program (Laursen et al., 2010). These types of benefits were also documented from other types of STEM professional work under the guidance of a mentor, such as internships or co-ops, yet only research experiences helped students to clarify whether a research career or pursuing a Ph.D. was the correct path for them, as indicated through structured interviews (Thiry et al., 2011).

Many studies have relied on the assertions of current URE students about the influence of the research experience on their future career and educational plans (Adedokun et al., 2012; Grimberg et al., 2008). Several of these studies have used comparisons with students without research experiences ("nonresearch students"), but it is often not clear whether students' career or educational goals differed prior to their research experience. For instance, Eagan and colleagues (2013) compared demographically matched groups of research and nonresearch students and found that students who had participated in apprentice-style UREs had stronger graduate school aspirations, but these differences may have existed prior to the experience. Likewise, a study of student researchers and nonresearchers reported that the former group felt that research increased their awareness of what graduate school is like and increased their aspirations for a Ph.D. degree, yet only 19 percent of students had a "new" expectation of receiving a Ph.D., which may reflect the selection bias inherent in students who are chosen for research experiences (Russell et al., 2007). Another study comparing apprentice-style student researchers and nonresearchers found that the research students held high expectations prior to their research experience that remained unchanged with respect to the value of research for facilitating their future career path (Craney et al., 2011). Other studies have reported that apprentice-style URE students felt that the experience prepared them for graduate school and STEM careers (Hunter et al., 2007; Sabitini, 1997; Seymour et al., 2004). Some studies found that students often enter UREs because they are interested in learning more about research or determining whether graduate school might be the right path for them. The results obtained show that research experiences played an important role in confirming or clarifying prior goals for these students (Gonzalez-Espada and LaDue, 2006; Hunter et al., 2007; Lopatto, 2004; Pacific and Thompson, 2011; Seymour et al., 2004).

Other studies have tracked URE participants' postbaccalaureate outcomes through retrospective accounts from apprentice-style URE alumni. Zydney and colleagues (2002) compared retrospective accounts of research and nonresearch alumni at a single institution and found that research students were more likely to go to graduate school and more likely to cite a faculty member as influential in their career choice. Alumni of a biosciences research program at Emory University were three times more likely to pursue a Ph.D. than nonresearch students (Junge et al., 2010). Likewise, students who conducted research in a formal research program had higher rates of graduate school attendance than students with individually reported research experiences that were not part of a formal program, suggesting that the professional development offered through programs can have an impact beyond the research experience itself (Bauer and Bennett, 2003). Taking these studies together, their retrospective approach does not control for initial motivation and interests. Those who initially selected UREs may have had greater interest in research careers. Thus, these findings may imply a correlational relationship that is not causal.

One of the few studies of UREs to use random assignment of students to research positions documented that URE participants were more likely to enroll in graduate school compared to nonresearch students who had applied for a research position and were not randomly selected (Hathaway et al., 2002). In fact, 82 percent of all research students enrolled in graduate degree programs, while only 65 percent of nonresearch students did so, although participation in UREs may have made the research students more competitive in their graduate school applications. This effect was even more pronounced for students of color, as underrepresented minority research students attended graduate school at rates similar to other research students, yet only 56 percent of nonresearch students of color attended graduate school.

Summary of Findings for Increased Retention and Participation of STEM Students

Students who participate in UREs are generally more likely to remain in STEM fields as undergraduates than are STEM students who do not participate. However, most of the studies cited in reaching this conclusion were not able to address differences in initial interest or motivation prior to the URE exposure (or lack thereof). Some studies have found higher grades and graduation rates for URE participants as well. Self-report data from students suggest that UREs can confirm the students' intention to attend graduate school in STEM and that these students perceive mentorship as an important component of the experience. Thus, supporting and maintaining student interest in a STEM major and subsequent career may be an important function of UREs.

PROMOTING STEM DISCIPLINARY KNOWLEDGE AND PRACTICES

The outcomes associated with promoting STEM disciplinary practices include what a student learns, understands, and knows regarding the state of his own knowledge of that STEM discipline through participation in a

URE. The specific content and concepts a student learns will vary, depending on the discipline or disciplines of that student's URE. However, in addition to learning traditional disciplinary content, a student in a URE is afforded an opportunity to engage in disciplinary practices common across STEM fields, such as analyzing and interpreting data, identifying the next steps in an experiment or research activity, and identifying gaps in knowledge that are worthy of further research.

Although this report considers a wide range of fields included within STEM, many of the studies reported in the literature examined a narrow range of fields, and much of the existing literature focuses heavily on bench science, rather than, for example, mathematics. Moreover, despite the fact that many of the findings focus on science and do not consider other STEM fields, the committee decided that these studies nevertheless provide useful insight for understanding the impact of UREs.

Content and Concepts

Several studies of apprentice-style summer research have documented that students perceive that they gained content knowledge, were able to relate their research projects to the larger field of study, and understood the context of the project (Craney et al., 2011; Kardash, 2000), yet these studies were conducted at a single site, relied on self-reports, and did not use a control or comparison group. Kardash (2000) also included research mentors' ratings of students' knowledge gains, which were similar to students' ratings of their own gains. In Kardash's study, female students rated their own cognitive gains from research as lower than male students rated their gains.

Because students in CUREs are exposed to standardized course content, CUREs may lend themselves to more uniform assessment of knowledge gains. Indeed, a study of one biosciences CURE found that students in the research-based laboratory section showed statistically significantly greater pre- and post gains on disciplinary content assessments than did students in the nonresearch-based lab sections (Russell et al., 2015), although this difference occurred only in the principles of biology and cell biology sections and not the ecology sections. Drew and Tiplett (2008) demonstrated that students made substantial increases in genomics knowledge from the beginning to the end of the CURE, though this study encompassed a single course with no comparison group.

One of the few studies to randomly assign students to either a research-based or traditional lab section and to use multiple methods to measure outcomes found that students in the research-based lab section believed that they were better able to explain the concepts in the experiment and had a better understanding of the research process than students in the traditional lab section (Szteinberg and Weaver, 2013). Two studies of the multi-institution Genomics Education Partnership (GEP) CURE found that CURE students made greater gains in content knowledge than comparison students from participating schools who completed prerequisites but had not engaged in the GEP curriculum. The content gains were larger when the faculty member devoted more class time to the CURE projects (Shaffer et al., 2010, 2014). Lopatto and colleagues (2008) found that those GEP students had larger increases in their positive attitude about research, as measured by the Survey of Undergraduate Learning Experiences, a learning survey (see Table 4-1). Shaffer and colleagues (2010) reported that GEP students also had higher scores on quizzes about the content and processes used in the course, compared to students not participating in the GEP program.

Research Skills

Students participating in UREs report that they gain experience with the practices and skills of conducting STEM research, such as data collection, analysis, and interpretation and understanding of research design. A comparative study of summer URE students and nonresearch students at Emory University found that the URE students felt more prepared to select appropriate data analysis strategies and apply research ethics principles than students who had not had research experience (Junge et al., 2010). In another study, URE alumni perceived greater growth in science, math, logic, and/or problem solving skills than did nonresearch alumni (Bauer and Bennett, 2003). These findings are consistent with the work of Lopatto (2004). Kardash (2000) reported that both students and faculty mentors in apprentice-style research experiences rated students' gains in collecting and analyzing data as some of the highest rated skills developed in UREs. In addition to these perceived gains in research skills, students' performance on exams revealed gains in the ability to analyze and interpret data—a goal of many CUREs.

In a performance-based assessment that was blindly scored, students in an introductory biology CURE were tested three times on their ability to design experiments and interpret data. Over the course of the exams, students showed significant increases in their ability to analyze and interpret data and describe their results (Brownell et al., 2015).[9] The authors argued that data analysis activities, collaboration, and discussion of research results within the course all promoted growth in students' STEM thinking and skills.

---

[9]It should be noted that although the participants are participating in a course required for all introductory biology students, there was no comparison sample for this study. Therefore, it is not certain whether the growth in ability to analyze and interpret data was any greater for the CURE students than it would have been in a traditional introductory biology course.

Knowledge of Experimental Design

Study authors have argued that students gain knowledge of experimental design from their work in apprentice-style UREs. A large study of research and nonresearch students across multiple institutions found that the research students (both sponsored and nonsponsored) reported gaining an understanding of experimental design at much higher rates than did the nonresearch students (Russell et al., 2007). A qualitative study of apprentice-style research at four liberal arts colleges found that students and faculty both reported student gains in understanding of experimental design, enhanced ability to connect their research experience to coursework, improved understanding of the role of theory in STEM research, and increased ability to troubleshoot research problems (Hunter et al., 2007; Seymour et al., 2004). Thiry and colleagues (2011) used interviews to gather data comparing outcomes from apprentice-style UREs with those from STEM coursework and other out-of-class STEM professional experiences. They found that undergraduate researchers who chose to enroll in UREs had developed a more sophisticated understanding of the research process and the nature of STEM knowledge than nonresearch students.

Research on student outcomes from CUREs has also documented gains in students' conceptions of experimental design. A pre and post study of research-based versus traditional course labs found that the only statistically significant difference between the groups was greater increases in the research students' perception of both their problem solving skills and their understanding of experimental design (Russell et al., 2015). Using a pre and post assessment of students performance, Kloser and colleagues (2013) documented that students made statistically significantly greater gains in understanding of experimental design and data interpretation. Open-ended surveys of students' self-confidence in research design showed similar gains.

Understanding Disciplinary Research Practices

One of the most widely discussed outcomes from UREs in the research literature is developing scientific thinking skills or habits of mind. Some studies have argued that UREs help students develop a scientific approach to problems; a general understanding of the nature of the research process; and an understanding of how disciplinary knowledge is constructed, debated, and evaluated. One study examined the development over time of students' abilities to perform tasks typical of STEM researchers, as well as their conceptions of STEM research (see Box 4-1).

Three in-depth ethnographic studies involving interviews, surveys, participant observation, and/or reflective journals have documented that students gain maturity in their beliefs about science from UREs, including a

---

BOX 4-1
Changes in Student Abilities with
Increasing Exposure to UREs

Duration of research experience in apprentice-style UREs has been linked to students' perceptions of their intellectual gains from the experience, as well as to greater maturity in their understanding of the research process (Adedokun et al., 2014; Bauer and Bennett, 2003; Feldman et al., 2009; Salsman et al., 2013; Thiry et al., 2012). In a study of students' intellectual development within research experiences, Thiry and colleagues (2012) found that students with less than 1 year of apprentice-style research were often able to carry out routine data collection and technical procedures, whereas students with multiyear research experiences were further able to identify the next steps in an experiment and perceived that they became more proficient at troubleshooting their project. Yet certain abilities seemed to take extensive time to develop; for instance, only a few advanced undergraduate researchers were able to generate a research question or design an experiment, even after multiple years of research experience. Finally, an assessment of students' proposal writing abilities and research design skills in graduate school found that duration of undergraduate research experience was linked to enhanced graduate school performance in all of the STEM thinking and research skills assessed. Autonomy in the research experience and collaboration within a research group were important in research alumni's outcomes, yet duration of experience was most strongly correlated with subsequent research skill development (Gilmore et al., 2015).

---

more sophisticated understanding of the validity of knowledge claims, the role of theory in shaping research questions, taking scientific approaches to problems, and understanding the practice of science as a collaborative and detail-oriented activity (Cartrette and Melro-Lehrman, 2012; Ryder et al., 1999; Thompson et al., 2016). However, none of these studies included a comparison group.

CUREs have been argued to contribute to students' understanding of the nature of scientific knowledge. Brownell and colleagues (2015) reported a change in students' conceptions of scientific thinking through a blindly scored pre and post open-ended survey. That is, students had a more expert-like conception of research that was more grounded in the research experience (focusing on collaboration and data analysis) rather than viewing research simply as the development of hypotheses and using the scientific method. A pre and post survey also found that these students also perceived that their scientific thinking had matured. Russell and Weaver (2011) compared traditional, inquiry-based and research-based labs at five universities and found that students in the research-based laboratory section demonstrated the most gains in understanding the nature of scientific knowledge, including more nuanced understandings of the role of creativity in science and their conceptions of science as a process. Other studies have also concluded that students learn about the scientific research process and the practice of science from CUREs (Harrison et al., 2011; Rowland et al., 2012).

Growth of Student Skills and Technical Knowledge

Another goal of UREs is growth in students' skills and technical knowledge. Through UREs, students are provided with an avenue for practicing application of knowledge as they address a research problem. Although UREs and CUREs are often touted as fostering important skills, such as technical or laboratory skills, critical thinking, teamwork, and communication skills, few if any studies have measured these outcomes beyond self-report methods. Other studies have reported that students engaged in apprentice-style research perceived that they have gained communication skills (Craney et al., 2011; Junge et al., 2010), with at least one of these studies reporting that Black and Latino students perceived higher communication skills gains than their counterparts (Craney et al., 2011).

Several studies have compared student and faculty reports of URE outcomes and have documented that the faculty and students both perceived that the students developed communication skills, organizational and time management skills, technical skills, collaboration skills, and the ability to read and interpret primary literature from apprentice-style UREs (Hunter et al., 2007; Kardash, 2000). Additionally, Kardash (2000) found that students' highest rated skills gains were in the oral communication of research results, such as presenting a poster, and their lowest rated skills gains were in writing a research paper for publication, suggesting the types of opportunities that students are likely to encounter during apprentice-style UREs. Few studies of CUREs have documented gains in skills, though students showed statistically significant increases in their comfort with reading and interpreting primary literature in a study of a CURE at a single institution (Drew and Tiplett, 2008).

Summary for Promoting an Understanding of
STEM Disciplinary Knowledge and Practices

Following UREs, students frequently report gains in understanding of STEM content, data analysis, the nature of experiments, and a range of skills. In some cases, these outcomes have been corroborated by various assessments and scoring rubrics that look at disciplinary knowledge or abilities in experimental design. However, most of the studies use self-reporting and few include comparison groups to document causal claims;

hence, they indicate *perceived* improvements. Assuming the reports reflect the students' true beliefs, this may be sufficient to bolster persistence in a STEM major (see below).

INTEGRATING STUDENTS INTO STEM CULTURE

Integration of students into STEM culture is another goal of participation in UREs. The following section describes some studies to date on students' feelings of autonomy and agency, belief in their own self-efficacy (i.e., feeling one "can" engage in a particular skill) and ability to act on their own, motivation, happiness, and commitment to persist in their field. For example, Healy and Rathbun (2013) reported that students developed more self-confidence in general as a result of their UREs. Estrada and colleagues (2011) showed that factors of self-efficacy, identity, and value endorsement may be important to the retention of historically underrepresented students' interest and persistence in STEM by creating a type of "inoculation effect" that prevents loss of interest among students already pursuing a STEM degree. These results can begin to provide insights into the mechanism of why one finds improvements in a wide range of other outcomes.

Student Confidence

UREs may foster an array of outcomes, such as increasing student confidence and self-efficacy; strengthening students' sense of belonging in the discipline; providing professional socialization experiences; and fostering the traits, attitudes, and temperament of scientists. For instance, a qualitative study of students and faculty in multiple summer research programs in computer science reported that UREs promoted a sense of belonging in the discipline, especially for women in a male-dominated field such as computing (Barker, 2009). Another study in computer science documented the positive influence of the Affinity Research Group model of research mentoring on students' identification with the larger professional community and the transformation of identity from student to researcher, especially for underrepresented minority students (Villa et al., 2013). The Affinity Research Group model outlines specific methods to socialize students into the research group through group orientation, scaffolding of students' responsibility within the group's work, and providing social and intellectual support within the group.

Several studies involving interviews or surveys have documented students' increased confidence in research abilities, general self-confidence, and increased independence gained from apprentice-style research experiences (John and Creighton, 2012; Russell et al., 2007). Interviews with students and faculty at four liberal arts colleges also elicited the influence of apprentice-style research on students' beliefs in their ability to contribute to science, sense of ownership of a project, patience and perseverance with research work, tolerance for ambiguity, sense of responsibility and maturity, and development of a scientific identity (Hunter et al., 2007; Seymour et al., 2004). A study of research interns and their mentors in two sponsored-research programs found that personal and professional dispositions fostered from research experiences were mentioned more often than other outcomes such as cognitive gains or research skills, suggesting the importance of these outcomes to students (Kardash and Edwards, 2012).

Chemers and colleagues (2011) conducted a study with 327 undergraduates and 338 graduate students and postdoctoral fellows to examine students' science support experiences (research experience, mentoring, and community involvement), psychological variables (science self-efficacy, leadership/teamwork self-efficacy, and identity as a scientist), and commitment to pursue a science career. They found that for the undergraduate students in this dataset, there was a strong relationship between science self-efficacy and both research experience and instrumental mentoring, suggesting that those who were more confident that they could perform the functions of a scientist (science self-efficacy) had more involvement in professional science activities (research experience) and with instrumental mentoring (helping students learn tasks of science career development). Moreover, students who were more likely to identify themselves as a scientist also stated that they were more likely to go on to work in scientific research (commitment to a science career). Estrada and colleagues (2011) found that science identity and endorsing the value of the scientific community were better predictors of persistence than was students' sense of self-efficacy.

A study by Raelin and colleagues (2014) of engineering undergraduates looked at reciprocal relationships between work self-efficacy and co-op participation and between academic self-efficacy and academic achievement to see whether these factors played a critical role in retention. Academic achievement and academic self-efficacy, as well as contextual support in all time periods, were found to be critical to retention. Work self-efficacy, developed by students between their second and fourth years, was also an important factor in retention, though it was strongly tied to the students' participation in co-op programs. The study also noted that higher retention was associated positively with the number of co-op experiences completed by students.

Several studies of CUREs have also documented enhanced positive attitudes and confidence of students enrolled in research-based courses. Shapiro and colleagues (2015) compared CURE students with students in traditional faculty-mentored research experiences on a single campus and concluded that in both types of experiences, students developed a sense of independence, interest, and ownership of their project when they perceived that they had agency and choice within the work. Several studies of CUREs have documented that students gained confidence in their ability to perform laboratory tasks (Kloser et al., 2013; Rowland et al., 2012). A study of CUREs found that students had more positive attitudes toward research, collaboration, and peer critique; higher self-confidence in research-based laboratory tasks; and increased interest in pursuing future research experiences, compared to students in a traditional lab section. However, career interests did not change for either the CURE students or the comparison group (Brownell et al., 2012). A comparative study of CURE versus traditional lab sections found that students in the experimental section reported positive attitudinal changes toward understanding inquiry and the nature of science; increasing problem-solving ability; designing experiments; understanding how to conduct research; and the likelihood of choosing a STEM career in pre and post testing, whereas students in the control sections experienced declines in attitudes from the beginning to the end of the semester (Russell et al., 2015).

One of the most widely studied predictors of academic perseverance is self-efficacy. This line of research emerges from Bandura (1997, p. 3), who described self-efficacy as "the belief in one's capabilities to organize and execute courses of action required to produce given attainments." Bandura found that a person's self-appraisal of ability is a strong predictor of the person's likelihood to perform those actions in the future. Estrada and colleague's (2011) research, using panel data from *TheScienceStudy*, found that when research experiences were more strongly correlated with perceived science self-efficacy, there was a greater intention to persist in biomedical careers.

Promoting Professional Identity

Another way that UREs promote identity development is by introducing students to the social and cultural processes underlying STEM practices, such as collaboration, critique, collegiality, mentorship, and peer review. An ethnographic study of student researchers and their faculty mentors found that students generated social ties with peers, postdocs, and faculty that they drew on for resources, information, and support (Thompson et al., 2016). Other qualitative studies have shown that apprentice-style research allowed students to enter into a community of practice where they learned the habits of mind, values, norms, and practices of researchers by working with experts who served as role models of STEM practices (Dolan and Johnson, 2010; Hunter et al., 2007; John and Creighton, 2012; Laursen et al., 2010; Thiry and Laursen, 2011). Apprentice-style research experiences, in particular, have been argued to strengthen student-faculty interactions and provide a mentoring relationship for students that exposes them to STEM thinking and practices, which boosts their confidence that they can be scientists (Hunter et al., 2007; Laursen et al., 2010; Seymour et al., 2004). Students who worked closely with peers and faculty in UREs were more likely to report that the research experience had increased their interest in graduate school (Craney et al., 2011).

Research with historically underrepresented students describes how UREs have increased a sense of belonging and inclusion. Strong evidence exists that historically underrepresented students' sense of belonging in academic environments is complex and often impeded (Hurtado and Carter, 1997). A sense of belonging influences the extent to which a student integrates into the academic community, which in turn affects intentions to persist (Hausmann et al., 2007). UREs designed specifically for promoting access for women and historically underrepresented students to engage in research have found that students describe an increasing sense of belonging and inclusion that may have been absent in the larger institution or STEM academic environments. Students who experience race-positive interactions[10] while pursuing a STEM degree report feeling a greater sense of belonging (Lee and Davis, 2000; Mendoza-Denton et al., 2002), and URE programs aimed toward historically underrepresented populations claim to counteract the effects of perceived exclusion (Hurtado et al., 1998).

Stereotype threat research has shown that when there are "signals" or context contingencies that communicate to historically underrepresented students that they do not belong in the academic or STEM community, the students' performances decline while cognitive vigilance increases (Murphy et al., 2007). Woodcock and colleagues (2012) found that participation in URE programs (specifically RISE and MARC) served to buffer students from the effects of stereotype threat, although they still experienced it.

Ownership

Project designs that encourage students to take ownership of their part of their URE's project have been associated with increased student retention in STEM (Hanauer and Dolan, 2014). Others have argued that facets of the research experience promote student development, such as a student's intellectual engagement in the project and in the opportunity to work independently with appropriate guidance (Laursen et al., 2010; Thiry et al.,

---

[10] In this context, Mendoza-Denton and colleagues (2002, p. 914) describe a race-positive experience as involving "interactions with same-race peers in settings where concern about the possibility of race-based rejection was absent."

2011). In addition, engaging in STEM practices for communicating results, such as preparing and presenting posters or attending conferences, has been linked to positive intellectual and psychosocial outcomes from apprentice-style research (Hunter et al., 2007; Laursen et al., 2010).

Within CUREs, Brownell and Kloser (2015) identified five critical components that serve to define CUREs and should be present in a research-based course: using the tools of a scientist, thinking and communicating like a scientist, collaboration, iteration, and discovery and relevance. Corwin and colleagues (2015a) developed a model from a review of the literature that identified project ownership, success in overcoming problems, and collaborative work with peers as additional critical components of CUREs. They also asserted that working with peers helps students to make improvements in technical skills—because peers may model or provide feedback about how to perform tasks—and that a sense of ownership over their work promotes students' sense of belonging to the STEM community (Corwin et al., 2015a; Hanauer et al., 2012).

Value of Teamwork

Working as part of a research group in a scientific community can lead to social benefits such as belonging and inclusion. This relationship suggests that research examining the value of teamwork and collaboration can provide mechanistic support for the benefits of UREs. A comparison of various approaches to collaboration found that requiring students to consider ideas of their peers that differ from their own is more effective than allowing students to consider only ideas that are consistent with their own (Matuk and Linn, 2015). The authors concluded that their results on collaboration provide support for a mechanism associated with the Knowledge Integration Framework, introduced by Linn and Eylon (2011).

The composition of the teams has also been shown to be important. Female engineering students were randomly assigned to one of three engineering groups of varying sex composition: 75 percent women, 50 percent women, or 25 percent women. For first-year students, group composition had a large effect: women in female-majority and sex-parity groups felt less anxious than women in female-minority groups. However, among advanced students, sex composition had no effect on anxiety. An important result was that group composition did have a statistically significant effect on verbal participation, regardless of women's academic seniority: women participated more in female-majority groups than in the sex-parity or female-minority groups (Dasgupta et al., 2015).

Carter and colleagues (2016) examined the impact of undergraduate research, broadly defined,[11] in engineering and focused on three specific learning outcomes: communication, teamwork, and leadership. They studied 5,126 students across 31 colleges of engineering. After propensity score adjustment, the study found no statistically significant effect on teamwork or leadership skills, but it did find that URE participation was a significant predictor of perceived communication skills. This study highlights the importance of taking into account selection bias when assessing the effect of co-curricular programs[12] on student learning. Implications of the study include expanding undergraduate research opportunities when possible and incorporating communication and leadership skill development into the required course curriculum.

Summary for Integrating Students into STEM Culture

Multiple studies indicate that students who participate in UREs feel more comfortable in STEM, have positive attitudes about STEM, and show increased confidence in being able to contribute to research after participation. Some work indicates that this feeling of confidence leads to greater engagement in STEM. The exposure to the culture, practices, and processes of STEM seems to increase students' feelings of belonging and sustain a professional identity, and such exposure may buffer students from the effects of stereotype threat. These increases in confidence, engagement, and identification with STEM, as well as endorsement of community values, may help provide some mechanistic explanation for why participation in UREs also improves outcomes such as retention and skills development.

PARTICIPATION OF WOMEN AND FIRST GENERATION COLLEGE STUDENTS IN URES

As discussed previously, there remain many unanswered questions about who participates in UREs and whether these experiences have a differential effect on specific subpopulations. While the committee was not able to find comprehensive data on the mix of men and women who did

---

[11] Carter and colleagues (2016) did not distinguish between the different types of undergraduate research in which a student could participate (e.g., research as part of the curriculum or a program of research such as in a faculty members lab).

[12] Co-curricular activities were measured as the months spent in: engineering internships, engineering cooperative education experiences, study abroad or international school-related tours, humanitarian engineering projects, student design projects/competitions beyond class requirements, involvement in an engineering club or student chapter of a professional society, engineering-related clubs or programs for women and/or minority students, and other clubs or activities (e.g., civic or church organizations, campus publications, student government, Greek life, sports) (Carter et al., 2016, p. 371).

undergraduate research, they did locate some studies on the topic. When taken as a group, the results of these studies appear inconsistent, with some reporting differential impacts by gender (Campbell and Skoog, 2004; Gregerman, 2008; Junge et al., 2010) but many others showing similar outcomes for both genders (Craney et al., 2011; McGee and Keller, 2007; Russell et al., 2007; Thiry et al., 2012).

The committee found a limited amount of data on first generation college students' participation in UREs, largely consisting of descriptive, qualitative studies that document the perceptions of the students who have engaged in UREs (Carpi and Lents, 2013; Ishiyama, 2007; Kwong Caputo, 2013; Stephens et al., 2014; Van Soom and Donche, 2014). Results from these studies suggest that programs of undergraduate research may be beneficial for women and first generation students, although it is not clear whether the benefits of participation are any different than for the majority of students. Nonetheless, if these students are at greater risk of leaving a STEM major, which appears to be the case in some fields, retention at the same rate as the average for all students would be a plus.

NEGATIVE OUTCOMES FROM URES

Although almost all of the research on UREs documents positive outcomes for research participants, several studies have noted less than desirable outcomes associated with poorly designed or poorly implemented research experiences, typically affecting only a small group of students (Craney et al., 2011; Harsh et al., 2011; Thiry et al., 2011). A poorly designed and/or implemented URE could involve students who have not received the proper training to do the work. It could also involve students lacking access to important resources due to an unexpected loss of research funds. Students could also be involved in projects that do not have the appropriate comparison samples built into the design. This could limit the types of claims that could be made about the research and reduce the quality of the work. Some studies have equated a lack of adequate mentoring with poor outcomes, such as loss of interest in graduate school or in the major (Barker, 2009; Thiry et al., 2011). Negative student-faculty interactions within research experiences can be particularly detrimental for students who are underrepresented in their fields, such as women in computing (Barker, 2009). These findings support the value of professional development for URE mentors. Other aspects of poorly designed research experiences, such as a lack of autonomy, inadequately selected projects (i.e., students take on an overly ambitious project given the time designated for the URE), or a general lack of structure have contributed to students' loss of confidence or loss of interest in STEM careers (Harsh et al., 2011; Thiry et al., 2011).

ASSESSMENT OF EVIDENCE AND NEED
FOR ADDITIONAL EVIDENCE

The evidence suggests that programs with research experience components are more likely to contribute to developing and sustaining student interest in STEM fields. The majority of studies cited here, however, have focused on persistence in biology or biomedical fields. More research concerning the impact of research experience in engineering, mathematics, other sciences, and technology fields is needed. At the same time, future research could examine how the duration of the URE, the timing of the experience in the academic career, and the quality of the research experience influences STEM interest and persistence.

It is clear that there is a need for additional evidence on the impacts of UREs. Perhaps most important is the need for more well-designed studies that can provide more than descriptive evidence about the effect of UREs. For example, there is a need for research that accounts for differences in URE and non-URE populations upon entering research experiences beyond simple demographic or GPA differences (e.g., differences in interest, motivation, aspirations, and confidence prior to the research experience). In turn, this points to the need for better instruments and a well-articulated experimental design, to measure these differences both before and after the URE. Although it may be difficult in most instances to design randomized controlled trial of UREs for students, it is certainly possible to improve the selection of the populations that are under study.

Educational and career outcomes have been among the most studied aspects of UREs or CUREs. However, many studies rely on students' self-report of aspirations or alumni retrospective accounts of the influence of research on their career or educational decisions, rather than longitudinally tracking students' educational or career outcomes. Such long-term studies can be logistically and financially challenging, but they would greatly enhance the claims that research experiences inspire students to enroll in graduate degree programs or strengthen their commitment to STEM careers.

There is also a need for more research on nontraditional populations (pre-service teachers or current teachers in research experiences, community college students in both workforce and transfer programs, students of nontraditional ages, veterans, students with disabilities, etc.), who typically do not have access to UREs. CUREs can provide one potential approach for understanding the potential benefits for these populations as students simply need to sign up for a course. This could effectively enable more students to engage in research opportunities beyond traditional apprentice-style programs (Bangera and Brownell, 2014). As more opportunities develop, it will become important to understand whether all populations benefit (or do not benefit) in the same ways as the populations on whom research has already been done. Additionally, there is a need for research on non-STEM majors in UREs to document whether outcomes for nonmajors differ from those of STEM majors.

Perhaps surprisingly, one of the least-documented effects of UREs is improvement in STEM thinking abilities for students. This includes improvements in disciplinary expertise, research design, and understanding of the research process. Most of the existing research has relied on self-report to document these important outcomes. Studies that include supplemental measures to self-report do not often include enough detail or description of what these instruments measure and how the instruments may have been piloted or validated. For example, whereas some studies of CUREs show improvement for students in course examinations, there is typically no discussion of what these examinations measure. Improvement in course grades is encouraging, but to be convincing such studies must provide information on what the course assessments are designed to measure and how and why a URE has changed student responses on these items.

SUMMARY

UREs are diverse in their structure and goals, so it is not surprising that the questions and methodologies used to investigate the effectiveness of UREs in achieving those goals are similarly diverse. Much of the published literature focuses on outcomes of participation, retention, and persistence. Additional research has examined the potential benefit of UREs on developing an understanding of STEM disciplinary practices (e.g., content knowledge, concepts, and corresponding research skills) and integrating students into the STEM culture (e.g., project ownership, sense of belonging, teamwork). The committee's review of the literature shows that most of the studies of UREs to date either are descriptive case studies or use correlational designs. Only a few studies have generated the causal evidence necessary to draw conclusions about the precise effects of UREs. However, the information currently available suggests that UREs may be beneficial for students due to their potential to improve participation and retention of students in STEM majors, as well as improving students' knowledge of career options, experimental design, and related disciplinary thinking (Graham et al., 2013; Rodenbusch et al., 2016). Multiple studies also indicate that students who participate in UREs feel more comfortable in STEM, have more positive attitudes, and show increased confidence in being able to contribute to research upon URE completion. A few studies have documented reliable improvements relating to degree completion and persistence of interest in STEM careers for historically underrepresented students (Byars-Winston et al., 2015; Chemers et al., 2011; Jones et al., 2010; Nagda et al., 1998; Rodenbusch et al., 2016; Schultz et al., 2011). Additional research is needed to better understand the mechanisms that explain why participation in UREs could lead to improved student outcomes.

REFERENCES

Adedokun, O.A., Zhang, D., Carleton Parker, L., Bessenbacher, A., Childress, A., and Burgess, W.D. (2012). Understanding how undergraduate research experiences influence student aspirations for research careers and graduate education. *Journal of College Science Teaching, 42*(1), 82-90.

Adedokun, O.A., Bessenbacher, A.B., Parker, L.C., Kirkham, L.L., and Burgess, W.D. (2013). Research skills and STEM undergraduate research students' aspirations for research careers: Mediating effects of research on self-efficacy. *Journal of Research in Science Teaching, 50*(8), 940-951.

Adedokun, O.A., Parker, L.C., Childress, A., Burgess, W., Adams, R., Agnew, C.R., Leary, J., Knapp, D., Shields, C., Lelievre, S., and Teegarden, D. (2014). Effect of time on perceived gains from an undergraduate research program. *CBE–Life Sciences Education, 13*, 139-148.

Bandura, A. (1997). *Self-Efficacy: The Exercise of Control.* New York: Freeman.

Bangera, G., and Brownell, S.E. (2014). Course-based undergraduate research experiences can make scientific research more inclusive. *CBE–Life Sciences Education, 14*, 602-606.

Barlow, A.E., and Villarejo, M. (2004). Making a difference for minorities: Evaluation of an educational enrichment program. *Journal of Research in Science Teaching, 41*(9), 861-881.

Bauer, K.W., and Bennett, J.S. (2003). Alumni perceptions used to assess undergraduate research experience. *The Journal of Higher Education, 74*(2), 210-230.

Barker, L. (2009). Student and faculty of undergraduate research experiences in computing. *ACM Transactions on Computing Education, 9*(1), 1-28.

Brownell, S.E., and Kloser, M.J. (2015). Toward a conceptual framework for measuring the effectiveness of course-based undergraduate research experiences in undergraduate biology. *Studies in Higher Education, 40*(3), 525-544.

Brownell, S.E., Kloser, M.J., Fukami, T., and Shavelson, R. (2012). Undergraduate biology lab courses: Comparing the impact of traditionally based "cookbook" and authentic research-based courses on student lab experiences. *Journal of College Science Teaching, 41*(4), 36-45.

Brownell, S.E., Wenderoth, M.P., Theobald, R., Okoroafor, N., Koval, M., Freeman, S., Walcher-Chevillet, C.L., and Crowe, A.J. (2014). How students think about experimental design: Novel conceptions revealed by in-class activities. *BioScience, 64*(2), 125-137.

Brownell, S.E., Hekmat-Scafe, D.S., Singla, V., Chandler Seawell, P., Conklin Imam, J.F., Eddy, S.L., Sterns, T., and Cyert, M.S. (2015). A high enrollment course-based undergraduate research experience improves student conceptions of scientific thinking and ability to interpret data. *CBE–Life Sciences Education, 41*, 1-14.

Byars-Winston, A.M., Branchaw, J., Pfund, C., Leverett, P., and Newton, J. (2015). Culturally diverse undergraduate researchers' academic outcomes and perceptions of their research mentoring relationships. *International Journal of Science Education, 37*(15), 2533-2554.

Campbell, A., and Skoog, G. (2004). Preparing undergraduate women for science careers. *Journal of College Science Teaching, 33*(5), 24-26.

Carpi, A., and Lents, N.H. (2013). Research by undergraduates helps underfinanced colleges as well as students. *Chronicle of Higher Education, 60*(9), B30-B31.

Carter, F.D., Mandell, M., and Maton, K.I. (2009). The influence of on-campus, academic year undergraduate research on STEM Ph.D. outcomes: Evidence from the Meyerhoff Scholarship Program. *Educational Evaluation and Policy Analysis, 31*(4), 441-462.

Carter, D.F., Ro, H.K., Alcott, B., and Lattuca, L. (2016). Curricular connections: The role of undergraduate research experiences in promoting engineering students' communication, teamwork, and leadership skills. *Research in Higher Education, 57*(3), 363-393.

Cartrette, D.P., and Melro-Lehrman, B.M. (2012). Describing changes in undergraduate students' preconceptions of research activities. *Research in Science Education, 42,* 1073-1100.

Chang, M.J., Sharkness, J., Hurtado, S., and Newman, C.B. (2014). What matters in college for retaining aspiring scientists and engineers from underrepresented racial groups. *Journal of Research in Science Teaching, 51*(5), 555-580.

Chemers, M.M., Zurbriggen, E.L., Syed, M., Goza, B.K., and Bearman, S. (2011). The role of efficacy and identity in science career commitment among underrepresented minority students. *Journal of Social Issues, 67*(3), 469-491.

Corwin, L.A., Graham, M.J., and Dolan, E.L. (2015a). Modeling course-based undergraduate research experiences: An agenda for future research and evaluation. *CBE–Life Sciences Education, 14,* es1. Available: http://www.lifescied.org/content/14/1/es1.full.pdf+html [January 2017].

Corwin, L.A., Runyon, C., Robinson, A., and Dolan, E.L. (2015b). The Laboratory Course Assessment Survey: A tool to measure three dimensions of research-course design. *CBE–Life Sciences Education, 14*(4), ar37. Available http://www.lifescied.org/content/14/4/ar37.abstract [November 2016].

Craney, C., McKay, T., Mazzeo, A., Morris, J., Prigodich, C., and de Groot, R. (2011). Cross-discipline perceptions of the undergraduate research experience. *The Journal of Higher Education, 82*(1), 92-113.

Dasgupta, A.P., Anderson, T.R., and Pelaez, N. (2014). Development and validation of a rubric for diagnosing students' experimental design knowledge and difficulties. *CBE–Life Sciences Education, 13*(2), 265-284.

Dasgupta, N., Scircle, M.M., and Hunsinger, M. (2015). Female peers in small work groups enhance women's motivation, verbal participation, and career aspirations in engineering. *Proceedings of the National Academy of Sciences, 112*(16), 4988-4993.

Deek, F., Briller, V., Friedman, R., and Joshi, K. (2003). Active research experience for undergraduates increases students' motivation and academic performance. Pp. 8.161.1-8.161.18. *Paper presented at 2003 ASEE Annual Conference and Exposition,* Nashville, TN. Available: https://peer.asee.org/12353 [November 2016].

Dolan, E. (2016). *Course-Based Undergraduate Research Experiences: Current Knowledge and Future Directions.* Paper commissioned for the Committee on Strengthening Research Experiences for Undergraduate STEM Students. Board on Science Education, Division of Behavioral and Social Sciences and Education. Board on Life Sciences, Division of Earth and Life Studies. Washington, DC: National Academies of Sciences, Engineering, and Medicine. Available: http://nas.edu/STEM_Undergraduate_Research_CURE. [February 2016].

Dolan, E., and Johnson, D. (2010). The undergraduate-postgraduate-faculty triad: Unique functions and tensions associated with undergraduate research at research universities. *CBE–Life Sciences Education, 9,* 543-553.

Drew, J.C., and Tiplett, E.W. (2008). Whole genome sequencing in the undergraduate classroom: Outcomes and lessons from a pilot course. *Journal of Microbiology & Biology Education, 9,* 3-11.

Eagan, M.K., Hurtado, S., Chang, M.J., Garcia, G.A., Herrara, F.A., and Garibay, J.C. (2013). Making a difference in science education: The impact of undergraduate research programs. *American Educational Research Journal, 50*(4), 683-713.

Estrada, M., Woodcock, A., Hernandez, P.R., and Schultz, P. (2011). Toward a model of social influence that explains minority student integration into the scientific community. *Journal of Educational Psychology, 103*(1), 206-222.

Fechheimer, M., Webber, K., and Kleiber, P. (2011). How well do undergraduate research programs promote engagement and success of students? *CBE–Life Sciences Education, 10*, 156-163.

Feldman, A., Divoll, K., and Rogan-Klyve, A. (2009). Research education of new scientists: Implications for science teacher education. *Journal of Research in Science Teaching, 46*(4), 442-459.

Gilmore, J., Vieyra, M., Timmerman, B., Feldon, D., and Maher, M. (2015). The relationship between undergraduate research participation and subsequent research performance of early career STEM graduate students. *The Journal of Higher Education, 86*(6), 834-863.

Graham, C.R., Woodfield, W., and Harrison, J.B. (2013). A framework for institutional adoption and implementation of blended learning in higher education. *The Internet and Higher Education, 18*, 4-14.

Gregerman, S. (2008). *Promising Practices in STEM Education.* Paper commissioned for the Workshop on Evidence on Promising Practices in Undergraduate STEM Education. National Research Council, Washington, DC. Available: http://sites.nationalacademies. org/cs/groups/dbassesite/documents/webpage/dbasse_072631.pdf [November 2016].

Grimberg, S.J., Langen, T.A., Compeau, L.D., and Powers, S.E. (2008). A theme-based seminar on environmental sustainability improves participant satisfaction in an undergraduate summer research program. *Journal of Engineering Education, 97*(1), 95-102.

Gonzalez-Espada, W.J., and LaDue, D.S. (2006). Evaluation of the impact of the NWC REU program compared with other undergraduate research experiences. *Journal of Geoscience Education, 54*(5), 541-549.

Hanauer, D.I., and Dolan, E.L. (2014). The Project Ownership Survey: Measuring differences in scientific inquiry experiences. *CBE–Life Sciences Education, 13*(1), 149-158.

Hanauer, D.I., and Hatfull, G. (2015). Measuring networking as an outcome variable in undergraduate research experiences. *CBE–Life Sciences Education, 14*(4), ar38. Available http://www.lifescied.org/content/14/4/ar38.full [November 2016].

Hanauer D.I., Frederick J., Fotinakes B., and Strobel S.A. (2012). Linguistic analysis of project ownership for undergraduate research experiences. *CBE–Life Sciences Education, 11*, 378–385.

Harrison, M., Dunbar, D., Ratmansky, L., Boyd, K., and Lopatto, D. (2011). Classroom-based science research at the introductory level: Changes in career choice and attitude. *CBE–Life Sciences Education, 10*, 279-286.

Harsh, J.A., Maltese, A.V., and Tai, R.H. (2011). Undergraduate research experiences from a longitudinal perspective. *Journal of College Science Teaching, 41*(1), 84-91.

Hathaway, R.S., Nagda, B.A., and Gregerman, S.R. (2002). The relationship of undergraduate research participation to graduate and professional education pursuit: An empirical study. *Journal of College Student Development, 43*(5), 1-18.

Hausmann, L.R., Schofield, J.W., and Woods, R.L. (2007). Sense of belonging as a predictor of intentions to persist among African American and White first-year college students. *Research in Higher Education, 48*(7), 803-839.

Healy, N., and Rathbun, L.C. (2013). *Developing Globally Aware Scientists and Engineers in Nanoscale Science and Engineering.* Paper presented at the 120th ASEE Annual Conference & Exposition [June 23-26, 2013) in Atlanta, GA. Available: http://www.asee.org/ public/conferences/20/papers/6264/download [November 2016].

Hunter, A.B., Laursen, S.L., and Seymour, E. (2007). Becoming a scientist: The role of undergraduate research in cognitive, personal and professional development. *Science Education, 91*(1), 36-74.

Hurtado, S., and Carter, D. F. (1997). Effects of college transition and perceptions of the campus racial climate on Latino college students' sense of belonging. *Sociology of Education, 70*(4), 324-345.

Hurtado, S., Milem, J.F., Clayton-Pedersen, A.R., and Allen, W.R. (1998). Enhancing campus climates for racial/ethnic diversity: Educational policy and practice. *The Review of Higher Education, 21*, 279-302.

Ishiyama, J. (2007). Expectations and perceptions of undergraduate research mentoring: Comparing first generation, low income white/Caucasian and African American students. *College Student Journal, 41*(3), 540-549.

John, J., and Creighton, J. (2012). 'In practice, it doesn't always work out like that.' Undergraduate experiences in a research community of practices. *Journal of Further and Higher Education, 37*(6), 1-19.

Jones, M., Amy, T., Barlow, E., and Villarejo, M. (2010). Importance of undergraduate research for minority persistence and achievement in biology. *Journal of Higher Education, 81*, 82-115.

Junge, B., Quiñones, C., Kakietek, J., Teodorescu, D., and Marsteller, P. (2010). Promoting undergraduate interest, preparedness, and professional pursuit in the sciences: An outcomes evaluation of the SURE program at Emory University. *CBE–Life Sciences Education, 9*(2), 119-132.

Kardash, C.M. (2000). Evaluation of an undergraduate research experience: Perceptions of undergraduate interns and their faculty mentors. *Journal of Educational Psychology, 92*(1), 191-201.

Kardash, C.M., and Edwards, O.V. (2012). Thinking and behaving like scientists: Perceptions of undergraduate science interns and their faculty mentors. *Instructional Science, 40*, 875-899.

Kloser, M.J., Brownell, S.E., Shavelson, R.J., and Fukami, T. (2013). Effects of a research-based ecology lab course: A study of nonvolunteer achievement, self-confidence, and perception of lab course purpose. *Journal of College Science Teaching, 42*(3), 72-81.

Kwong Caputo, J.J. (2013). *Undergraduate Research and Metropolitan Commuter University Student Involvement: Exploring the Narratives of Five Female Undergraduate Students.* [Dissertation]. Available at http://pdxscholar.library.pdx.edu/open_access_etds/1006/ [November 2016].

Laursen S.L., Hunter A.B., Seymour E., Thiry H., and Melton G. (2010). *Undergraduate Research in the Sciences: Engaging Students in Real Science.* San Francisco: Jossey-Bass.

Lee, R.M., and Davis III, C. (2000). Cultural orientation, past multicultural experience, and a sense of belonging on campus for Asian American college students. *Journal of College Student Development, 41*(1), 110-115.

Linn, M.C., and Eylon, B.S. (2011). *Science Learning and Instruction: Taking Advantage of Technology to Promote Knowledge Integration.* New York: Routledge.

Litzinger, T.A., Lattuca, L.R., Hadgraft, R.G., and Newstetter, W.C. (2011). Engineering education and the development of expertise. *Journal of Engineering Education, 100*(1), 123-150.

Lopatto, D. (2004). Survey of Undergraduate Research Experiences (SURE): First findings. *Cell Biology Education, 3*, 270-277.

Lopatto, D., Alvarez, C., Barnard, D., Chandrasekaran, C., Chung, H., Du, C., Eckdahl, T., Goodman, A. Hauser, C., Jones, C.J., Kopp, O.R., Kuleck, G.A., McNeil, G., Morris, R., Myka, J.L., Nagengast, A., Overvoorde, P.J., Poet, J.L., Reed, K., Regisford, G., Revie, D., Rosenwald, A., Saville, K., Shaw, M., Skuse, G.R., Smith, C., Spratt, M., Stamm, J., Thomspon, J.S., Wilson, B.A., Witkowski, C., Youngblom, J., Leung, W., Shaffer, C.D., Buhler, J., Mardis, E., and Elgin, S.C.R. (2008). Genomics Education Partnership. *Science, 322*(5902), 684-685.

Matuk, C., and Linn, M.C. (2015). Examining the real and perceived impacts of a public idea repository on literacy and science inquiry. *CSCL'15: Proceedings of the 11th International Conference for Computer Supported Collaborative Learning, Gothenburg, Sweden*. International Society of the Learning Sciences. Available at https://www.isls.org/cscl2015/papers/MC-0178-FullPaper-Matuk.pdf [November 2016].

McGee, R., and Keller, J.L. (2007). Identifying future scientist: Predicting persistence into research training. *CBE–Life Sciences Education, 6*, 316-331.

Mendoza-Denton, R., Downey, G., Purdie, V.J., Davis, A., and Pietrzak, J. (2002). Sensitivity to status-based rejection: Implications for African American students' college experience. *Journal of Personality and Social Psychology, 83*(4), 896-918.

Murphy, T.J., Shehab, R.L., Reed-Rhoads, T., Foor, C.E., Harris, B.J., Trytten, D.A., Walden, S.E., Besterfield-Sacre, M., Hallbek, M.S., and Moor, W.C. (2007). Achieving parity of the sexes at the undergraduate level: A study of success. *Journal of Engineering Education, 96*(3), 241-252.

Nagda, B.A., Gregerman, S.R., Jonides, J., von Hippel, W., and Lerner, J.S. (1998). Undergraduate student-faculty research partnerships affect student retention. *The Review of Higher Education, 21*(1), 55-72.

Pacific, L.B., and Thompson, N. (2011). Undergraduate science research: A comparison of influences and experiences between premed and non-premed students. *CBE–Life Sciences Education, 10*, 199-208.

Raelin, J.A., Bailey, M.B., Hamann, J., Pendleton, L.K., Reisberg, R., and Whitman, D.L. (2014). The gendered effect of cooperative education, contextual support, and self-efficacy on undergraduate retention. *Journal of Engineering Education, 103*(4), 599-624.

Rodenbusch, S.E., Hernandez, P.R., Simmons, S.L., and Dolan, E.L. (2016). Early engagement in course-based research increases graduation rates and completion of science, engineering, and mathematics degrees. *CBE–Life Sciences Education, 15*(2), ar20. Available at http://www.lifescied.org/content/15/2/ar20 [November 2016].

Rowland, S.L., Lawrie, G.A., Behrendorff, J.B.Y.H., and Gillam, E.M.J. (2012). Is the undergraduate research experience (URE) always best? *Biochemistry and Molecular Biology Education, 40*(1), 46-62.

Russell, C.B., and Weaver, G.C. (2011). A comparative study of traditional, inquiry-based, and research-based laboratory curricula: Impacts on understanding of the nature of science. *Chemistry Education Research & Practice, 12*, 57-67.

Russell, J.E., D'Costa, A.R., Runck, C., Barnes, D.W., Barrera, A.L., Hurst-Kennedy, J., Sudduth, E.B., Quinlan, E.L., and Schlueter, M. (2015). Bridging the undergraduate curriculum using an integrated course-embedded undergraduate research experience (ICURE). *CBE–Life Sciences Education, 14*, 1-10

Russell, S.H., Hancock, M.P., and McCullough, J. (2007). Benefits of undergraduate research experiences. *Science, 316*, 548-549.

Ryder, J., Leach, J., and Driver, R. (1999). Undergraduate science students' images of science. *Journal of Research in Science Teaching, 36*(2), 201-219.

Sabitini, D.A. (1997). Teaching and research synergism: The undergraduate research experience. *Journal of Professional Issues in Engineering Education and Practice, 123*(3), 98-102.

Salsman, N., Dulaney, C., Chinta, R., Zascavage, V., and Joshi, H. (2013). Student effort in and perceived benefits from undergraduate research. *College Student Journal, 47*(1), 202-211.

Schultz, P.W., Hernandez, P.R., Woodcock, A., Estrada, M., Chance, R.C., Aguilar, M., and Serpe, R.T. (2011). Patching the pipeline: Reducing educational disparities in the sciences through minority training programs. *Educational Evaluation and Policy Analysis, 33*(1), 95-114.

Seymour, E., Hunter, A.B., Laursen, S.L., and DeAntoni, T. (2004). Establishing the benefits of research experiences for undergraduates in the sciences: First findings from a three-year study. *Science Education, 88*, 493-534.

Shaffer, C.D., Alvarez, C., Bailey, C., Barnard, D., Bhalla, S., Chandrasekaran, C., Chandrasekaran, V., Chung, H.M., Dorer, D.R., Du, C., Eckdahl, T.T., Poet, J.L., Frohlich, D., Goodman, A.L., Gosser, Y., Hauser, C., Hoopes, L.L., Johnson, D., Jones, C.J., Kaehler, M., Kokan, N., Kopp, O.R., Kuleck, G.A., McNeil, G., Moss, R., Myka, J.L., Nagengast, A., Morris, R., Overvoorde, P.J., Shoop, E., Parrish, S., Reed, K., Regisford, E.G., Revie, D., Rosenwald, A.G., Saville, K., Schroeder, S., Shaw, W., Skuse, G., Smith, C., Smith, M., Spana, E.P., Spratt, M., Stamm, J., Thompson, J.S., Wawersik, M., Wilson, B.A., Youngblom, J., Leung, W., Buhler, J., Mardis, E.R., Lopatto, D., and Elgin, S.C. (2010). The Genomics Education Partnership: Successful integration of research into laboratory classes at a diverse group of undergraduate institutions. *CBE–Life Sciences Education, 9*, 55-69.

Shaffer, C.D., Alvarez, C.J., Bednarski, A.E., Dunbar, D., Goodman, A.L., Reinke, C., Rosenwald, A.G., Wolyniak, M.J., Bailey, C., Barnard, D., Bazinet, C., Beach, D.L., Bedard, J.E.J., Bhalla, S., Braverman, J., Burg, M., Chandrasekaran, V., Chung, H.-M., Clase, K., DeJong, R.J., DiAngelo, J.R., Du, C., Eckdahl, T.R., Eisler, H., Emerson, J.A., Frary, A., Frohlich, D., Gosser, Y., Govind, S., haberman, A., Hark, A.T., Hauser, C., Hoogewerf, A., Hooper, L.L.M., Howell, C.E., Johnson, D., Jones, C.J., Kadlec, L., Kaehler, M., Silver Key, S.C., Kleinschmit, A., Kokan, N.P., Kopp, O., Kuleck, G., Leatherman, J., Lopilato, J., MacKinnon, C., Martinez-Cruzado, J.C., McNeil, G., Mel, S., Mistry, H., Nagengast, A., Overvoorde, P., paetkau, D.W., Parrish, S., Peterson, C.N., Preuss, M., Reed, L.K., Revie, D., Robic, S., Roecklein-Canfield, J., Rubin, M.R., Saville, K., Scjrpeder, S., Sharif, K., Shaw, M., Skuse, G., Smith, C.D., Smith, M.A., Smith, S.T., Spana, E., Spratt, M., Sreenivasan, A., Stamm, J., Szauter, P., Thompson, J.S., Wawersik, M., Youngblom, J., Zhou, L., Mardis, E.R., Buhler, J., Leung, W., Lopatto, D., and Elgin, S.C.R. (2014). A course-based research experience: How benefits change with increased investment of instructional time. *CBE–Life Sciences Education, 13*, 111-130.

Shapiro, C., Moberg-Parker, J., Toma, S., Ayon, C., Zimmerman, H., Roth-Johnson, E.A., Hancock, S.P., Levis-Fitzgerald, M., and Sanders, E.R. (2015). Comparing the impact of a course-based and apprentice-based research experiences in a life sciences laboratory curriculum. *Journal of Microbiology & Biology Education, 16*(2), 189-197.

Sirum, K., and Humburg, J. (2011). The Experimental Design Ability Test (EDAT). *Bioscene: Journal of College Biology Teaching, 37*(1), 8-16.

Stephens, N.M., Hamedani, M.G., and Destin, M. (2014). Closing the social-class achievement gap a difference-education intervention improves first-generation students' academic performance and all students' college transition. *Psychological Science, 25*(4), 943-953.

Szteinberg, G.A., and Weaver, G.C. (2013). Participants' reflections two and three years after an introductory chemistry course-embedded research experience. *Chemistry Education Research and Practice, 14*, 23-35.

Thiry, H., and Laursen, S.L. (2011). The role of student-advisor interactions in apprenticing undergraduate researchers into a scientific community of practice. *Journal of Science Education and Technology, 20*(6), 771-784.

Thiry, H., Laursen, S.L., and Hunter, A.B. (2011). What experiences help students become scientists? A comparative study of research and other sources of personal and professional gains for STEM undergraduates. *Journal of Higher Education, 82*(4), 358-389.

Thiry, H., Weston, T.J., Laursen, S.L., and Hunter, A.B. (2012). The benefits of multi-year research experiences: Differences in novice and experienced students' reported gains from undergraduate research. *CBE–Life Sciences Education, 11,* 1-13.

Thompson, J.J., Conaway, E., and Dolan, E.L. (2016). Undergraduate students' development of social, cultural, and human capital in a networked research experience. *Cultural Studies of Science Education, 11*(4), 959-990.

Van Soom, C., and Donche, V. (2014). Profiling first-year students in STEM programs based on autonomous motivation and academic self-concept and relationship with academic achievement. *PloS One, 9*(11), e112489. Available at http://dx.doi.org/10.1371/journal.pone.0112489 [November 2016].

Villa, E.Q., Kephart, K., Gates, A.Q., Thiry, H., and Hug, S. (2013). Affinity research groups in practice: Apprenticing students in research. *Journal of Engineering Education, 102*(3), 444-466.

Villarejo, M., and Barlow, A.E. (2007). Evolution and evaluation of a biology enrichment program for minorities. *Journal of Women and Minorities in Science and Engineering, 13*(2), 119-144.

Weston, T.J., and Laursen, S.L. (2015). The Undergraduate Research Student Self-Assessment (URSSA): Validation for use in program evaluation. *CBE–Life Sciences Education, 14,* ar33. Available at http://www.lifescied.org/content/14/3/ar33.long [November 2016].

Woodcock, A., Graziano, W.G., Branch, S.E., Ngambeki, I., and Evangelou, D. (2012). Engineering students' beliefs about research: Sex differences, personality, and career plans. *Journal of Engineering Education, 101*(3), 495-511.

Zydney, A.L., Bennett, J.S., Shahid, A., and Bauer, K. (2002). Faculty perspectives regarding the undergraduate research experience in science and engineering. *Journal of Engineering Education, 91*(3), 291-297.

5

The Role of Mentoring

Students participating in undergraduate research experiences (UREs) in science, technology, engineering, and mathematics (STEM) might be faced with a number of engaging and challenging situations during their research experience. The success of students in UREs depends upon the support structures in place. Often this means having available and accessible mentors, although not all undergraduates will have access to mentors.[1] There are more than 50 definitions of mentoring: mentoring can be defined as a concept, a process, a developmental experience, or a set of activities (Crisp and Cruz, 2009). Moreover, mentoring interactions can be informal or formal, short or long, spontaneous or planned. Mentors can also play a variety of roles. These can include relatively simple activities such as offering a name or well-timed introduction, or mentoring may involve more complex activities such as providing advice or guidance and answering complex questions. Furthermore, mentors can help students by bringing together ideas from different contexts to promote deeper learning. The roles played by mentors can change across the experience and can be accomplished by different individuals or a team of individuals. Although most studies tend to report that mentoring has a positive impact on academic success, the variability in terms of the defining roles and types of interactions has made it difficult to fully evaluate the impact of mentoring on UREs (Crisp and Cruz, 2009).

---

[1] This chapter includes content from a paper commissioned by the committee, titled *Studying the Role and Impact of Mentoring on Undergraduate Research Experiences*, by Christine Pfund (2016).

This chapter examines the role of mentors in undergraduate research by defining "mentor," the mentoring relationship, and who can serve as a mentor and then examining the research on mentoring. The chapter then goes into a discussion of the various roles that mentors can play and presents a summary of some of the associated outcomes of mentoring from the perspective of the mentor and the mentee. The last section reviews some of the existing URE mentoring programs, including programs to train mentors for success with undergraduate mentees.

MENTOR DEFINED

"Mentor" has been defined in many ways dating back to Greek mythology (Kram, 1985). In the simplest sense, mentorship, or the act of mentoring, describes an experienced person (mentor) guiding a less experienced person (mentee/protégé) (Eby et al., 2007). Mentoring has also been used to describe many different types of relationships in the research training context. These relationships include academic advising, research or laboratory supervision, evaluation, informal support, personal support, and career coaching. Mentors provide support beyond teaching and learning to include social and personal elements (Galbraith, 2003; Johnson and Zlotnick, 2005; Mullen, 2005; Waldeck et al., 1997). After reviewing usage in the literature, the committee adopted the following functional definition: *Mentoring is a collaborative learning relationship that proceeds through stages over time and has the primary goal of helping a less experienced person acquire the essential competencies needed for success in that person's chosen career.*

As stated previously, mentoring interactions can be informal or formal, short or long, spontaneous or planned. Mentoring relationships can occur naturally in a spontaneous manner, and the development of the relationship may be gradual and informal in nature (Johnson, 2002). This kind of mentoring role contrasts with formal mentoring that is more structured, with the mentee assigned to the mentor (Johnson and Ridley, 2004), as occurs in some wrap-around programs (see Chapter 2 on URE program types) that have an institutionalized mentoring structure in which specific types of mentoring (e.g., research, academic, personal) are carried out by trained, qualified mentors (Twale and Kochan, 2000). However, more informal mentoring relationships can allow for a closer interpersonal bond to form, as they are not limited to the length of the program and frequently persist over a longer period of time (Mullen, 2005).

Ideally, mentees and mentors engage as partners through reciprocal activities such as planning, acting, reflecting, questioning, and problem solving (Pfund et al., 2016). *Mentoring competency* is then defined as having the skills and knowledge to effectively support mentee development and facilitate the attainment of the transferable "competencies" necessary to meet individual mentees' goals. This requires the ability to come to a clear understanding of each mentee's unique needs and desires and the flexibility and humility to adjust one's approach to support a mentee's success. Thus, *mentoring success*, which can be an ongoing and adaptive experience, occurs when the mentee has gained (1) the personal and professional competencies necessary to define his/her career goals, (2) the experience needed for that career, and (3) the ability and opportunity to progress toward that chosen career goal (Pfund et al., 2016). Alignment of the goals of the mentor and mentee is crucial, whether or not the mentee aspires to become a STEM professional.

WHO IS MENTORING IN URES?

Students in apprentice-style research experiences, particularly at research-intensive universities, are typically mentored by postdoctoral scholars or graduate students; these novice mentors may vary in their ability to provide appropriate guidance and support and in their commitment to advising an undergraduate (Dolan and Johnson, 2009; Thiry and Laursen, 2011). In the case of course-based UREs, lab instructors or teaching assistants may play the role of mentors. For co-ops and internships, in addition to the faculty sponsor, industry researchers take on many of the responsibilities of mentorship. Moreover, in more structured programs, peer-to-peer mentoring programs are common, drawing on peers who are at the same grade level but may have more experience or junior/senior undergraduates. In some instances, this form of "mutual mentoring" can happen informally as students work together to solve problems. There is no training for this type of mentoring, but it can have benefits for research that is designed to be carried out in team settings (Ryser et al., 2009). Box 5-1 highlights the beneficial role that peer-to-peer mentoring can have in increasing retention in STEM. Moreover, mentoring carried out by graduate students can provide undergraduates with an "insider's" perspective into the next step in pursuing a research career: the graduate training program. For example, a grad-undergrad mentoring program developed at the University of Pennsylvania[2] has shown that grad-undergrad mentoring has helped undergraduate students broaden and deepen their understanding of educational and career opportunities in STEM fields.

Finally, in many cases a single individual does not serve all of the mentoring functions (described in the subsequent section). Mosaic mentoring—mentoring that is carried out through a network of mentors—is becoming a more prevalent approach in order to provide a circle of support for undergraduates (Bartlett, 2012; Darling, 1986; Head et al., 1992;

---

[2] See http://www.gsc.upenn.edu/mentoring [February 2017].

BOX 5-1
Peer-to-Peer Mentoring Programs

The Division of Undergraduate Education at the University of California, Santa Barbara, has developed a peer-to-peer mentorship program to connect freshmen students with an upper-level peer mentor.[a] The goal of this program is to help create an increased self-awareness, enhanced sense of belonging and self-esteem, and academic skill development for the mentee. Peer mentors are experienced undergraduates who have participated in mentor training, which provides a foundation for how to have intentional conversations with their mentees. Mentors meet with support staff and academic advising for guidance on various questions asked by the mentee. Mentees in the program receive advice regarding study skills, test taking strategies, accessing key campus resources, setting and achieving goals, and time management.

University of Central Florida has developed a peer-to-peer mentoring program to increase the number of students obtaining STEM degrees.[b] The Girls Exceling in Math and Science (GEMS) program includes peer-to-peer mentoring for female freshman. Each upper-division female mentor is assigned 4-5 freshmen mentees. In addition to connecting students with opportunities to engage in research and industrial experiences, GEMS activities include networking events featuring female faculty and industry professionals, mentee group meetings, and socials.

---

[a]See the program's description at http://www.duels.ucsb.edu/academics/academic-success/mentor [February 2017].
[b]See http://stem.ucf.edu/stem-programs-at-ucf [November 2016].

Mullen, 2007). For example, in the Girls Exceling in Math and Science (GEMS) program described in Box 5-1, students have a peer support group (the cohort of mentees) that meets on a regular basis in addition to the mentoring provided by the upper-division peer and faculty mentors. As the example highlights, this level of support provided by a network of mentors has resulted in significant benefits. However, this approach is not always practical within a particular institution or in certain disciplines. In these cases, mentoring may be fulfilled in a variety of ways by individuals within the institution from other departments or from individuals outside the institution.

The quality of mentoring and support within the research experience is essential in facilitating students' technical and intellectual proficiency, as well as in shaping their understanding of the professional work and practice of science (Feldman et al., 2009, 2012; Thiry and Laursen, 2011). Regardless of who is serving in the role(s) of mentor, there are rarely criteria for selecting or evaluating them, and it is not clear that all professionals will make good mentors. In some circumstances, there can be conflict and dysfunction; however, this is not frequently investigated (Johnson, 2002). Also, mentors often do not participate in training to obtain a baseline knowledge about and skills in mentoring. Traditionally, the only experience required for being a research mentor is having been mentored, regardless of whether the experience was negative or positive (Handelsman et al., 2005).

ROLES THAT MENTORS MAY PLAY

Mentors can play many roles. On a practical level, mentors can assign research tasks and construct research experiences that are appropriate to the mentees' skills and understanding of disciplinary content. Mentors can introduce relevant concepts and skills, as well as provide a way for thinking about research. The responsibility of a mentor includes monitoring progress of the student's research experience (this can be done informally or through formal assessment), facilitating their participation within the lab or other research environment, and providing guidance on the student's future educational or career pathways. This guidance can include assisting students with gaining employment. Moreover, mentors can help students develop a variety of skills through the mentor-mentee relationship. The development of these skills may be different for students in community college settings, as students often face different obstacles and may enter with lower levels of academic preparation (Bailey and Alfonso, 2005; Crisp, 2010). As shown in Figure 5-1, these skills include such things as research skills, interpersonal skills, diversity-focused/culturally focused skills, psychosocial skills, and sponsorship skills (Abedin et al., 2012; Pfund et al., 2016; Ragins and Kram, 2007).

A primary goal of many mentoring programs is to encourage persistence in STEM through the development of a set of attributes such as STEM identity, research self-efficacy, and acceptance of cultural diversity, which can be accomplished through the mentor-mentee relationship (Byars-Winston et al., 2015; Chang et al., 2011; Chemers et al., 2011; Estrada et al., 2011; Hurtado et al., 2009; McGee and Keller, 2007; Seymour et al., 2011). Figure 5-1 lists some general roles that mentors can play to help students develop these skills; however, not all mentors work to develop these skills. For instance, for students to develop psychosocial skills, mentors need to show students the positive aspects of participating in STEM research and being a part of the group of people who work together to research a particular topic. Being part of a team environment could provide social incentives to students to become more engaged, enabling students to develop an identity as a STEM researcher.

The research on faculty mentoring in general has focused on the development of skills through the lens of three main domains: career functions,

FIGURE 5-1 Goals for students in UREs and the roles mentors play.
SOURCE: Adapted from commissioned paper (Pfund, 2016).

psychosocial functions, and role-modeling. Career functions refer to the roles mentors play to prepare an individual for advancement within an organization or along a career path, making sure that the student has the appropriate educational background and training for that path. For example, mentors may help undergraduates develop research presentations for local student symposia or national conferences and include them in the preparation of manuscripts for publication, as well as fostering the professional and networking skills that will help them gain employment (Dinham and Scott, 2001; Mullen et al., 2000; Young et al., 2004). Psychosocial functions include the emotional roles a mentor plays to build an interpersonal relationship with the mentee, to help that mentee grow professionally and personally. For example, implicit acceptance of the student by the mentor into the STEM disciplinary community will build the self-confidence of the mentee. Research has suggested that mentees judge this form of mentoring as crucial and assign it greater value than mentoring that focuses on career functions (Young et al., 2004). Role modeling is demonstrating effective attitudes and behaviors that can help a mentee succeed in a given context, making sure that the student is aware of the social norms for the STEM community or other group that the mentee plans to join (Ragins and Kram, 2007).

For mentors working with undergraduates engaged in research, roles have been described across all three of these domains. Thiry and Laursen (2011) described three sets of roles that emerged from their qualitative studies: professional socialization, intellectual support, and personal/emotional support. They found that mentors provided professional socialization by helping mentees learn disciplinary knowledge and skills, setting and aligning expectations, and modeling behaviors and norms. They also reported that mentors provide intellectual support to their mentees on their research project, helping them learn the methods of research and applying those methods. Finally, Thiry and Laursen (2011) stated that undergraduates reported valuing the personal/emotional support the mentor provided while becoming a trusted advisor, consistent with the earlier study by Young and colleagues (2004).

The need for mentors to play specific roles varies with each individual relationship and across the phases of the relationship (Kram, 1985). Moreover, as stated previously, it is unlikely that any single mentor can tackle all of these roles within a given mentoring relationship; it is more likely that multiple mentors will serve the roles needed to meet the targeted goals for a given individual at a given point in their life. Yet, little is known about which specific roles are related to particular outcomes across student populations, as UREs do not generally carry out an assessment of the mentors or mentoring relationships (Lunsford et al., 2017). Given the variability across mentoring roles with URE type, institution, and discipline, the generalizability of results can be limited (Crisp, 2010; Eagan et al., 2013). However, in recent years, there have been calls from funding agencies to evaluate and improve mentoring relationships for trainees (i.e., National Institute of General Medical Sciences [NIGMS], National Science Foundation, Howard Hughes Medical Institute, and Sloan Foundation). For example, an initiative led by NIGMS seeks "to develop, implement, assess and disseminate innovative and effective approaches to engaging, training and mentoring students; enhancing faculty development, and strengthening institutional research training infrastructure to enhance the participation and persistence of individuals from underrepresented backgrounds in biomedical research careers."[3]

---

[3] See https://www.nigms.nih.gov/training/dpc/Pages/default.aspx [February 2017].

IMPACTS OF EFFECTIVE MENTORING RELATIONSHIPS

Faculty-Related Outcomes

The bulk of the research on mentoring has focused on the mentee's perception and outcomes, with only a few studies discussing the effects on the mentor. In general, this research on mentors is predominantly on faculty mentors and indicates that mentoring has a positive impact on the mentor's perception of career success, career satisfaction, and career commitment (see Cox, 1997). Though there is less research about the benefits of being a mentor, a productive mentee may lead to increased productivity for research mentors (Campbell and Campbell, 2000; Dolan and Johnson, 2009). An important finding is that faculty members often volunteer as undergraduate research mentors, and their interest in volunteering includes achieving satisfaction, attracting good students, developing a professional network, and extending one's contributions (National Academy of Sciences, National Academy of Engineering, and Institute of Medicine, 1997). Examples of other benefits to mentors include a sense of personal fulfillment through knowledge and skill sharing, sharpening of leadership skills, career preparation, and cognitive growth (Dolan and Johnson, 2009; Eagan et al., 2013; Laursen et al., 2010). Although the bulk of the research on effects on mentors applies to faculty members, it is possible that many of these same outcomes could apply to other mentors, such as research scientists and engineers, corporate professionals, postdoctoral fellows, graduate students, lecturers, and lab managers.

Student Outcomes

The frequency and quality of mentee-mentor interactions has been positively correlated with students' persistence in STEM degree programs (Nagda et al., 1998), and mentoring has been found to improve, directly or indirectly, GPA and persistence in college (Bordes-Edgar et al., 2011; Campbell and Campbell, 1997). The associations were even stronger for students from underrepresented racial and ethnic groups than for students in general. For undergraduates, engagement in mentored research experiences in STEM has been positively correlated with self-reported gains in research skills and productivity as well as with retention in STEM (see Linn et al., 2015, for a recent review).

Crisp (2010) used structural equation modeling to examine the different factors that were predictive of persistence in community college settings. This analysis found that mentoring was an integral part of the theoretical framework predicting student persistence, and there was a direct positive relationship with mentoring experience and the student's ability to integrate socially and academically at the institution. Although, Crisp found no significant predictors of student persistence, including mentoring, which suggests that the current perspectives used regarding mentoring within four-year institutions may not be relevant for community college students, additional research is still needed to identify the role and effectiveness of mentoring in community college settings.

In addition to persistence in STEM, mentoring has also been positively associated with students' identity and confidence as a STEM professional and their sense of belonging (Byars-Winston et al., 2015; Chemers et al., 2011; Dolan and Johnson, 2009; Eagan et al., 2013; Hernandez et al., 2016; Lopatto, 2007; Paglis et al., 2006; Thiry and Laursen, 2011). These outcomes have primarily been documented in historically underrepresented groups (Hathaway et al., 2002; Junge et al., 2010; Nagda et al., 1998; Thiry and Laursen, 2011) and may result from exposing students to an affirming experience in the context and the culture of STEM and its community of practice (Hunter et al., 2007; Laursen et al., 2010). Chapter 4 has additional discussion of the reported outcomes.

Effective mentoring relationships that focus on the psychosocial components have been associated with an increase in the mentee's perception and satisfaction with the relationship (Tenenbaum et al., 2001; Waldeck et al., 1997). That is, students perceived themselves as more competent, identified as a STEM researcher, and saw value in the work (Walkdeck et al., 1997). Other studies have concluded that the quality of the mentoring relationship, as well as the attributes of the mentor, can have a significant impact on the student's perception of the URE and ultimately on persistence in STEM (Johnson, 2002; Johnson and Huwe, 2003; Liang et al., 2002; Nagda et al., 1998). For example, mentors who intentionally model ethical behavior, kindness, and competence are perceived as exhibiting outstanding mentor qualities (Johnson, 2002; Mullen et al., 2000; Rice and Brown, 1990). Moreover, negative student-faculty interactions can be detrimental and result in a loss of interest in persisting in STEM (Barker, 2009; Thiry and Laursen, 2011).

Byars-Winston and colleagues (2015) used archival data from more than 400 protégés, collected from 2005 through 2011 from several undergraduate biology research programs at a large, Midwestern research university. Path analysis of a subset of the data (which included 77 percent underrepresented racial/ethnic minorities) showed that perceived mentor effectiveness indirectly predicted enrollment in science-related doctoral or medical degree programs through research self-efficacy as the intermediate factor.

Different mentoring functions, such as socioemotional (e.g., psychological support) and instrumental (e.g., research task support), have been positively associated with both students' identity as a STEM professional, specifically their sense of belonging in the discipline, and their confidence in functioning as STEM professionals (research self-efficacy) (Byars-Winston et al., 2015; Chemers et al., 2011; Dolan and Johnson, 2009; Lopatto, 2007; Paglis et al., 2006; Thiry and Laursen, 2011). These factors have also been associated with increased interest in and commitment to research careers (Hunter et al., 2007). UREs have been associated with an increase in undergraduate student interest, motivation, and preparedness for research careers, with a positive mentoring relationship often cited as a key factor in these outcomes (Eagan et al., 2013; Hernandez et al., 2016; Lopatto, 2007; Seymour et al., 2011).

Student Outcomes for Historically Underrepresented Groups

For students from underrepresented racial and ethnic groups, mentorship has been positively correlated with enhanced recruitment into graduate school and research-related career pathways (Hathaway et al., 2002; Junge et al., 2010; Nagda et al., 1998; Thiry and Laursen, 2011). Interestingly, the effect of whether or not a student is matched with a mentor of the same race and gender is not clear (Russell et al., 2007); Hernandez and colleagues (2016) found no effect. In another study, students ranked having a mentor in their field with higher importance than race or gender concordance (Lee, 1999). However, some research suggests that underrepresented undergraduate and graduate students experience more positive attitudes toward research when they are mentored by female faculty or faculty of color (Frierson et al., 1994; Gandara and Maxwell-Jolly, 1999). Blake-Beard and colleagues (2011) found that female and racial/ethnic minority mentees in STEM reported experiencing more psychosocial and instrumental help, as well as more role model support, when paired with a mentor with whom they had race or gender concordance. The value of concordant mentoring relationships simply by gender has also been reported (Johnson-Bailey and Cervero, 2004). However, the ability to match students with mentors who share cultural similarities and come from the same field would require a level of cultural diversity among STEM mentors that does not yet exist.

Recent research indicated that cultural diversity must be considered in mentoring relationships. For example, Byars-Winston and colleagues (2015) found that historically underrepresented students were more likely than their ethnic-majority mentors to agree that cultural diversity matters should be addressed in research mentoring relationships. This is supported by research showing that mentors of historically underrepresented mentees needed to recognize the potential for colorblind attitudes, which could lead to a better understanding of underlying biases, and seek to better incorporate nondominant views into the research mentoring relationship (Prunuske et al., 2013).

NEED FOR ADDITIONAL RESEARCH

The studies described provide insight into how mentoring works. However, they do not fully examine the complex nature of research mentoring relationships and their impact on undergraduates. Therefore, theoretically grounded, validated measures are needed to assess the quality and effectiveness of research mentoring relationships and to identify factors that shape a successful research mentoring experience (Byars-Winston et al., 2015; Pfund et al., 2016). Currently, there are few metrics available to assess the effectiveness of research mentoring relationships at various career stages, with diverse mentees, across varied types of research mentoring relationships and across career stages. A handful of scales have been developed that are designed to assess the mentor's self-reported knowledge and skills as a mentor (e.g., Fleming et al., 2012; Pfund et al., 2006, 2014); to assess a mentor's skills, knowledge, and behaviors from the mentees' perspective (e.g., Berk et al., 2005; Byars-Winston et al., 2015; Eagan et al., 2013; Hunter et al., 2009; Lopatto, 2004; Weston and Laursen, 2015); and to assess the effectiveness or quality of the mentoring relationship overall (e.g., Berk et al., 2005; Hernandez et al., 2016). Although these scales hold some promise, there is much work to be done to develop and validate metrics that can be used to identify causal links between the quality of mentoring and the career outcomes of mentees.

DEVELOPING URE MENTORING PROGRAMS

In the absence of solid evidence for how to be a good mentor, decisions must be made based on the available information and resources. Many mentoring programs in support of UREs are developed to promote retention of STEM students from their freshmen year to their sophomore year, as well as to increase retention of historically underrepresented students (Campbell, 2007). Box 5-2 presents an evaluation of the Undergraduate Research Opportunity Program (UROP), developed by the University of Michigan (Nagda et al., 1998). This program uses mentoring by both peers and faculty as a mechanism to ameliorate high attrition rates and has shown promising results specifically for African American students and for sophomores.

Practical approaches to improving the quality of mentoring programs include making prospective mentors aware of the many dimensions of this role, as described above. In particular, programs have been developed to coach peers and near-peers in how to be better mentors to beginners in research. For example, with support from the Howard Hughes Medical Institute, Handelsman and colleagues (2005) developed and disseminated a program called Entering Mentoring: A Seminar to Train a New

---

BOX 5-2
Evaluation of University of Michigan's UROP

The University of Michigan's Undergraduate Research Opportunity Program (UROP) received funding through the U.S. Department of Education, the National Science Foundation, and the State of Michigan's Office of Equity to conduct a longitudinal assessment of the university's mentoring program. UROP provides research partnerships between undergraduate students and University of Michigan researchers. Students in their first and second year experience a year-long supervised research project and attend mandatory research seminars. A summer research fellowship program provides 10 weeks for students to participate in an independent research experience. The program includes more than 1,300 students and 800 faculty.[a]

An assessment was performed of the program and its impact on student retention and engagement, academic performance, and pursuit of higher education. Results showed that retention effects were strongest for African American students and for sophomore students over first year students. A significantly positive effect on male African American student degree completion was found; that is, 75.3 percent of UROP students completed their degree compared to 56.3 percent of students not enrolled in the program. In general, African American students whose academic performance was below average for their race/ethnic group appeared to benefit most from participation. Although white students showed some benefit from the program, the benefits were not as strong as for African Americans. Interestingly, there was no retention difference observed for Hispanic students. Taken all together, participation in the program increased degree completion rates for male African American and white students, with no impact on male Hispanic students or female students. Overall, UROP has shown positive influences on academic achievement, retention, behavior, and postgraduate educational and professional activities. The benefits for African American students' on retention and academic achievement may stem from a program designed to integrate students into research and pursuit of knowledge.

---

[a]See https://lsa.umich.edu/urop/about-us/evaluation-assessment.html [February 2017].

Generation of Scientists. In addition, Packard (2016) published a guide, *Successful STEM Mentoring Initiatives for Underrepresented Students: A Research-Based Guide for Faculty and Administrators*, which provides readers with practical questions and case studies to guide those who wish to develop programs through the process. Colleges and universities (e.g., see Boston University's Mentoring Training in the Sciences and Engineering program[4]) have also developed and disseminated mentoring training programs throughout various networks, such as the Center for the Integration

---

[4] Available at http://www.bu.edu/stem/mentoring-training [February 2017].

of Research, Teaching and Learning Network.[5] Workshops hosted by colleges and universities could be another avenue to support the development of mentoring skills for their faculty.

SUMMARY

Mentees and mentors engage as partners through reciprocal activities such as planning, acting, reflecting, questioning, and problem solving. The success of each relationship can be defined as achieving alignment in goals toward a desired career outcome for the mentee, whether or not that career aspiration is to become a STEM professional, and a sense of accomplishment for the mentor in having provided valuable guidance. Mentors can range from peers to very senior professionals; each has important insights to bring to the relationship. Consequently, mentees should be encouraged to seek out multiple mentors. Moreover, mentors can play many roles. The need for mentors to play specific roles varies with each individual relationship and across the phases of the relationship. Little is known about which specific roles have the greatest impact, and mentors may need to seek out opportunities for professional development to ensure a high-quality mentoring relationship. However, in some cases these opportunities may be difficult to find or may still need to be developed for dissemination. Although there is limited causal evidence to show the effects mentoring has on persistence in STEM, there is significant descriptive data showing the many positive effects that mentoring can have on academic success and persistence in STEM, as well as developing a sense of belonging and confidence to function as a STEM researcher.

REFERENCES

Abedin, Z., Biskup, E., Silet, K., Garbutt, J.M., Kroenke, K., Feldman, M.D., McGee Jr, R., Fleming, M., and Pincus, H.A. (2012). Deriving competencies for mentors of clinical and translational scholars. *Clinical and Translational Science. 5*, 273-280.

Bailey, T.R., and Alfonso, M. (2005). *Paths to persistence: An analysis of research on program effectiveness at community colleges.* Lumina Foundation for Education New Agenda Series 6(1). Indianapolis, IN: Lumina Foundation for Education.

Barker, L. (2009). Student and faculty of undergraduate research experiences in computing. *ACM Transactions on Computing Education, 9*(1), 1-28.

Bartlett, J. (2012). *A Model Role Evaluation of Mosaic Mentoring Programmes.* London: Demos.

Berk, R.A., Berg, J., Mortimer, R., Walton-Moss, B., and Yeo, T.P. (2005). Measuring the effectiveness of faculty mentoring relationships. *Academic Medicine, 80*, 66-71.

---

[5] See http://www.cirtl.net [February 2017].

Blake-Beard, S., Bayne, M.L., Crosby, F.J., and Muller, C.B. (2011). Matching by race and gender in mentoring relationships: Keeping our eyes on the prize. *Journal of Social Issues, 67,* 622-643.

Bordes-Edgar, V., Arredondo, P., Kurpius, S.R., and Rund, J. (2011). A longitudinal analysis of Latina/o students' academic persistence. *Journal of Hispanic Higher Education, 10,* 358-368.

Byars-Winston, A.M., Branchaw, J., Pfund, C., Leverett, P., and Newton, J. (2015). Culturally diverse undergraduate researchers' academic outcomes and perceptions of their research mentoring relationships. *International Journal of Science Education, 37,* 2533-2554.

Campbell, C. (2007). Best practices for student-faculty mentoring programs. Pp. 325-344 in T. Allen and L. Eby (Eds.), *The Blackwell Handbook of Mentoring: A Multiple Perspectives Approach.* Malden, MA: Blackwell.

Campbell, D.E., and Campbell, T.A. (2000). The mentoring relationship: Differing perceptions of benefits. *College Student Journal, 34,* 516-523.

Campbell, T.A., and Campbell, D.E. (1997). Faculty/student mentor program: Effects on academic performance and retention. *Research in Higher Education, 38,* 727-742.

Chang, M., Eagan, M.K., Lin, M., and Hurtado, S. (2011). Considering the impact of racial stigmas and science identity: Persistence among biomedical and behavioral science aspirants. *Journal of Higher Education, 82,* 564-596.

Chemers, M., Zurbriggen, E., Syed, M., Goza, B., and Bearman, S. (2011). The role of efficacy and identity in science career commitment among underrepresented minority students. *Journal of Social Issues, 67,* 469-491.

Cox, M.D. (1997). Long-term patterns in a mentoring program for junior faculty: Recommendations for practice. Pp. 225-268 in D. DeZure (Ed.) *To Improve the Academy, Vol. 16.* Stillwater, OK: New Forums Press and the Professional and Organizational Development Network in Higher Education.

Crisp, G. (2010). The impact of mentoring on the success of community college students. *Review of Higher Education, 34*(1), 39-60.

Crisp, G., and Cruz, I. (2009). Mentoring college students: A critical review of the literature between 1990 and 2007. *Research in Higher Education. 50,* 525-545.

Darling, L.W. (1986). The mentoring mosaic: A new theory of mentoring. Pp. 1-7 in W.A. Gray and M.M. Gray (Eds), *Mentoring: Aid to Excellence in Career Development, Business, and the Professions* (Vol. 2). Vancouver, BC: International Association for Mentoring.

Dinham, S., and Scott, C. (2001). The experience of disseminating the results of doctoral research. *Journal of Further and Higher Education, 25*(1), 45-55.

Dolan, E., and Johnson, D. (2009). Toward a holistic view of undergraduate research experiences: An exploratory study of impact on graduate/postdoctoral mentors. *Journal of Science Education and Technology, 18*(6), 487-500.

Eagan, M.K., Hurtado, S., Chang, M.J., Garcia, G.A., Herrera, F.A., and Garibay, J.C. (2013). Making a difference in science education the impact of undergraduate research programs. *American Education Research Journal, 50,* 683-713.

Eby, L.T., Rhodes, J.E., and Allen, T.D. (2007). Definition and evolution of mentoring. Pp. 1-20 in T.D. Allen and L.T. Eby (Eds.) *Blackwell Handbook of Mentoring.* Oxford: Blackwell Publishing.

Estrada, M., Woodcock, A., Hernandez, P.R., and Schultz, P. (2011). Toward a model of social influence that explains minority student integration into the scientific community. *Journal of Educational Psychology, 103,* 206-222.

Feldman, M.D., Huang, L., Guglielmo, B.J., Jordan, R., Kahn, J., Creasman, J.M., Wiener-Kronish, J.P., Lee, K.A., Tehrani, A., Yaffe, K., and Brown, J.S. (2009). Training the next generation of research mentors: The University of California, San Francisco, clinical & translational science institute mentor development program. *Clinical and Translational Science, 2*(3), 216-221.

Feldman, M.D., Steinauer, J.E., Khalili, M., Huang, L., Kahn, J.S., Lee, K.A., Creasman, J., and Brown, J.S. (2012). A mentor development program for clinical translational science faculty leads to sustained, improved confidence in mentoring skills. *Clinical and Translational Science, 5*(4), 362-367.

Fleming, M., Burnham, E., and Huskins, W. (2012). Mentoring translational science investigators. *Journal of the American Medical Association, 308,* 1981-1982.

Frierson, H.T., Hargrove, B.K., and Lewis, N.R. (1994). Black summer research students' perceptions related to research mentors' race and gender. *Journal of College Student Development, 35*(6), 475-480.

Galbraith, M. (2003). Celebrating mentoring. *Adult Learning, 14*(1), 2-3.

Gandara, P., and Maxwell-Jolly, J. (1999). *Priming the Pump: A Review of Programs That Aim to Increase the Achievement of Underrepresented Minority Undergraduates.* New York: College Board.

Handelsman, J., Pfund, C., Lauffer, S., and Pribbenow, C. (2005). *Entering Mentoring: A Seminar to Train a New Generation of Scientists.* Madison, WI: The Wisconsin Program for Scientific Teaching. Available: http://www.hhmi.org/sites/default/files/Educational%20 Materials/Lab%20Management/entering_mentoring.pdf [September 2016].

Hathaway, R.S., Nagda, B.A., and Gregerman, S.R. (2002). The relationship of undergraduate research participation to graduate and professional education pursuit: An empirical study. *Journal of College Student Development, 43,* 614-631.

Head, F.A., Reiman, A.J., and Thies-Sprinthall, L. (1992). The reality of mentoring: Complexity in its process and function. Pp. 5-24 in T.M. Bey and C.T. Holmes (Eds.), *Mentoring: Contemporary Principles and Issues.* Reston, VA: Association of Teachers.

Hernandez, P.R., Estrada, M., Woodcock, A., and Schultz, P.W. (2016). Protégé perceptions of high mentorship quality depend on shared values more than on demographic match. *Journal of Experimental Education.* Available: http://www.tandfonline.com/doi/full/10. 1080/00220973.2016.1246405 [November 2016].

Hunter, A.B., Laursen, S.L., and Seymour, E. (2007). Becoming a scientist: The role of undergraduate research in students' cognitive, personal, and professional development. *Science Education, 91,* 36-74.

Hunter, A.B., Weston, T.J., Laursen, S.L., and Thiry, H. (2009). URSSA: Evaluating student gains from undergraduate research in the sciences. *Council on Undergraduate Research Quarterly, 29,* 315-319.

Hurtado, S., Cabrera, N.L., Lin, M.H., Arellano, L., and Espinosa, L.L. (2009). Diversifying science: Underrepresented student experiences in structured research programs. *Research in Higher Education, 50,* 189-214.

Johnson, W. (2002). The intentional mentor: Strategies and guidelines for the practice of mentoring. *Professional Psychology: Research and Practice, 33,* 89-96.

Johnson, W.B., and Huwe, J.M. (2003). *Getting Mentored in Graduate School.* Washington, DC: American Psychological Association.

Johnson, W., and Ridley, C. (2004). *The Elements of Mentoring.* New York: Oalgrave MacMillan.

Johnson, W., and Zlotnik, S. (2005). The frequency of advising and mentoring as salient work roles in academic job advertisements. *Mentoring and Tutoring, 12*(1), 7-21.

Johnson-Bailey, J., and Cervero, R.M. (2004). Mentoring in black and white: The intricacies of cross-cultural mentoring. *Mentoring & Tutoring: Partnership in Learning, 12,* 7-21.

Junge, B., Quinones, C., Kakietek, J., Teodorescu, D., and Marsteller, P. (2010). Promoting undergraduate interest, preparedness, and professional pursuit in the sciences: An outcomes evaluation of the SURE Program at Emory University. *CBE–Life Sciences Education, 9,* 199-132.

Kram, K.E. (1985). *Mentoring at Work: Developmental Relationships in Organizational Life.* Glenview, IL: Scott, Foresman.

Laursen, S., Seymour, E., Hunter, A.B., Thiry, H., and Melton, G. (2010). *Undergraduate Research in the Sciences: Engaging Students in Real Science.* San Francisco: Jossey-Bass.

Lee, W.Y. (1999). Striving toward effective retention: The effect of race on mentoring African American students. *Peabody Journal of Education, 74,* 27-43.

Liang, B., Tracy, A.J., Taylor, C.A., and Williams, L.M. (2002). Mentoring college-age women: A relational approach. *American Journal of Community Psychology, 30*(2), 271-288.

Linn, M.C., Palmer, E., Baranger, A., Gerard, E., and Stone, E. (2015). Undergraduate research experiences: Impacts and opportunities. *Science, 347,* 1261757. Available: http://science.sciencemag.org/content/347/6222/1261757 [February 2017].

Lopatto, D. (2004). Survey of Undergraduate Research Experiences (SURE): First findings. *Cell Biology Education, 3,* 270-277.

Lopatto, D. (2007). Undergraduate research experiences support science career decisions and active learning. *CBE–Life Sciences Education, 6,* 297-306.

Lunsford, L.G., Crisp, G., Dolan, E., and Wutherick, B. (2017). Mentoring in higher education. In D.A. Clutterbuck, F.K. Kochan, L.G. Lunsford, N. Dominguez, and J. Haddock-Millar (Eds.), *SAGE Handbook of Mentoring.* Thousand Oaks, CA: SAGE Publishing.

McGee, R., and Keller, J.L. (2007). Identifying future scientists: Predicting persistence into research training. *CBE–Life Sciences Education, 6,* 316-331.

Mullen, C.A. (2005). *The Mentorship Primer.* New York: Peter Lang.

Mullen, C.A. (2007). Naturally occurring student-faculty mentoring relationships: A literature review. Pp. 119-138 in T.A. Allen and L.T. Eby (Eds.), *Blackwell Handbook of Mentoring: A Multiple Perspectives Approach.* Oxford: Blackwell Publishing Ltd.

Mullen, C.A., Whatley, A., and Kealy, W. (2000). Widening the circle: Faculty-student support groups as innovative practice in higher education. *Interchange: A Quarterly Review of Education, 31*(1), 35-60.

Nagda, B.A., Gregerman, S., Jonides, J., von Hippel, W., and Lerner, J. (1998). Undergraduate student-faculty research partnerships affect student retention. *The Review of Higher Education, 22,* 55-72.

National Academy of Sciences, National Academy of Engineering, and Institute of Medicine. (1997). *Adviser, Teacher, Role Model, Friend: On Being a Mentor to Students in Science and Engineering.* Committee on Science, Engineering, and Public Policy of the National Academy of Sciences, National Academy of Engineering, and Institute of Medicine. Washington, DC: National Academies Press. Available: http://www.nap.edu/read/5789/chapter/1 [January 2017].

Packard, B. (2016). *Successful STEM Mentoring Initiatives for Underrepresented Students: A Research-Based Guide for Faculty and Administrators.* Sterling, VA: Stylus.

Paglis, L.L., Green, S.G., and Bauer, T.N. (2006). Does adviser mentoring add value? A longitudinal study of mentoring and doctoral student outcomes. *Research in Higher Education, 47,* 451-476.

Pfund, C. (2016). *Studying the Role and Impact of Mentoring on Undergraduate Research Experiences.* Paper commissioned for the Committee on Strengthening Research Experiences for Undergraduate STEM Students. Board on Science Education, Division of Behavioral and Social Sciences and Education. Board on Life Sciences, Division of Earth and Life Studies. National Academies of Sciences, Engineering, and Medicine. Available: http://nas.edu/STEM_Undergraduate_Research_Mentoring.

Pfund, C., Pribbenow, C.M., Branchaw, J., Lauffer, S.M., and Handelsman, J. (2006). The merits of training mentors. *Science, 311,* 473-474.

Pfund, C., Branchaw, J., and Handelsman, J. (2014). *Entering Mentoring.* New York: W.H. Freeman & Co.

Pfund, C., Byars-Winston, A., Branchaw, J.L., Hurtado, S., and Eagan, M.K. (2016). Defining attributes and metrics of effective research mentoring relationships. *AIDS and Behavior, 20,* 238-248.

Prunuske, A., Wilson, J., Walls, M., Marrin, H., and Clarke, B. (2013). Efforts at broadening participation in the sciences: An examination of the mentoring experiences of students from underrepresented groups. *CBE–Life Sciences Education, 15,* ar26. Available: http://www.lifescied.org/content/15/3/ar26.long [February 2017].

Ragins, B., and Kram, K. (2007). *The Handbook of Mentoring at Work: Theory, Research, and Practice.* Thousand Oaks, CA: Sage Publications, Inc.

Rice, M., and Brown, R. (1990). Developmental factors associated with self-perceptions of mentoring competence and mentoring needs. *Journal of College Student Development, 31,* 293-299.

Russell, S.H., Hancock, M.P., and McCullough, J. (2007). Benefits of undergraduate research experiences. *Science, 316*(5824), 548-549.

Ryser, L., Halseth, G., and Thien, D. (2009). Strategies and intervening factors influencing student social interaction and experiential learning in an interdisciplinary research team. *Research in Higher Education, 50*(3), 248-267.

Seymour, E., Hunter, A., Laursen, S., and DeAntoni, T. (2011). Establishing the benefits of undergraduate researchers into a scientific community of practice. *Journal of Science Education and Technology, 20,* 771-784.

Tenenbaum, H., Crosby, F., and Gliner, M. (2001). Mentoring relationships in graduate school. *Journal of Vocational Behavior, 59,* 326-341.

Thiry, H., and Laursen, S.L. (2011). The role of student-advisor interactions in apprenticing undergraduate researchers into a scientific community of practice. *Journal of Science Education and Technology, 20,* 771-784.

Twale, D., and Kochan, F. (2000). Assessment of an alternative cohort model for part-time students in an educational leadership program. *Journal of School Leadership, 10*(2), 188-208.

Waldeck, J., Orrego, V., Plax, T., and Kearney, P. (1997). Graduate student/faculty mentoring relationships: Who gets mentored, how it happens, and to what end. *Communication Quarterly, 45,* 93-109.

Weston, T.J., and Laursen, S.L. (2015). The Undergraduate Research Student Self-Assessment (URSSA): Validation for use in program evaluation. *CBE–Life Sciences Education, 14,* ar33. Available: https://www.ncbi.nlm.nih.gov/pmc/articles/PMC4710391/ [February 2017].

Young, J., Alvermann, D., Kaste, J., Henderson, S., and Many, J. (2004). Being a friend and a mentor at the same time: A pooled case comparison. *Mentoring and Tutoring, 12*(1), 23-36.

6

Faculty Impact and Needs

An important aspect of the undergraduate research experience (URE) is the participation of faculty, as they are responsible for most UREs (with the exception of apprenticeships in industry or other off-campus UREs). The faculty member will typically set the goals of the experience, design the overall experimental approach, gather relevant materials to introduce students to the questions to be addressed, organize the workflow, and serve as mentor. Although the hands-on training of students may be done by the faculty member, it may also be carried out under supervision of staff members, postdoctoral fellows, graduate students, other undergraduates in the URE, or combinations of these. The type of support the faculty member receives—financial, administrative, and access to facilities—can vary dramatically, depending on the type of URE (see Chapter 2 for an overview of program types), on the type of institution (community college versus four-year college versus research university), and the traditions and resources of the particular institution.

This chapter examines the impact of UREs on faculty beyond their role as mentor (see Chapter 5 for a discussion of mentoring). It situates UREs within the faculty context by describing the teaching-research nexus (TRN), which highlights the tension between teaching responsibilities and research productivity. The chapter then provides a more nuanced discussion of the impacts of UREs on faculty with respect to tenure and promotion, productivity, and motivation. Building upon these impacts, the final section addresses the support systems and needs of faculty to ensure their involvement and success in UREs.

TEACHING-RESEARCH NEXUS

One of the primary complicating factors associated with understanding the impact on faculty of participation in UREs is the tension in the relationship between teaching activities and research activities. Although there is not consensus on the precise definition of the TRN (Jenkins, 2004; Wareham and Trowler, 2007), this concept attempts to describe the multiple links between teaching and research that can benefit student learning and outcomes.[1] The typical conceptualization is to consider the relationship between teaching and research within an institution and the alignment between institutional priorities, mission, and expectation of faculty work. But a broader view of how to enhance teaching and learning could examine the relationship at multiple levels—institution, faculty, and student—to better understand how these factors interact and then how UREs might fit into this framework. The breakdown of the different factors includes:

- How the institution views the relationship between teaching and research (level of integration into the curriculum): for example, emphasizing the results from research versus emphasizing research processes and problems;
- The role of the student in the teaching-research relationship: students are treated as the audience versus students are treated as participants; and
- The role of the faculty member in the teaching-research relationship: teaching is teacher-focused versus teaching is student-focused.

A considerable amount of the extant TRN research literature has focused on how research enhances teaching (Prince et al., 2007). In practice, the faculty are impacted by curricular demands (i.e., whether the focus is purely on content versus emphasizing the research process) and the role of the student (i.e., whether students are treated as audience or participants). The campus climate impacts the relationship between teaching and research, which in turn shapes the choices faculty make in planning and implementing UREs. The TRN literature has primarily focused on two types of programs: "research-based" and "research-led," although Healy (2005) has identified a few other approaches and the URE literature suggests a continuum rather than a strict dichotomy (Auchincloss et al., 2014). In a research-based program, the curriculum emphasizes students as participants, as well as placing emphasis on the research process and problems. Research-based programs would likely be considered a URE. Alternatively, in a research-led program, the curriculum is structured around

---

[1]See http://trnexus.edu.au [November 2016].

teaching subject content and students are treated as the audience. So there is more emphasis on content rather than the experience of research. For example, a research-led program is similar to a "cookbook" course that relies heavily on examples from the research literature and prespecified research methods to facilitate learning the content. With a focus on subject content, the research-led design is most closely associated with a traditional "information transmission" academic model. This type of teaching model is often seen as being in direct conflict with research productivity as it takes time away from engaging in research; however, some view the research-based model as a way for students to learn while contributing to the faculty member's research productivity (Brew, 2013; Kim et al., 2003; Layzell, 1996; Presley and Engelbride, 1998; Verburgh et al., 2007). Another potential issue with a "research-based" class is the role of the faculty member as a mentor guiding the student's learning, engagement in the field, and identity as a science, technology, engineering, and mathematics (STEM) researcher. This mentoring function may conflict with the goal of having the student help maximize the faculty member's research productivity. In a "research-led" class the faculty member's research is not involved and this potential conflict is avoided.

In addition to curricular demands and faculty motivations, the variability across institutions and departments with respect to the TRN is also important (Elsen et al., 2009; Marsh and Hattie, 2002). To illustrate how the TRN might differ depending upon the type of university, consider the role of the faculty member at a typical community college and the role of a faculty member at a research-intensive university. The role that these two faculty members play may be very different with respect to their institution's demands on teaching and research productivity, which influences their views on participating in UREs. At most community colleges, in addition to lack of resources (i.e., facilities and capital), heavy teaching expectations have been identified as a significant barrier for faculty interested in providing UREs (Hewlett, 2009; Langley, 2015; Perez, 2003), and research productivity (as it is traditionally defined) is not a significant priority. However, as the Community College Undergraduate Research Initiative highlights, there are many community colleges that are increasingly incorporating undergraduate research into the standard curriculum.[2]

A very different scenario may exist for the early career scientist at a research-intensive university, where actual and perceived conflicts between teaching responsibilities and research productivity can lead to some unique tensions associated with the URE (Brownell and Tanner, 2012; Dolan and Johnson, 2010; Laursen et al., 2012). Where tensions are high, faculty may look toward engaging in courses that are more "research-based," as they

---

[2]For additional information on this initiative, see http://www.ccuri.org [November 2016].

may offer a better opportunity for contributions to the faculty member's research program, compared to spending time teaching "research led" courses on potentially unrelated topics. When faculty identify themselves not as *either* a teacher *or* a researcher but as both and institutions adopt strategies that encourage a balance between teaching and research, opportunities exist that have the potential to benefit not only the student, but also the faculty member and the institution (Zubrick et al., 2001).

IMPACTS ON FACULTY

Faculty impacts must be considered within the context of the academic environment, including the type of institution, the faculty appointment and rank, the departmental culture, and the STEM discipline. There is currently a relative paucity of data with respect to the impact of UREs on faculty beyond the role as mentor. Research to improve understanding of how UREs affect faculty is needed because of the potential for unintended impacts to jeopardize the success of efforts to develop and sustain UREs (see Chapters 7 and 9 for a discussion of recommendations for research). Where studies have examined faculty perspectives, the impacts under study are often faculty perceptions of student outcomes and not necessarily direct effects on the individual faculty mentor (Cox and Andriot, 2009; Hunter et al., 2006; Kardash, 2000; Zydney et al., 2002) or the effects that faculty research in general has on teaching, undergraduate education, and institutional metrics (Grunig, 1997; Prince et al., 2007).

The limited research literature on faculty has primarily considered the effects of UREs on promotion and tenure, productivity, and motivation. Moreover, from our review of the literature, the committee was unclear as to how much faculty use the existing literature in designing and implementing UREs. This stems from the committee members' experiences of a disconnect between the accessibility of the research literature and how that translates to practice. Despite the lack of data across the multitude of UREs, one area that has garnered attention and is gaining some traction is understanding the challenges and benefits for faculty associated with teaching course-based undergraduate research experiences (CUREs) (Brownell and Kloser, 2015; Dolan, 2016; Shortlidge et al., 2016). Thus, a portion of the research described throughout the following sections emphasizes CUREs.

Promotion and Tenure

One area of considerable interest is the impact of URE engagement on the promotion and tenure process. For large research universities, this has been a topic of considerable discussion since the release of the Boyer Commission Report, which called upon large research universities to take a critical look at how they educate undergraduate students (Boyer Commission on Education of Undergraduates in the Research University, 1998). The report specifically identified "research-based learning" as an approach that these universities should consider as an education standard. Institutional efforts to address this report faced the challenge of a promotion and tenure process that focuses heavily on faculty research productivity. Whereas the Boyer Commission Report encourages the integration of faculty research and undergraduate education, subsequent studies suggest that considerable challenges still exist with respect to providing incentives for faculty, including critically needed reforms of the typical tenure and promotion process (Anderson et al., 2011; Brownell and Tanner, 2012; Elgren and Hensel, 2006; Evans, 2010; Gibbs and Coffey, 2004; Hernandez-Jarvis et al., 2011; Laursen et al., 2012; Schultheis et al., 2011; Weiss et al., 2004).

Very little work has been done on the effect of undergraduate research on the tenure and promotion process (Evans, 2010; Hernandez-Jarvis et al., 2011). One possible reason for this is that a relatively small number of research institutions have made the move toward making engagement in undergraduate research a significant component of tenure and promotion decisions (Chapdelaine, 2012; Schultheis et al., 2011). There are some notable exceptions that exist at primarily undergraduate institutions, as well as some larger research universities. For example, on October 9, 2015, the Purdue University Board of Trustees adopted a modification to the tenure and promotion process to include components that are very specific to faculty engagement in student mentoring and undergraduate research.[3]

Although involving undergraduate students in faculty research is often mentioned in tenure and promotion policies and procedures (Chapdelaine, 2012), very few research institutions consider mentoring undergraduate researchers as a critical component of the process. Providing a URE for students either in the summer or during the academic year is often an unpaid "voluntary" activity. This treatment has led faculty to perceive their involvement in UREs as undervalued or even unrecognized (Cooley et al., 2008; Hu et al., 2008; Laursen et al., 2012). And it may be a source of tensions associated with working with undergraduate researchers (Dolan and Johnson, 2010; Laursen et al., 2012). Indeed, the lack of focus at the institutional level on URE engagement as a component of tenure and promotion may suggest that engagement in UREs leads to a negative impact on the faculty involved in them (Buddie and Collins, 2011; Mervis, 2001). However, the structure of the URE may influence faculty perceptions on

---

[3]For additional information, see the press announcement at http://www.purdue.edu/ newsroom/releases/2015/Q4/trustees-change-purdue-polytechnic-department-name-to-reflect-enhancements.html and more specific information about policies at http://www.purdue.edu/ policies/academic-research-affairs/ib2.html [November 2016].

tenure and promotion. For example, in an analysis of CUREs, Shortlidge and colleagues (2016) found that 68 percent of the faculty respondents indicated that the CURE had a positive impact on tenure and promotion decisions at their institution (see below).

Productivity

Another area of focus with respect to faculty impact is the effect that the URE has on faculty research productivity. However, the impact on faculty productivity may vary according to the structure of the research experience itself. When working with undergraduates on research is considered an educational activity distinct from the faculty member's research program, the actual and perceived impact on research productivity may be negative (Dolan and Johnson, 2010; Engelbride and Presley, 1998; Harvey and Thompson, 2009; Layzell, 1996; Laursen et al., 2012; Prince et al., 2007).

In light of this potential for conflict, undergraduate research programs structured to integrate teaching and research may offer unique opportunities for faculty research programs to benefit from the effort (Brownell and Kloser 2015; Kloser et al., 2011; Lopatto et al., 2014; Shortlidge et al., 2016; Wayment and Dickson, 2008). CUREs are an example of this type of experience. In a study by Shortlidge and colleagues (2016), faculty members who had developed a CURE were invited to be interviewed to share their experiences. Thirty-one faculty members were interviewed, and several themes were identified. Results revealed that 61 percent of the faculty respondents reported that the CURE provided opportunities to publish not only the results obtained with the students, but also results obtained in educational research. Another 61 percent reported that the data collected by the students in the CURE offered direct benefits to the faculty research program. The benefits may be extended when the CURE is part of a national network because the data feeding into the faculty member's research program are collected across multiple sites (Dolan, 2016; Lopatto et al., 2014). Moreover, 42 percent of the faculty respondents reported that student research projects opened up new directions in the faculty research program that would otherwise have gone unexplored (Shortlidge et al., 2016).

One of the key features of CUREs that are part of a national network is that they often provide support in the form of professional development, online resources, and peer mentors, all of which contribute to supporting the course and the faculty member. Research has shown that the lack of faculty time to develop the research project, training materials, etc., is the most significant barrier when it comes to engaging undergraduates in a research experience (Benvenuto, 2002; Brownell and Tanner, 2012; Desai et al., 2008; Dolan, 2016; Dolan and Johnson, 2010; Eagan et al., 2011; Laursen et al., 2012; Lopatto et al., 2014; Wood, 2003; Zydney et al., 2002).

A potential added benefit relates directly to the connection between teaching and research—the two primary competitors for faculty time. With an understanding that these two aspects of a faculty member's professional identity are often perceived to be in direct conflict (Kim et al., 2003; Layzell, 1996; Presley and Engelbride, 1998; Verburgh et al., 2007), the CURE has the potential to strengthen the TRN and relieve the tensions associated with these conflicting interests.

Motivation

As with other high-impact practices and educational reform efforts, the URE can be seen as a novel pedagogical approach that requires a significant investment of time to be effective. Studies focused on faculty change have shown that the time required for investing in change, the incentives to do so, and a lack of focused training are the three most cited barriers (American Association for the Advancement of Science, 2011; Henderson et al., 2010, 2011). Institutions interested in reforming their STEM educational practices to add or strengthen UREs must consider the many factors that motivate faculty. Research has shown that faculty interest in pedagogical change may not be well aligned with the incentive and reward structure for spurring change (Anderson et al., 2011; Brownell and Tanner, 2012; Gibbs and Coffey, 2004; Hativa, 1995; Weiss et al., 2004). Blackburn and Lawrence (1995) concluded that motivation toward pedagogical change involves an interaction of faculty interests, their expectations of success, and the rewards associated with the change. Whereas there are likely to be a large number of external factors that influence the interactions of these variables, the faculty member's prior education experience, preparation and training, STEM discipline, stage of career, and type of faculty appointment are all critical elements that influence a faculty member's decision to adopt a specific pedagogical reform (Austin, 2011).

In gaining a better understanding of faculty motivations, an important point is that faculty members often volunteer to be undergraduate research mentors (Linn et al., 2015). Faculty interest in volunteering includes achieving satisfaction, attracting good students, developing a professional network, and extending one's contributions (National Academy of Sciences, National Academy of Engineering, and Institute of Medicine, 1997). When an external reward structure is lacking, faculty may see investing their own limited resources as a potentially risky venture and therefore will turn their focus toward strong or "high-reward" students. Bangera and Brownell (2014) discussed what they call the "rising star hypothesis," which posits that faculty members tend to prefer students who are predicted to do well and become stars. This preference is attributed to the limited incentive for faculty members to take risks by selecting more shy or modest students.

The creation of institutional awards has also been discussed as incentive or motivation for faculty members to become mentors (National Academy of Sciences, National Academy of Engineering, and Institute of Medicine, 1997).

Unfortunately, there are relatively few studies that focus specifically on what motivates faculty members to include undergraduates in their research programs. Not surprisingly, faculty who work primarily with undergraduates as part of teaching undergraduate coursework are more likely to include undergraduates in their research than faculty who work primarily with graduate students and teach graduate-level courses (Einarson and Clarkberg, 2004).

Eagan and colleagues (2011) discussed faculty motivations to include undergraduates in research through the lens of social exchange theory. Although social exchange theory is most often associated with understanding the underlying psychological components of romantic relationships, the basic premise can be applied to understanding the mentor-mentee relationship. In social exchange theory, the participants in the relationship weigh the costs and benefits of the relationship as they exchange something of value (Emerson, 1981). In the case of the URE, the student receives the knowledge and skills offered by the mentor, while the faculty member receives a student contribution to the research program and the satisfaction and social benefits associated with working with student researchers. Eagan and colleagues (2011) found a higher probability of engaging undergraduates in a research program if faculty stated that they were motivated by a desire to improve student learning outcomes, had higher levels of interactions with undergraduates, were well-funded, and were valued by their colleagues. In addition, the study revealed that the type of institution was a statistically significant factor in determining the probability of a faculty member working with undergraduate researchers. Faculty who worked at liberal arts colleges, historically black colleges and universities, or at more selective institutions were much more likely to be engaging undergraduates in research when compared to their peers at other institution types.

It appears that opportunities for UREs may be smaller at institutions where research and teaching are perceived to compete for faculty time (a weak TRN). Future studies may help clarify whether there are multiple factors affecting this decreased opportunity. If a lack of an incentive and reward structure is considered a primary barrier to faculty engaging with undergraduates in their research programs, then it is critical to have a clear understanding of faculty motivations as they exist within multiple contexts. For example, historically black colleges and universities are known to have student-centered missions and may offer students an academic environment that is more supportive and collaborative than other institution types (Allen, 1992; Hurtado, 2003; Hurtado et al., 2009; Nelson Laird et al.,

2007). The unique character of this type of institution may help explain why faculty are more likely to include undergraduates in their research program when compared to their peers at institutions serving primarily white and Hispanic student populations.

FACULTY NEEDS

Most studies of faculty needs have taken a deficit-model approach through an analysis of barriers and disincentives that exist with respect to faculty involvement in undergraduate research. In summary, the four areas of focus have been faculty time, faculty incentives, funding, and faculty training and development.

By far, the biggest barrier, and therefore the greatest need for faculty in mentoring undergraduate researchers is time (Benvenuto, 2002; Brown, 2001; Brownell and Tanner, 2012; Chapman, 2003; Coker and Davies, 2006; Cooley et al., 2008; Desai et al., 2008; Dolan and Johnson, 2010; Eagan et al., 2011; Einarson and Clarkberg, 2004; Hewlett, 2009; Hu et al., 2008; Jones and Davis, 2014; Karukstis, 2004; Langley, 2015; Laursen et al., 2012; Mateja and Otto, 2007; McKinney et al., 1998; Merkel, 2001; Perez, 2003; Spell et al., 2014; Wood, 2003; Zydney et al., 2002). Research has shown that uncommitted faculty time has become increasingly scarce, and finding time to focus on anything other than their core responsibilities has become increasingly more difficult (Eagan et al., 2011). Issues with faculty time allocation have come about as the result of an ever-expanding workload, which studies suggest has been increasing across all institutions (Milem et al., 2000; Schuster and Finkelstein, 2006; Townsend and Rosser, 2007).

Successful undergraduate research programs have incorporated models and solutions that address this critical need. Although often the solution is to incorporate release time or reassigned time, that solution has been found to be unsustainable at many institutions, including community colleges (Hewlett, 2009). Whereas there are some well-known time allocation strategies for faculty who are engaged in mentoring undergraduate researchers (Coker and Davies, 2006; Karukstis, 2004), what faculty often need are strategies that include the "blending" of their professional roles to allow for multitasking. Institutions can support faculty by supporting academic structures where teaching and research are integrated and where faculty involvement with undergraduates is seen as a service to the institutional mission (Downs and Young, 2012).

One strategy that institutions adopt to address issues of faculty time is to embed the research experience in the curriculum through the use of independent studies, credit-bearing summer research programs, academic year seminars, and CUREs (Free et al., 2015). Successful models for integrating the research experience into the curriculum exist (Gates et al., 1999; Hakim, 2000; Kierniesky, 2005; Kortz and van der Hoeven Kraft, 2016; Lopatto et al., 2014; Merkel, 2001; Pukkila et al., 2007; Reinen et al., 2007; Rueckert, 2007; Russell et al., 2009; Temple et al., 2010; Weaver et al., 2006). In the case of the community college, where faculty are burdened with very high teaching loads, the embedded model most likely offers the most effective solution to issues with faculty time (Hewlett, 2009; Langley, 2015; Perez, 2003). As previously mentioned, the time saving benefits may be extended when the research experience is part of a national network of CUREs, which generally feature shared curriculum, reducing preparation time.

Embedding student research may involve significant pedagogical change to an existing course or development of a novel course. Successful models for integrating the experience often require faculty training and development, which may come at an additional cost with respect to faculty time allocation (Brownell and Tanner, 2012). CURE networks have the potential to provide much needed support in the form of training, "plug and play" curriculum and course materials, and mentoring from experienced peers. All of these features have the potential to significantly reduce the amount of upfront time required by faculty who are engaging undergraduates in their own CUREs (Lopatto et al., 2014).

SUMMARY

Faculty members play a key role in UREs, from setting the disciplinary goals to designing the initial workflow. The literature on the impact on faculty from participating in UREs is limited; however, there is evidence showing faculty benefits in rewards such as satisfaction, enjoyment, and a sense of fulfilling an obligation to their students. For example, faculty might integrate their research into their teaching responsibilities through the use of CUREs.

Research suggests that the current reward structures for allocating time and training to provide opportunities for undergraduate research may not be supportive of faculty needs. Colleges and universities need to be mindful of the impact of a URE program on their faculty and need to consider how they can and should support such a program. UREs address a variety of educational challenges such as improving completion and retention in STEM programs, preparedness for graduate studies, and general science literacy. Although limitations of time, incentives, and training are perceived to be significant barriers to faculty engaging in pedagogical change, undergraduate research programs continue to grow and thrive.

The diversity of undergraduate research program structures—institution type, level of curriculum integration, faculty motivations, length of the URE, role of the student researcher, incentive and reward structure, and availability of professional development—makes it difficult to fully evaluate the impact on faculty. In order to develop a better understanding of the impacts of participation in providing UREs on faculty, studies are needed that clearly identify and take into account the various types of research programs and available support structures. This understanding is important because much can be learned by a well-designed study examining faculty situations before and after a significant change in campus goals, support structures, etc., related to UREs.

REFERENCES

Allen, W. (1992). The color of success: African-American college student outcomes at predominantly White and historically Black public colleges and universities. *Harvard Educational Review, 62*(1), 26-45.

American Association for the Advancement of Science (2011). *Vision and Change in Undergraduate Biology Education: A Call to Action* (C. Brewer and D. Smith, Eds.). Washington, DC: American Association for the Advancement of Science.

Anderson, W.A., Banerjee, U., Drennan, C.L., Elgin, S.C.R., Epstein, I.R., Handelsman, J., Hatfull, F., Losick, R., O'Dowd, D.K., Olivera, B.M., Strobel, S.A., Walker, G.C., and Warner, I.M. (2011). Changing the culture of science education at research universities. *Science, 331*(6014), 152-153.

Auchincloss, L.C., Laursen, S.L., Branchaw, J.L., Eagan, K., Graham, M., Hanauer, D.I., Lawrie, G., McLinn, C.M., Pelaez, N., Rowland, S., Towns, M., Trautmann, N.M., Varma-Nelson, P., Weston, T.J., and Dolan, E.L. (2014). Assessment of course-based undergraduate research experiences: A meeting report. *CBE–Life Sciences Education, 13,* 29-40.

Austin, A.E. (2011). *Promoting Evidence-Based Change in Undergraduate Science Education.* Paper commissioned by the Board on Science Education of the National Research Council. Available: http://sites.nationalacademies.org/cs/groups/dbassesite/documents/webpage/dbasse_072578.pdf [September 2016].

Bangera, G., and Brownell, S.E. (2014). Course-based undergraduate research experiences can make scientific research more inclusive. *Life Sciences Education, 13,* 602-606.

Benvenuto, M. (2002). Educational reform: Why the academy doesn't change. *Thought & Action, 18*(1/2), 63-74.

Blackburn. R.T., and Lawrence, J.H. (1995). *Faculty at Work: Motivation, Expectation, Satisfaction.* Baltimore, MD: The Johns Hopkins Press.

Boyer Commission on Education of Undergraduates in the Research University. (1998). *Reinventing Undergraduate Education: A Blueprint for America's Research Universities.* New York. Available: http://files.eric.ed.gov/fulltext/ED424840.pdf [November 2016].

Brew, A. (2013). Understanding the score of undergraduate research: A framework for curricular and pedagogical decision-making. *Higher Education, 66,* 603-618.

Brown, K. (2001). Time, money, mentors: Overcoming the barriers to undergraduate research. *HHMI Bulletin, 14,* 30-33.

Brownell, S.E., and Kloser, M.J. (2015). Toward a conceptual framework for measuring the effectiveness of course-based undergraduate research experiences in undergraduate biology. *Studies in Higher Education, 40*(3), 525-544.

Brownell, S.E., and Tanner, K.D. (2012). Barriers to faculty pedagogical change: Lack of training, time, incentives, and... tensions with professional identity?. *CBE–Life Sciences Education, 11*(4), 339-346.

Buddie, A.M., and Collins, C.L. (2011). Faculty perceptions of undergraduate research. *Perspectives on Undergraduate Research and Mentoring 1.1.* Available: http://blogs. elon.edu/purm/2011/10/11/faculty-perceptions-of-undergraduate-research-purm-1-1/ [November 2016].

Chapdelaine, A. (2012). Including undergraduate research in faculty promotion and tenure policies. Pp. 115-132 in N. Hensel and E. Paul (Eds.), *Faculty Support and Undergraduate Research: Innovations in Faculty Role Definition, Workload, and Reward.* Washington, DC: Council on Undergraduate Research.

Chapman, D.W. (2003). Undergraduate research: Showcasing young scholars. *Chronicle of Higher Education, 50*(3), B5. Available at http://www.chronicle.com/article/Undergraduate-Research-/9284 [November 2016].

Coker, J.S., and Davies, E. (2006). Ten time-saving tips for undergraduate research mentors. *Journal of Natural Resources and Life Sciences Education, 35,* 110-112.

Cooley, E.L., Garcia, A.L., and Hughes, J.L. (2008). Undergraduate research in psychology at liberal arts colleges: Reflections on mutual benefits for faculty and students. *North American Journal of Psychology 10*(3), 463-471.

Cox, M.F., and Andriot, A. (2009). Mentor and undergraduate student comparisons of students' research skills. *Journal of STEM Education: Innovations and Research, 10*(1-2), 31-39.

Desai, K.V., Gatson, S.N., Stiles, T.W., Stewart, R.H., Laine, G.A., and Quick, C.M. (2008). Integrating research and education at research-extensive universities with research-intensive communities. *Advances in Physiology Education, 32*(2), 136-141.

Dolan, E. (2016). *Course-Based Undergraduate Research Experiences: Current Knowledge and Future Directions.* Paper commissioned for the Committee on Strengthening Research Experiences for Undergraduate STEM Students. Board on Science Education, Division of Behavioral and Social Sciences and Education. Board on Life Sciences, Division of Earth and Life Studies. National Academies of Sciences, Engineering, and Medicine. Available: http://nas.edu/STEM_Undergraduate_Research_CURE [February 2016].

Dolan, E.L., and Johnson, D. (2010). The undergraduate–postgraduate–faculty triad: Unique functions and tensions associated with undergraduate research experiences at research universities. *CBE–Life Sciences Education, 9*(4), 543-553.

Downs, D., and Young, G. (2012). What faculty need and want. Pp. 115-132 in N. Hensel and E. Paul (Eds.), *Faculty Support and Undergraduate Research: Innovations in Faculty Role Definition, Workload, and Reward.* Washington, DC: Council on Undergraduate Research.

Eagan, M.K., Sharkness, J., Hurtado, S., Mosqueda, C.M., and Chang, M.J. (2011). Engaging undergraduates in science research: Not just about faculty willingness. *Research in Higher Education, 52*(2), 151-177.

Einarson, M.K., and Clarkberg, M.E. (2004). *Understanding Faculty Out-of-class Interaction with Undergraduate Students at a Research University* (CHERI Working Paper #57). Available: http://digitalcommons.ilr.cornell.edu/cheri/20/ [February 2016].

Elgren, T., and Hensel, N. (2006). Undergraduate research experiences: Synergies between scholarship and teaching. *Peer Review, 8*(1), 4-7.

Elsen, M.G., Visser-Wijnveen, G.J., Van der Rijst, R.M., and Van Driel, J.H. (2009). How to strengthen the connection between research and teaching in undergraduate university education. *Higher Education Quarterly, 63*(1), 64-85.

Emerson, R.M. (1981). Social exchange theory. Pp. 30-65 in M. Rosenberg and R.H. Turner (Eds.), *Social Psychology: Sociological Perspectives.* New York: Basic Books, Inc.

Engelbride, E., and Presley, J.B. (1998). Accounting for faculty productivity in the research university. *Review of Higher Education, 22*(1), 17-37.

Evans, D.R. (2010). The challenge of undergraduate research. *Peer Review 12*(2), 31. Available: https://www.aacu.org/publications-research/periodicals/challenge-undergraduate-research [November 2016].

Free, R., Griffith, S., and Spellman, B. (2015). Faculty workload issues connected to undergraduate research. *New Directions for Higher Education, 2015*(169), 51-60.

Gates, A.Q., Teller, P.J., Bernat, A., Delgado, N., and Della-Piana, C.K. (1999). Expanding participation in undergraduate research using the Affinity Group model. *Journal of Engineering Education, 88*(4), 409-414.

Gibbs, G., and Coffey, M. (2004). The impact of training of university teachers on their teaching skills, their approach to teaching and the approach to learning of their students. *Active Learn Higher Education, 5*, 87-100.

Grunig, S.D. (1997). Research, reputation, and resources: The effect of research activity on perceptions of undergraduate education and institutional resource acquisition. *Journal of Higher Education, 68*(1), 17-52.

Hakim, T.M. (2000). *How to Develop and Administer Institutional Undergraduate Research Programs*. Washington, DC: Council on Undergraduate Research.

Harvey, L., and Thompson, K. (2009). Approaches to undergraduate research and their practical impact on faculty productivity in the natural sciences. *Journal of College Science Teaching, 38*(5), 12-13.

Hativa, N. (1995). The department-wide approach to improving faculty instruction in higher education: A qualitative evaluation. *Research in Higher Education, 36*, 377-413.

Healy, M. (2005). Linking research and teaching exploring disciplinary spaces and the role of inquiry-based learning. Pp. 67-78 in R. Barnett (Ed.), *Reshaping the University: New Relationships Between Research, Scholarship and Teaching*. New York: McGraw-Hill/Open University Press.

Henderson, C., Finklestein, N., and Beach, A. (2010). Beyond dissemination in college science teaching: An introduction to four core change strategies. *Journal of College Science Teaching, 39*, 18-25.

Henderson, C., Beach, A., and Finkelstein, N. (2011). Facilitating change in undergraduate STEM instructional practices: An analytic review of the literature. *Journal of Research in Science Teaching, 48*(8), 952-984.

Hernandez-Jarvis, L., Shaughnessy, J.J., Chase-Wallar, L.A., and Barney, C.C. (2011). Integrating undergraduate research into faculty responsibilities: The impact of tenure and promotion decisions. *CUR Quarterly, 31*(4), 7-9.

Hewlett, J. (2009). The search for synergy: Undergraduate research at the community college. Pp. 9-18 in B.D. Cejda and N. Hensel (Eds.), *Undergraduate Research at Community Colleges*. Washington, DC: Council on Undergraduate Research.

Hu, S., Scheuch, K., Schwartz, R.A., Gayles, J.G., and Li, S. (2008). Reinventing undergraduate education: Engaging college students in research and creative activities. *ASHE Higher Education Report, 33*(4), 1-103.

Hunter, A.B., Laursen, S.L., and Seymour, E. (2006). Becoming a scientist: The role of undergraduate research in students' cognitive, personal, and professional development. *Science Education, 91*(1), 36-74.

Hurtado, S. (2003). *Preparing College Students for a Diverse Democracy* (presentation made within the Chet Peters lecture series). Manhattan, KS: Kansas State University.

Hurtado, S., Cabrera, N.L., Lin, M.H., Arellano, L., and Espinosa, L.L. (2009). Diversifying science: Underrepresented student experiences in structured research programs. *Research in Higher Education, 50*, 189-214.

Jenkins, A. (2004). *A Guide to the Research Evidence on Teaching-Research Relations*. York, UK: The Higher Education Academy.

Jones, R.M., and Davis, S.N. (2014). Assessing faculty perspectives on undergraduate research: Implications from studies of two faculties. *CUR Quarterly, 34*, 37-42.

Kardash, C.M. (2000). Evaluation of undergraduate research experience: Perceptions of undergraduate interns and their faculty mentors. *Journal of Educational Psychology, 92*(1), 191-201.

Karukstis, K.K. (2004). Creating time for research: Recommendations from faculty at predominantly undergraduate institutions. *Journal of Chemical Education, 81*, 1550-1551.

Kierniesky, N.C. (2005). Undergraduate research in small psychology departments: Two decades later. *Teaching of Psychology, 32*(2), 84-90.

Kim, M.M., Rhoades, G., and Woodard Jr., D.B. (2003). Sponsored research versus graduating students? Intervening variables and unanticipated findings in public research universities. *Research in Higher Education, 44*(1), 51-81.

Kloser, M.J., Brownell, S.E., Chiariello, N.R., and Fukami, T. (2011). Integrating teaching and research in undergraduate biology laboratory education. *PLoS Biology, 9*(11), e1001174. Available: http://journals.plos.org/plosbiology/article?id=10.1371/journal.pbio.1001174 [November 2016].

Kortz, K.M., and van der Hoeven Kraft, K.J. (2016). Geoscience Education Research Project: Student benefits and effective design of a course-based undergraduate research experience. *Journal of Geoscience Education, 64*(1), 24-36.

Langley, W. (2015). Undergraduate research at a two-year college: A team approach. *Journal of College Science Teaching, 45*(2), 16-17.

Laursen, S., Seymour, E., and Hunter, A.B. (2012). Learning, teaching and scholarship: Fundamental tensions of undergraduate research. *Change: The Magazine of Higher Learning, 44*(2), 30-37.

Layzell, D.T. (1996). Faculty workload and productivity: Recurrent issues with new imperatives. *Review of Higher Education, 19*(3), 267-81.

Linn, M.C., Palmer, E., Baranger, A., Gerard, E., and Stone, E. (2015). Undergraduate research experiences: Impacts and opportunities. *Science* 347(6222), 1-6.

Lopatto, D., Hauser, C., Jones, C.J., Paetkau, D., Chandrasekaran, V., Dunbar, D., MacKinnon, C., Stamm, J., Alvarez, C., and Barnard, D. (2014). A central support system can facilitate implementation and sustainability of a classroom-based undergraduate research experience (CURE) in genomics. *CBE–Life Sciences Education, 13*, 711-723.

Marsh, H.W., and Hattie, J. (2002). The relation between research productivity and teaching effectiveness: Complementary, antagonistic, or independent constructs? *Journal of Higher Education, 73*(5), 603-641.

Mateja, J., and Otto, C. (2007). Undergraduate research: Approaches to success. Pp. 269-272 in K.J. Denniston (Ed.), *Invention and Impact: Building Excellence in Undergraduate Science, Technology, Engineering and Mathematics (STEM) Education*. Washington, DC: American Association for the Advancement of Science. Available: http://www.aaas.org/sites/default/files/09_Prep_Grad_Mateja.pdf [November 2016].

McKinney, K., Saxe, D., and Cobb, L. (1998). Are we really doing all we can for our undergraduates? Professional socialization via out-of-class experiences. *Teaching Sociology, 26*(1), 1-13.

Merkel, C.A. (2001). *Undergraduate Research at Six Research Universities: A Pilot Study for the Association of American Universities*. Pasadena: California Institute of Technology. Available: http://www.aau.edu/education/Merkel.pdf [February 2016].

Mervis, J. (2001). Student research: What is it good for? *Science, 293*, 1614-1615.

Milem, J.F., Berger, J.B., and Dey, E.L. (2000). Faculty time allocation: A study of change over twenty years. *Journal of Higher Education, 71*(4), 454-475.

National Academy of Sciences, National Academy of Engineering, and Institute of Medicine. (1997). *Adviser, Teacher, Role Model, Friend: On Being a Mentor to Students in Science and Engineering.* Committee on Science, Engineering, and Public Policy of the National Academy of Sciences, National Academy of Engineering, and Institute of Medicine. Washington, DC: National Academies Press. Available: http://www.nap.edu/read/5789/chapter/1 [February 2017].

Nelson Laird, T.F., Bridges, B.K., Morelon-Quainoo, C.L., Williams, J.M., and Holmes, M.S. (2007). African American and Hispanic student engagement at minority serving and predominantly White institutions. *Journal of College Student Development, 48*(1), 39-56.

Perez, J.A. (2003). Undergraduate research at two-year colleges. *New Directions for Teaching and Learning, 93*, 69-77.

Presley, J.B., and Engelbride, E. (1998). Accounting for faculty productivity in the research university. *Review of Higher Education, 22*(1), 17-37.

Prince, M.J., Felder, R.M., and Brent, R. (2007). Does faculty research improve undergraduate teaching? An analysis of existing and potential synergies. *Journal of Engineering Education, 96*(4), 283-294.

Pukkila, P., DeCosmo, J., Swick, D.C., and Arnold, M.S. (2007). How to engage in collaborative curriculum design to foster undergraduate inquiry and research in all disciplines. Pp. 321-357 in K.K. Karukstis and T.E. Elgren (Eds.), *Developing and Sustaining a Research-Supportive Curriculum: A Compendium of Successful Practices.* Washington, DC: Council of Undergraduate Research.

Reinen, L., Grasfils, E., Gaines, R., and Hazlett, R. (2007). Integrating research into a small geology department's curriculum. Pp. 331-339 in K.K. Karukstis and T.E. Elgren (Eds.), *Developing and Sustaining a Research-supportive Curriculum: A Compendium of Successful Practices.* Washington, DC: Council on Undergraduate Research.

Rueckert, L. (2007). Flexible curricular structures to provide time for research within the classroom. Pp. 285-294 in K.K. Karukstis and T.E. Elgren (Eds.), *Developing and Sustaining a Research-supportive Curriculum: A Compendium of Successful Practices.* Washington, DC: Council on Undergraduate Research.

Russell, C.B., Bentley, A.K., Wink, D.J., and Weaver, G.C. (2009). Materials development for a research-based undergraduate laboratory curriculum. *The Chemical Educator, 14*, 55-60.

Schultheis, A.S., Farrell, T.M., and Paul, E.L. (2011). Promoting undergraduate research through revising tenure and promotion policy. *Council on Undergraduate Research Quarterly, 31*(4), 25-31.

Schuster, J.H., and Finkelstein, M.J. (2006). *The American Faculty: The Restructuring of Academic Work and Careers.* Baltimore, MD: Johns Hopkins University Press.

Shortlidge, E.E., Bangera, G., and Brownell, S.E. (2016). Faculty perspectives on developing and teaching course-based undergraduate research experiences. *BioScience, 66*(1), 54-62.

Spell, R.M., Guinan, J.A., Miller, K.R., Beck, C.W. (2014). Redefining authentic research experiences in introductory biology laboratories and barriers to their implementation. *CBE–Life Sciences Education, 13*, 102-110.

Temple, L., Sibley, T., and Orr, A.J. (2010). *How to Mentor Undergraduate Research.* Washington, DC: Council on Undergraduate Research.

Townsend, B., and Rosser, V. (2007). Workload issues and measures of faculty productivity. *Thought & Action, 23*, 7-19.

Verburgh, A., Elen, J., and Lindblom-Ylänne, S. (2007). Investigating the myth of the relationship between teaching and research in higher education: A review of empirical research. *Studies in Philosophy and Education, 26*(5), 449-465.

Wareham, T., and Trowler, P. (2007). *Deconstructing and Reconstructing the "Teaching-Research Nexus": Lessons from Art and Design.* Paper presented at the AISHE annual conference, August 2007. Available: http://paul-trowler.weebly.com/uploads/4/2/4/3/42439197/deconstructing_and_reconstructing_the_teaching-research_nexus-_lessons_from_art_and_design.pdf [November 2016].

Wayment, H.A., and Dickson, K.L. (2008). Increasing student participation in undergraduate research benefits students, faculty, and department. *Teaching of Psychology, 35*(3), 194-197.

Weaver, G.C., Wink, D., Varma-Nelson, P., Lytle, F., Morris, R., Fornes, W., Russell, C., and Boone, W.J. (2006). Developing a new model to provide first and second-year undergraduates with chemistry research experience: Early findings of the Center for Authentic Science Practice in Education (CASPiE). *The Chemical Educator, 11,* 125-129.

Weiss, T.H., Feldman, A., Pedevillano, D.E., and Copobianco, B. (2004). The implications of culture and identity: A professor's engagement with a reform collaborative. *International Journal of Science and Math Education, 1,* 333-356.

Wood, W.B. (2003). Inquiry-based undergraduate teaching in the life sciences at large research universities: A perspective on the Boyer Commission report. *CBE–Life Sciences Education, 2,* 112-116.

Zubrick, A., Reid, I., and Rossiter, P.L. (2001). *Strengthening the Nexus between Teaching and Research* (Vol. 6499). Washington, DC: U.S. Department of Education. Available: http://citeseerx.ist.psu.edu/viewdoc/download?doi=10.1.1.214.8309&rep=rep1&type=pdf [November 2016].

Zydney, A.L., Bennett, J.S., Shahid, A., and Bauer, K. (2002). Faculty perspectives regarding the undergraduate research experience in science and engineering. *Journal of Engineering Education, 91*(3), 291-297.

7

Need for Research About UREs

During the course of the committee's review of the existing literature, numerous opportunities for research were identified that could deepen understanding of undergraduate research experiences (UREs). This chapter identifies priorities for research and discusses multiple methodological approaches needed to answer questions about UREs, especially questions about the value-added of these experiences over programs that lack such experiences. This research is challenging due to the heterogeneity of research experiences. It will benefit from a clear conceptual framework that guides researchers to identify key questions and mechanisms for further investigation.

Conducting research can be expensive and time consuming, so it is important to consider the cost-effectiveness of the various research approaches and the relative importance of the questions so that resources can be targeted appropriately. Although all URE programs should conduct some type of evaluation to measure whether they are meeting their goals, not all UREs must or should be part of a research study. However, it is critical that some research studies are conducted to collect and analyze information that will allow the community to better define and describe UREs and their features and to clarify their mechanisms and effects. The results of the research about UREs would provide information to inform planning of future UREs.

Based on the committee's review of dozens of empirical studies, we have found a rich descriptive foundation for testable hypotheses about the effects of UREs on student outcomes. The descriptive evidence, predominantly from self-reports, suggests that research on URE participation should focus on its impact on disciplinary and research understanding, identity as a researcher; persistence in a science, technology, engineering, and mathematics (STEM) major; and increased enrollment in graduate programs in STEM (Blockus, 2016; Dolan, 2016; Hathaway et al., 2002; Hunter et al., 2007; Nagda et al., 1998; Sadler, 2010; Seymour et al., 2004). Since few studies employ research designs that allow for strong causal inferences about the effects on students of participating in UREs compared to programs without UREs, the next step for research on UREs is to gather this information. This chapter provides recommendations to create a firmer research base and address numerous gaps, as well as ideas for other types of research that would be beneficial to the field.

In approaching the task of creating a research agenda for strengthening UREs, this committee found it useful to build on an earlier National Research Council (2002) report, *Scientific Research in Education*. As discussed in Chapter 2, that report distinguished among three types of research questions in education research: descriptive, causal, and mechanistic. Research intended to answer descriptive, causal, and mechanistic questions requires a combination of theory, method, measurement, and analysis, ideally based on a shared conceptual framework. Researchers seeking to address complex questions about the underlying mechanisms and outcomes of UREs need to use the tools of the social sciences, build on prior research, and draw from existing information about learning and teaching. At the start of their projects, investigators need to identify appropriate and feasible ways to document impacts; this involves planning studies with appropriate comparison groups, creating ways to measure important elements of research and course experiences, using valid, reliable measures of the outcomes of interest, and when possible acquiring longitudinal data. As discussed later in the chapter, there can be logistical and financial challenges to some of these approaches.

All three types of research are necessary to provide the information needed to improve undergraduate training and experiences in STEM fields. The three types must proceed along parallel tracks. Given the paucity of strong causal evidence about the effects of UREs and about the mechanisms that are most effective in achieving desired outcomes, the committee urges funding agencies to provide funding for research projects intended to generate causal and mechanistic evidence. Such evidence will be useful in guiding investments. The evidence need not come from large-scale, multisite randomized controlled trials (RCTs). Small-scale experiments at individual campuses or well-designed quasi-experimental studies across courses within a college or department can provide important building blocks for the evidentiary foundation needed. If the evidence is consistent with the many descriptive studies already available and with experiences of faculty, then it can be used to advocate for greater resources for UREs that build upon this strengthened body of research. To successfully carry out research on the individual characteristics (e.g., collaboration and reflection) and potential impacts (e.g., retention in STEM and integration into the STEM culture) of UREs, including the mechanisms by which those impacts are realized, the field needs testable hypotheses about what, why, and for whom UREs work best and about how to improve the structure and provision of UREs to reach a larger and more diverse pool of students. These ends are best accomplished through design-based and mixed methods research.

The following section introduces two key challenges to understanding the effects of UREs: nonrandom selection into UREs (as a function of student, faculty, or mentor choice) and high-quality measures of outcomes. Based on the needs of the field, we then present potential approaches that meet these challenges for research on UREs.

STEM practitioners and researchers may find that forming or joining multidisciplinary teams/partnerships with researchers who have expertise in the behavioral/social sciences, education research, and program evaluation can provide a rich opportunity for collaboration to investigate and strengthen UREs for students. For example, the multidisciplinary community of Understanding Interventions has been focused for years on creating dialogue among members of the education community participating in STEM intervention programs.

CHALLENGES TO RESEARCH ABOUT URES

To build a stronger research literature that informs the community about the effects that UREs can have, researchers need to be aware of the advantages and limitations inherent in various research designs. In addition, researchers need to be aware of issues and challenges related to selection and measurement. This section discusses the challenges, and the next section focuses on approaches to the research about UREs.

Nonrandom Selection into UREs

Selection bias is a bias in which the characteristics of the students and faculty/mentors participating in any given URE are collected in such a way that they are not equivalent to other potentially URE-eligible participants. This makes the comparisons across UREs difficult. There are at least three common ways that selection bias can creep into the research process and affect the estimated effects of UREs: (1) student self-selection, (2) program-based selection, and (3) selective attrition (e.g., weaker students or those for whom STEM research is not a good fit may be less likely to complete URE projects, remain as STEM majors, or elect to participate in longitudinal surveys about their experiences).

First, with respect to self-selection, students who do or do not pursue opportunities for UREs likely differ from one another in important ways. Those students who seek out or take advantage of opportunities to engage in research may be better prepared academically, more motivated, or more interested in and/or more committed to STEM fields than otherwise similar students who choose not to participate in UREs.

Second, in many instances, students are not the only people involved in the URE choice process. Faculty and program staff may choose to recruit students who share similar interests and values as the faculty member or are deemed as having the greatest likelihood of success in college in general or STEM fields in particular (program-based selection). Such a process would, again, lead to a group of students participating in UREs who would be more likely to succeed (e.g., stay in a STEM major, graduate in STEM) than nonparticipants, even absent the URE participation.

Finally, attrition is another form of selection bias. Students who continue to participate in UREs and/or studies of UREs until outcomes are measured may consistently differ in outcome-relevant ways from students who withdraw or fail to respond to a survey. Students who are not satisfied with their experience in undergraduate research, who struggle academically, or who confront challenges outside of school that hinder their academic progress are more likely than other students to withdraw from courses or from the university itself. As a result, students who persist in the URE may on average be more successful by other measures as well, leading to a falsely inflated estimate of the effect of the URE on the selected outcome measures.

There are at least two ways to deal with this challenge: (1) Demonstrate the equivalence of the URE and non-URE groups (e.g., the control and experimental groups) as measured by their performance on a dependent variable (e.g., knowledge, motivation, attitudes) before and after the implementation of the URE so claims about the impact of UREs can be based on the functional equivalence between the groups. If the comparison groups are different from one another at the beginning of the study the results of the study are biased. (2) Keep track of the characteristics of the students (e.g., grade point average, previous research experience, gender) to determine the equivalence with non-URE students. This last strategy enables accumulation of knowledge about *for whom* UREs with certain characteristics (including the mentors' characteristics) work; that is, which characteristics of students and mentors are associated with positive outcomes. Tracking can be more easily done within an institution but potentially it could be done across institutions.

High-Quality Measures of Outcomes

Measurement can simply reflect the process by which one observes and records the observations as part of a research study. It is important to ensure that the instruments employed to investigate the subject/object of the research are reliable and accurately capture the construct of interest. Some measures, such as graduation rates, are readily obtained and objectively defined. However, careful consideration needs to be given to selecting appropriate measures of learning gains and/or acquisition of content knowledge and skills by students who do, and those who do not, participate in UREs. The committee's review of the literature in Chapters 2 through 6 showed that future studies need more rigorous measurement and more-valid indicators. Validation of self-reported information, for example, can be improved by cross-referencing analysis of research products, such as presentations and reports, essay examinations, or other observations of student activities.

Researchers studying URE outcomes often call for assessments that measure a student's ability to form arguments using evidence from research in the student's field of study, such as analyses of primary scientific literature (Dasgupta et al., 2014; Gormally et al., 2012; National Research Council, 2007). Although the use of such indicators appears to be rare in the context of UREs, the approach has proven successful in assessing learning in some courses (e.g., Brownell et al., 2014).

Many studies rely on student self-reports to measure constructs such as identity as a STEM professional, interest, and motivation to study STEM, and career plans. Even though these constructs are inherently subjective, relying on self-reports to measure them poses some challenges. One limitation of self-reports is that student's responses may be influenced by recent events: a failed experiment, an unpleasant interaction with a collaborator, or an unexpected high grade. Self-report measures may mean different things to different students, depending on their perspectives and experiences. Students from different parts of the country or different parts of the world may not choose the same words to describe similar experiences. Students who have never met an engineer, for example, may respond differently from those whose family friends include engineers. Finally, self-report measures can be influenced by situational factors such as the expectations of the person administering the test or interview or the feeling that it is socially desirable to express interest in STEM. With these caveats noted, there are existing self-report measures that have been shown to be reliable across time, predictive of long-term persistence, and valid.

To establish the validity of new self-report measures, researchers can use multiple indicators to ensure that the intended construct is accurately measured. Promising indicators include observations of participation in experiments; logs of student activities on a project; analysis of transcripts;

analysis of journals that capture responses across weeks or months; and interviews that probe for individual characteristics such as perspectives on prior STEM activities, personal details (such as anecdotes about mentors), and confusions or conundrums about their possible futures. Additional cross-validating indicators are perceptions of peers, instructors, or advisors. Researchers can strengthen the evidence base for self-report measures by using one or more of these indicators, along with the self-report measure, to form an input construct. Moreover, by following students longitudinally, researchers can see how well their chosen indicators predict future decisions and career paths.

In order to characterize, assess, and compare student learning in different laboratory contexts (that use a wide variety of discipline-specific research questions and experimental methods), researchers need to identify appropriate measurement instruments. A recent paper (Shortlidge and Brownell, 2016) provides a table of possible assessment tools for CURE instructors; some of these tools will also be useful for running other types of URE programs. In some cases instruments will need to be generalizable across different fields and scalable for use with a large number of students. Possible areas for development of such instruments include poster presentations or similar reports, notebooks and journals, responses to a challenge requiring data analysis, and other measures of STEM-specific activities. For example, recent efforts to develop rubrics to assess undergraduate writing across courses offer promise (Timmerman et al., 2011).

APPROACHES TO RESEARCH ABOUT URES

To establish causal findings requires analytic strategies that can rule out alternative explanations for impacts of UREs. Causal questions related to learning outcomes could include the following: Did URE participation increase STEM literacy? Did URE participation alter the ability to navigate uncertainty or professional STEM efficacy? Causal questions about longer term career pathways might include: Did a specific URE help to sustain a student interested in STEM in the path a student was on? Did it support her and enable her to change in some way that she would not have changed, absent the experience? Did the effect vary depending on the students' expectations or specific experiences in the laboratory?

To answer these central questions regarding the gains from URE participation in learning and persistence, studies need rigorous comparisons to alternatives and may require nuanced analysis of (multiple) outcomes. Thoughtful attention to the organization of the study before the implementation of new UREs would allow for robust conclusions to be made about UREs and how they work.

Experimental and Quasi-Experimental Designs

Whenever possible, the use of experimental designs is recommended, as these approaches may be particularly useful for those seeking to document the added value of UREs. Randomization is possible in instances of excess demand (e.g., by using lottery). Scholars at the University of Michigan successfully employed this approach to study the causal effect of Michigan's Undergraduate Research Opportunity Program (Nagda et al., 1998). This approach requires that demand exceed supply; another study attempting to employ this design was unsuccessful because too few students signed up for the course (Brownell et al., 2012). However, more students were enrolled the next year, and a randomized assignment was possible (Brownell et al., 2013). Randomization is also possible when students accept to be randomized into experimental and control classes and/or when balancing across sections/groups is feasible (Schultz, 2004). When programs have small numbers of students, studies sometimes attempt to cluster data across sites in a consortium (Reardon, 2013).

Quasi-experimental designs provide causal evidence in the absence of RCTs. Although the RCT is a gold standard in many research fields for establishing causal evidence for efficacy of a particular intervention (e.g., pharmaceutical clinical trials), the use of RCTs in educational research is often limited by practical, political, and ethical constraints. Absent successful random assignment, researchers can pursue a number of quasi-experimental approaches to establish that subjects (students) experiencing different treatments (courses/experiences) are on average the same and that prior to treatment, nothing about either the subjects or the treatments predicted who would end up in what treatment. For example, one approach might be to match students in the treatment pool with students in the nontreatment pool on relevant variables (e.g., preparation, ethnicity). Any quasi-experimental solution to the problem of group comparability, however, requires an additional set of assumptions. For example, as an initial step, researchers might statistically adjust (or control) for students' high school grades and SAT or ACT math scores or for student performance on a pre-test measure of achievement and assume that *conditional* on these pre-existing differences, students were more or less the same on average.

Both experimental and quasi-experimental designs benefit from planning for assessment of longitudinal effects. Panel attrition can undermine the validity of panel studies to the extent that those who persist in a study are different from those who drop out. Gaining consent from research subjects at the beginning of the study to link to their administrative records (e.g., grades, final major, degree attainment) is critically important. Use of such records can help to minimize the harm done by sample attrition. In addition, there is evidence that the technique of tailored panel management can help retain panels with a higher response rate (Estrada et al., 2014).

Design-Based Studies

Research experiences occur in complex contexts and often have differential impacts on students due to the students' prior experiences and expectations. Box 7-1 provides some examples. These factors may undermine the utility of large-scale comparative studies for course developers. Research that has value for the developers of the innovations and also has potential to reveal mechanisms that might be of use to others are promising alternatives. Instructors/directors of UREs who engage in evidence-based practices in their own programs can study their programs in order to identify features and elements for improvement. Courses and programs can then be improved via iterative refinement. Research comparing successive versions of a course can shed light on the impacts of the improvements (Cobb et al., 2003).

Design-based research provides a methodology, common among researchers in learning sciences, wherein interventions are conceptualized and implemented iteratively in a natural setting to test a hypothesis (Barab and Squire, 2004). The methodology applied to education can effectively capture the effect of an innovation in a complex, local system (Johri and Olds, 2011). Design-based research may result in plausible causal accounts, assist in the identification of contextual factors and mechanisms that alter program impacts, and deepen the understanding of the nature of the intervention/feature. Iterative cycles of development, implementation, and study allow researchers to gauge how an intervention is or is not succeeding in ways that may then inform an improved approach (Barab and Squire, 2004). In all such studies, the researcher (or program director) will need to

---

BOX 7-1
Examples of Design-Based Research

- Randomly assign students taking UREs to weekly structured mentoring sessions or to informal mentoring to explore the effects of structured mentoring.
- Randomly assign URE students to writing a weekly journal reflecting on their insights or to keeping a typical research notebook.
- Randomly assign students to receive online guidance or to meet an instructor in person.

obtain Institutional Review Board approval and the informed consent of participating students, prior to the start of the study.

Other Considerations in Research About UREs

Mixed method approaches integrate quantitative and qualitative approaches to research. For example, qualitative data can inform a RCT. A well-constructed mixed method study might include collecting quantitative measures of student learning outcomes (e.g., surveys or tests such as the Force Concept Inventory or ETS's Major Field Test for Physics) and qualitative evidence from observations, interviews with participants, and collection of artifacts (e.g., reports, lab notebooks, presentations). The combination of these data can uncover "links between theory and empirical findings, challenge theoretical assumptions and develop new theory" (Östlund et al., 2011). Because social phenomena are very complex, mixed method designs can help to elucidate critical factors in the phenomenon of interest (Creswell et al., 2003; Greene et al., 1989). Mixed method design studies should be considered when planning studies aimed at understanding the roles and impacts that various features have on the outcomes of UREs.

Longitudinal studies provide the opportunity to track students from entrance into a URE to completion of the experience and beyond. These studies provide additional insight into the impact of UREs and may identify the impact of participation in UREs on student persistence, completion of STEM degrees, enrollment in graduate school, entrance into the STEM workforce, participation in the STEM community through publication or presentation, or other career or educational outcomes. Mixed methods experimental or quasi-experimental approaches should be used that account for the influence of students' incoming interest, motivation, expectations, and academic background on student outcomes.

Longitudinal studies will require researchers to document the number and types of UREs that students participate in, the characteristics of those UREs, and the duration and timing of the UREs within the students' educational experience. Longitudinal studies measuring the development of students' knowledge and skills, such as scientific thinking or experimental design abilities, argumentation skills, STEM communication abilities, or problem-solving skills, from participation in UREs would also be valuable, after valid, reliable assessments of these outcomes are developed. These longitudinal studies are not trivial tasks but are necessary to fully understand the way UREs impact career choices.

RECOMMENDATIONS FOR FUTURE STUDIES

To strengthen UREs, the committee has identified a series of high-priority study areas that merit careful consideration by URE program directors, education researchers, faculty, and funding agencies. More general recommendations about the use of UREs in undergraduate education are presented in Chapter 9, which also contains a recommendation about the importance of conducting quality research about UREs that takes a bigger-picture view and is therefore included with the general recommendations of the report and not in this chapter.

In order to meet the call for expanded research tools and active research to study the impacts of UREs, funding agencies that typically support UREs will need to examine their research portfolios and priorities, as well as funding practices (such as length of grants, which can affect the ability to carry out longitudinal studies). Well-designed summative cross-site external evaluations and studies of URE programs and their features are of potential value to the nation's students and the national STEM education community. Optimally, the studies outlined below would be conducted by teams composed of members with strengths in the design and analysis of behavioral science and educational research, members with strengths in URE program implementation, and members who are STEM practitioners. This type of research should not be expected of every faculty member who runs a URE, but the community should work together to ensure that these questions are addressed and the results disseminated to the community in order to inform future UREs. As is always the case, studies should be designed in ways that respect the needs of students, and any necessary Institutional Review Board approval should be established before studies begin.

RESEARCH RECOMMENDATION 1 *Researchers should develop and validate tools that can be readily used by people who direct undergraduate research experiences to assess student outcomes. Assessment should address both conceptual knowledge and development of skills important to STEM professionals. Some of these tools will be useful to those studying UREs in many different disciplines, whereas others will focus on concepts and content of a particular discipline.*

Formative assessment by research mentors, program directors, and instructors can be used to monitor student development and achievement through a URE and to make appropriate adjustments along the way. If researchers are able to develop validated, theoretically informed tools, such tools could be used by faculty running UREs to better assess the impact of UREs on students and to identify the most influential and beneficial factors in UREs. Tools intended to assess content knowledge need to be developed with input from subject matter experts. Potential tools would include scoring rubrics for posters, presentations, or laboratory notebooks. Instruments need to be made broadly accessible to leaders and developers of undergraduate research programs.

Tools need to be reliable and valid for various types of UREs and populations of students. For example, validated measures of student growth in knowledge and skills should work similarly for men and women, for students from historically underrepresented racial/ethnic groups, and for those who are not part of those groups. This uniformity is important for determining the broad impact of UREs across student populations. It may entail developing tools that are readily customized to the discipline, student population, or research experience goals. Tools need to be in a form readily used by program directors without social science training, and they must be relatively inexpensive to score. Research is needed to develop valid and reliable measures of important outcomes of UREs in order to allow for comparisons between UREs and other types of experiences, such as typical courses.

RESEARCH RECOMMENDATION 2 *Future studies should seek to identify and measure the variables that explain why specific aspects of UREs have impact (or not) on the students participating in a URE. Researchers should consider a range of student outcomes (e.g., improved persistence, development of STEM identity, understanding of the nature of research, and development of specific skills or disciplinary knowledge). The number of UREs that a student participates in, the duration of the experience, and the timing of those experiences within the student's undergraduate education should also be examined.*

Proponents of UREs believe that they have an impact on student trajectories that is superior to that of traditional courses of instruction. While the available evidence is consistent with these beliefs, few studies have been sufficiently rigorous to offer a strong test of them. For example, does participation in a URE impact performance in future upper-division courses? Evaluation of how UREs enhance student outcomes when compared to other experiences is needed and can be informed by research on inquiry instruction and identity processes. (Further information about these approaches can be found in Furtak et al., 2012, and Nasir and Cooks, 2009.) Specific objectives of UREs may include improvements in students' understanding of the nature of STEM, of the process of research and associated skills, or of scientific and technical communication. Other objectives may include skill development for career preparation, collaboration, and teamwork.

Researchers should characterize the type of value the URE will add for those who participate and document the mechanisms that enable the value to be delivered. The evidence required will come from comparing UREs to other experiences and other learning approaches, including traditional courses. Research on UREs needs to take into consideration the duration of these activities, as well as their variety and goals. Many students participate in multiple UREs, so studies that compare the presence or absence of a URE in a student's education may not adequately reflect today's environment. Studies should attempt to identify the value added of the different types of experiences, including the importance of the scheduling/timing of the experience in the educational progression and pathway of a student, characterizing how the nature and characteristics of the URE affect the student, and the role that research experience(s) play in contributing to student outcomes.

To make conclusions about a particular outcome, multiple measures are needed. These measures may include self-report on some psychosocial measures (potentially including efficacy, identity, values, belongingness, stereotype threat, micro-aggression, and micro-affirmations), analysis of research products, and documentation of research experiences (potentially including type of URE, timing and duration of the experience, type of mentoring, opportunity for autonomous investigation and decision making, and development of research techniques). Not all of these measures would be relevant to every study, but a combination of measures would likely be required for each study.

Beyond measuring the impact of UREs on learning and student retention, studies should be undertaken that seek to answer the question of why these programs have (or have not) achieved successful outcomes. Results that explain "why" have the potential to advance theory in both educational and behavioral sciences. Further, these sorts of results inform science educators about how to refine and increase the effectiveness of their programs. For example, if UREs result in the development of a professional identity and it is found that URE students who develop a professional identity are more likely to go to graduate school in a STEM field, then educators might actively foster activities that help student's grow their professional identity. Research that seeks to measure the "why" will benefit from large numbers of study participants, longitudinal data collection methods, and measurement (both self-report and objective measures) of URE experience, as well as measures of STEM career engagement. Because these types of studies are expensive and time consuming, there should be no expectation that all faculty who run UREs would conduct research meeting these requirements as a matter of course. Such studies should be carefully designed by teams of researchers with appropriate training in the relevant skills. A small number of well-designed and carefully executed studies will be of greater value than a large number of partial studies.

RESEARCH RECOMMENDATION 3 *Future studies should systematically analyze the impact that various characteristics of UREs have on different student populations, to better identify what works for whom and under what conditions.*

Descriptive research suggests that individual responses to UREs may vary depending on a student's prior experience and academic preparation, the student's sense of belonging to the STEM enterprise, URE goals, the timing and duration of the experience, and other factors. There is little empirical evidence showing which student characteristics moderate the effects of UREs. The sheer number of possible variables makes it impossible to investigate how all possible combinations of student cultural and experiential characteristics fare in each of the variations in UREs. Research in this area needs to be informed by prior research, theoretical frameworks, and policy priorities. For example, data on student participation could be used to analyze demographics of the participants to better understand access issues relating to barriers to participation, disciplinary differences, trends in engaging underclassmen, and information on students participating in more than one opportunity.

For this research question, it would be valuable to collect participant demographic information (race/ethnicity, age, generation, and socioeconomic status) in combination with URE characteristics (see conceptual framework) and to conduct carefully designed comparisons between specific UREs. For example, a study comparing mentoring practices could examine possible interactions of those practices with cultural or experiential background characteristics of the protégé and mentor. Such studies might identify possible mentoring mechanisms that could be recommended for broad implementation. It is possible that even with such findings, instructors will need to customize the mentoring mechanism to the characteristics of their protégés/mentees.

A major research priority is to understand the critical factors that contribute to the success of diverse groups engaged in UREs. For example, longitudinal research on the role and impact that mentors have on the persistence of diverse groups in STEM fields could help shape mentor-mentee interactions (see Research Recommendation 5). Any research design needs to pay attention to how theoretically derived factors associated with student persistence, including self-efficacy, science identity, and values, vary as a function of gender, racial/ethnic group membership, and their intersection (e.g., Byars-Winston et al., 2016).

RESEARCH RECOMMENDATION 4 *Researchers should study in a systematic manner the impact of a URE's characteristics on faculty and other* *mentors to better know the diversity of benefits obtained by faculty and mentors.*

While an evidentiary foundation for causal effects of UREs on students is just now beginning to be established, a foundation for causal effects on faculty and mentors is almost nonexistent. Hypotheses have been offered that UREs can increase or decrease faculty productivity depending on the circumstances at the institution, the structure of the URE, and the particular students involved. The value placed on UREs, and on teaching in general, on a particular campus may have an effect on the incentives and rewards that alter faculty decisions regarding UREs.

Although there is a long tradition of mentoring in STEM education, there is limited empirical evidence to explain specific ways that mentoring affects URE students (Pfund, 2016). More methodologically rigorous studies of mentoring are needed. The research community lacks a set of refined common variables; a first step would be for the field to define a set of common input and output variables, after which there would be a better chance of generating reproducible results when investigating mentoring.

RESEARCH RECOMMENDATION 5 *Additional research should examine the specific role(s) of the mentor and the impact of the mentoring relationship on the undergraduate mentee, compared to the immersive URE itself.*

Using theoretical models to understand the mechanisms contributing to persistence is one promising approach for providing insights into how and why mentoring relationships contribute to success (Byars-Winston et al., 2015; Estrada et al., 2011; Hurtado et al., 2009; Packard, 2016; Pfund, 2016). Mentoring has been proposed as a critical factor affecting the persistence of STEM students, and it offers a potential target for further investigation. Good mentoring is potentially a key way to provide an intervention that benefits students.

Research is also needed to uncover the mechanisms by which mentoring relationships foster particular outcomes and how these outcomes may differ, based on the mentoring model or student population. Potentially relevant factors include persistence, engagement in or commitment to the discipline, belonging, and educational and career decision making.

ROLE FOR FUNDERS OF RESEARCH ON URES

Progress on these research questions will require financial support. The results will increase knowledge of the ways that UREs affect students and provide guidance for design of future UREs that may have a more significant impact on students. Teams of researchers with strengths in the design and analysis of experimental and quasi-experimental educational research, as well as those with strengths in URE program implementation working in concert with STEM researchers, may be needed to make progress on the research agenda identified here. Funding agencies may want to coordinate and/or pool their efforts in this regard to achieve maximum return per dollar spent.

Well-designed summative cross-site external evaluations and research on URE programs and their design features are of potential value to the nation's students and the national STEM education community. Using rigorous research approaches for studying UREs will cost more than small outcome-centric evaluation, but it is important that some in-depth research studies be conducted.

In addition to considering research about UREs, funding agencies may want to assemble guidelines for effective assessments of funded programs that are not part of a research study. These guidelines might suggest some key elements to consider when designing and choosing assessments. Or funding agencies could focus some resources on development of an overall assessment unit that all funded projects must use. The limitation with the second approach is that funding agencies will want to allow for some flexibility so that at least part of the assessment could take into account the specifics of the URE under study, in terms of its structure, setting, organization, and population of students served. Nonetheless, a shared rubric can enable a study encompassing a larger number of students and provide greater opportunity to discern differences between implementations that matter. Many prior studies of UREs have been conducted at a single institution, and multisite studies would enhance the understanding of URE programs, their characteristics, and their outcomes in different institutional contexts and for various populations of students.

SUMMARY

Institutions of higher education are looking for effective methods to maximize educational impact on students while minimizing cost during a time when information systems and technology are rapidly changing. Careful and well-designed research has the potential to illuminate mechanisms that could help designers make informed decisions. As discussed above, three areas of research are needed. First, research that measures outcomes and tracks types of URE engagement would be very useful. For example, research is currently needed on the components of apprentice-style UREs, how they differ from the components of CUREs and other types of UREs, and comparative outcomes. Second, research is needed to assess how the same URE affects students differently because of their prior experiences, expectations, cultural commitments, and stage in their education. Third, there is a need to evaluate why a given URE has the outcomes it does. Researchers need to be clear about which outcomes they are studying, and they need to make sure that they use previous knowledge on the topic, as well as consider evidence that comes from discipline-based education research and from studies on topics such as retention and persistence. Multidisciplinary teams are critical to conducting this research, which bridges the expertise of education researchers, STEM educators, social scientists, natural scientists, and engineers.

Whether the goal is to evaluate an existing program or to modify a program to better achieve a particular student outcome, funders, program administrators, and faculty need to keep in mind the importance of rigorous method design and identify the specific set of questions of interest. This may include validating existing tools and/or developing better tools before questions that are more causal can be addressed. Moreover, the state of the existing evidence may suggest that additional descriptive studies are needed before a theory or model can be developed that identifies potential mechanisms for further investigation in that setting.

REFERENCES

Barab, S., and Squire, K. (2004). Design-based research: Putting a stake in the ground. *Journal of the Learning Sciences, 13*(1), 1-14.

Blockus, L. (2016). *Strengthening Research Experiences for Undergraduate STEM Students: The Co-Curricular Model of the Research Experience.* Paper commissioned for the Committee on Strengthening Research Experiences for Undergraduate STEM Students. Board on Science Education, Division of Behavioral and Social Sciences and Education. Board on Life Sciences, Division of Earth and Life Studies. National Academies of Sciences, Engineering, and Medicine. Available: http://nas.edu/STEM_Undergraduate_Research_Apprentice.

Brownell, S.E., Kloser, M.J., Fukami, T., and Shavelson, R. (2012). Undergraduate biology lab courses: Comparing the impact of traditionally based "cookbook" and authentic research-based courses on student lab experiences. *Journal of College Science Teaching, 41*(4), 36-45.

Brownell, S.E., Price, J.V., and Steinman, L. (2013). A writing-intensive course improves biology undergraduates' perception and confidence of their abilities to read scientific literature and communicate science. *Advances in Physiology Education, 37*(1), 70-79.

Brownell, S.E., Wenderoth, M.P., Theobald, R., Okoroafor, N., Koval, M., Freeman, S., Walcher-Chevillet, C.L., and Crowe, A.J. (2014). How students think about experimental design: Novel conceptions revealed by in-class activities. *BioScience, 64*(2), 125-137.

Byars-Winston, A.M., Branchaw, J., Pfund, C., Leverett, P., and Newton, J. (2015). Culturally diverse undergraduate researchers' academic outcomes and perceptions of their research mentoring relationships. *International Journal of Science Education, 37,* 2533-2554.

Byars-Winston, A., Rogers, J., Branchaw, J.L., Pribbenow, C.M., Hanke, R., and Pfund, C. (2016). New measures assessing predictors of academic persistence for historically underrepresented racial/ethnic undergraduates in STEM fields. *CBE–Life Sciences Education, 15*(3), ar32. Available: https://www.ncbi.nlm.nih.gov/pmc/articles/PMC5008879/pdf/ar32.pdf [February 2017].

Cobb, P., Confrey, J., diSessa, A., Lehrer, R., and Schauble, L. (2003). Design experiments in education research. *The Educational Researcher, 32*(1), 9-13.

Creswell, J.W., Plano Clark, V.L., Gutmann, M.L., and Hanson, W.E. (2003). Advanced mixed methods research designs. Pp. 209-240 in A. Tahakkori and C. Teddlie (Eds.), *Handbook of Mixed Methods in Social and Behavioral Research.* Thousand Oaks, CA: Sage Publication, Inc.

Dasgupta, A.P., Anderson, T.R., and Pelaez, N. (2014). Development and validation of a rubric for diagnosing students' experimental design knowledge and difficulties. *CBE–Life Sciences Education, 13*(2), 265-284.

Dolan, E. (2016). *Course-Based Undergraduate Research Experiences: Current Knowledge and Future Directions.* Paper commissioned for the Committee on Strengthening Research Experiences for Undergraduate STEM Students. Board on Science Education, Division of Behavioral and Social Sciences and Education. Board on Life Sciences, Division of Earth and Life Studies. National Academies of Sciences, Engineering, and Medicine. Available: http://nas.edu/STEM_Undergraduate_Research_CURE [February 2016].

Estrada, M., Woodcock, A., Hernandez, P.R., and Schultz, P. (2011). Toward a model of social influence that explains minority student integration into the scientific community. *Journal of Educational Psychology, 103*, 206-222.

Estrada, M., Woodcock, A., and Schultz, P. (2014). Tailored panel management: A theory-based approach to building and maintaining participant commitment to a longitudinal study. *Evaluation Review, 38*(1), 3-28.

Furtak, E.M., Seidel, T., Iverson, H., and Briggs, D.C. (2012). Experimental and quasi-experimental studies of inquiry-based science teaching: A meta-analysis. *Review of Educational Research, 82*(3), 300-329.

Gormally, C., Brickman, P., and Lutz, M. (2012). Developing a Test of Scientific Literacy Skills (TOSLS): Measuring undergraduates' evaluation of scientific information and arguments. *CBE–Life Sciences Education, 11*(4), 364-377.

Greene, J.C., Caracelli, V.J., and Graham, W.F. (1989). Toward a conceptual framework for mixed-method evaluation designs. *Educational Evaluation and Policy Analysis, 11*(3), 255-274.

Hathaway, R., Biren. S., Nagda, A., and Gregerman, S. (2002). The relationship of undergraduate research participation to graduate and professional education pursuit: An empirical study. *Journal of College Student Development, 43*, 614-31. Available: http://www.eric.ed.gov/ERICWebPortal/detail?accno=EJ653327 [February 2017].

Hunter, A.B., Laursen, S.L., and Seymour, E. (2007). Becoming a scientist: The role of undergraduate research in cognitive, personal and professional development. *Science Education, 91*(1), 36-74.

Hurtado, S., Cabrera, N.L., Lin, M.H., Arellano, L., and Espinosa, L.L. (2009). Diversifying science: Underrepresented student experiences in structured research programs. *Research in Higher Education, 50*, 189-214.

Johri, A., and Olds, B.M. (2011). Situated engineering learning: Bridging engineering education research and the learning sciences. *Journal of Engineering Education, 100*(1), 151-185.

Nagda, B.A., Gregerman, S.R., Jonides, J., von Hippel, W., and Lerner, J.S. (1998). Undergraduate student-faculty research partnerships affect student retention. *Review of Higher Education, 22*, 55-72. Available: http://scholar.harvard.edu/files/jenniferlerner/files/nagda_1998_paper.pdf [February 2017].

Nasir, N.S., and Cooks, J. (2009). Becoming a hurdler: How learning settings afford identities. *Anthropology and Education Quarterly, 40*(1), 41-61. doi:10.1111/j.1548-1492.2009.01027.x

National Research Council. (2002). *Scientific Research in Education*. Committee on Scientific Principles for Education Research, Center for Education, Division of Behavioral and Social Sciences and Education. Washington, DC: National Academy Press.

National Research Council. (2007). *Rising Above the Gathering Storm: Energizing and Employing America for a Brighter Economic Future*. Committee on Prospering in the Global Economy of the 21st Centruy: An Agenda for American Science and Technology. Committee on Science and Engineering Policy. Washington, DC: The National Academies Press.

Östlund, U., Kidd, L., Wengström, Y., and Rowa-Dewar, N. (2011). Combining qualitative and quantitative research within mixed method research designs: A methodological review. *International Journal of Nursing Studies, 48*(3), 369-383.

Packard, B. (2016). *Successful STEM Mentoring Initiatives for Underrepresented Students: A Research-Based Guide for Faculty and Administrators*. Sterling, VA: Stylus.

Pfund, C. (2016). *Studying the Role and Impact of Mentoring on Undergraduate Research Experiences*. Paper commissioned for the Committee on Strengthening Research Experiences for Undergraduate STEM Students. Board on Science Education, Division of Behavioral and Social Sciences and Education. Board on Life Sciences, Division of Earth and Life Studies. National Academies of Sciences, Engineering, and Medicine. Available: http://nas.edu/STEM_Undergraduate_Research_Mentoring.

Reardon, S.F. (2013). The widening income achievement gap. *Educational Leadership, 70*(8), 10-16.

Sadler, D.R. (2010). Beyond feedback: Developing student capability in complex appraisal. *Assessment and Evaluation in Higher Education, 35*(5), 535-550.

Schultz, P.T. (2004). School subsidies for the poor: Evaluating the Mexican Progresa poverty program. *Journal of Development Economics, 74*, 199-250. Available: http://www.sciencedirect.com/science/article/pii/S0304387803001858 [February 2017].

Seymour, E., Hunter, A.B., Laursen, S.L., and DeAntoni, T. (2004). Establishing the benefits of research experiences for undergraduates in the sciences: First findings from a three-year study. *Science Education, 88*, 493-534.

Shortlidge, E., and Brownell, S. (2016). How to assess your CURE: A practical guide for instructors of course-based undergraduate research experiences. *Journal of Microbiology and Biology Education, 17*(3), 399-408.

Timmerman, B.E.C., Strickland, D.C., Johnson, R.L., and Payne, J.R. (2011). Development of a "universal" rubric for assessing undergraduates' scientific reasoning skills using scientific writing. *Assessment and Evaluation in Higher Education, 36*(5), 509-547.

8

Considerations for Design and Implementation of Undergraduate Research Experiences

This report describes an ongoing conversation in the education community that claims that the benefits of undergraduate research experiences (UREs) justify the expansion of such programs. Yet Chapter 7 (Need for Research About UREs) has pointed out many areas where increased research is needed to better understand the impact of UREs and the potential tradeoffs among design choices. This situation created noticeable tension for the committee, as we are charged with working from the evidence base but also want to provide actionable guidance to educators. Given that many schools are moving now to increase their efforts to support undergraduate research, the committee has prepared this chapter to address issues of design and implementation of UREs, drawing on both the currently available evidence base and the expert opinion of the committee. We aim to present a structure for considering relevant aspects of UREs as part of a design and decision making process embedded in the conceptual framework described in Chapter 3.

This chapter is designed to serve as a guide to readers who wish to support the development of UREs on their campus—primarily faculty, URE program designers/directors, and institutional leaders. The committee identifies important questions to ask and issues to address during the process. Keep in mind that URE design and implementation can be a time-consuming process: key players should be provided with adequate time and resources to achieve their program goals, and they should be recognized when that is accomplished. In some situations, however, people must initiate a URE and carry out large amounts of work before getting buy-in from their department or institution. In this case it can be even more crucial that there is an institutional mechanism to reward their efforts after the fact. The mission, priorities, and resources of the institution will influence many practical decisions of the department and faculty. Many of the questions presented here must be dealt with on an institutionwide basis, whereas others are the purview of departments, the primary concern of the URE designer, or the primary concern of the individual faculty mentor.

Several considerations need to be kept in mind when designing and implementing UREs, whether the intent is to create a new program, refine an existing one, or broaden (scale up) the access to a specific URE. These include the make-up of the student body, the types of programs that can be offered, the envisioned goals and outcomes of the experience, who will implement and who will serve as mentor, and the departmental and institutional constraints that might impact the design and implementation of the experience. Considering the goals of all participants will help ensure that the program can be successful and sustainable with adequate participants and human resources. Understanding the goals of the students will help in designing programs that keep the students engaged and motivated.

As discussed in various places throughout this report, and specifically addressed both within the research agenda in Chapter 7 and in the final chapter detailing the committees' conclusions and recommendations, there is insufficient *causal* evidence to develop and support a comprehensive set of guidelines to promote *specific* best practices or to contrast the effectiveness of different mechanisms and programs. However, based upon the available descriptive evidence, the collective beliefs of the community, and emerging research that supports the utility of UREs in providing unique learning opportunities for students, we provide this chapter as a resource for design, implementation, and evaluation of UREs. In preparing the guidance reported here, the committee draws from best practices that have emerged from education research on the science of learning, published research evidence on UREs, resources and research syntheses by national organizations that support UREs, presentations made during the committee meetings, and the expertise of the committee members.

This chapter begins with some initial considerations to keep in mind when considering the type of URE program that will be institutionally appropriate. It then moves on to discuss goals, resources, implementation (including using the existing evidence and knowledge of how people learn), and improvement (evaluating UREs and resources available). Finally, the chapter concludes with a section that speaks to campus leaders about the importance of campus culture, systemic change, and rewards/incentives.

PRACTICAL QUESTIONS

Many factors need to be considered when trying to determine either the appropriate URE program(s) to implement or whether a new type of URE might be desirable and possible. To facilitate the process, answers to several questions can help to narrow down the potential formats. Some of these questions should be addressed on the departmental or institutional level, to ensure that adequate resources are available to the URE designers and that the tradeoffs that need to be made align with departmental and institutional priorities. The answers to other questions are in the purview of the faculty members guiding the research. The questions provided below are intended to be not an exhaustive list but a starting point.

- What is the overall goal of the program? For example, does it aim to provide research experiences for some or all students in a given STEM major, for students in the beginning courses for the major, or for some other overarching end?
- Is this an expansion of an existing program or a new program?
- How will the new program fit with any current programs? How will it fit within the existing curriculum and major academic requirements?
- What strategies will be used to reach the goals? Do they fit best with an apprentice-style model, a course-based undergraduate research experience (CURE), an internship, etc.? How much active time do the students need to reach the goals? How many hours per week should the students expect to participate? How much total time is needed, and how many weeks will the experience last? Is there already an experience on campus or at a nearby school with the proposed format?
- What are the program costs and how will participants be covered? Will internal and/or external funding be required? Can existing funds be used or repurposed, or will new sources of revenue be needed? If the program is initiated with grant funding, how will it transition to a sustainable mode of operation after the grant period?
- Do faculty members have the resources they need: access to knowledge about designing and assessing UREs and access to necessary financial and logistical resources?
- Is there appropriate space currently available or would modifications be necessary?
- How much faculty time will be needed? Will this require changes to existing responsibilities? How will participating faculty be rewarded or compensated for their time and energy spent on design and over-

sight of the research project? Will time for faculty participation be provided within the normal workload? If extra hours or summer participation will be required, how will that be compensated?

- Who will serve as research mentor(s), and what role will the mentor(s) play? How will the mentor(s) be prepared for that role?
- Who will provide hands-on training to the students, and how will the trainers be prepared for that role?
- Will students be given increased decision making opportunities and responsibility for formulating and designing the content of their research as their experience increases? Are there opportunities for students to take on increasing ownership of the project?
- Is one of the goals to ensure equity and access or to specifically broaden participation? How will students from populations of interest be recruited to the program? Is the recruitment and selection process equitable? Does it promote broadening participation?
- How will participation be documented and participants tracked?
- How will research ethics and standards of research documentation be taught?
- How will the students be rewarded/compensated? If graded, will the grade be pass/fail or a letter grade? How will grades be assigned? If students will be compensated, will they receive a stipend or hourly wage? If a summer program, will room and board be provided?
- How long is the intended research experience? What is the weekly (or monthly) time commitment expected of participants?
- What are the research expectations? Are there steps along the way where expectations must be documented? Do they include keeping a research notebook? Do they include presenting at a conference? How will they be clearly communicated to the students?
- Are there novel questions for students to tackle?
- Are students expected to present or publish on their research?
- Are there plans to help the students gain a sense of belonging?
- Are there opportunities for students to collaborate and discuss their research activities, as well as to reflect on the activities' wider implications and connections in the field and to broader life issues? Do the students have the resources they need (e.g., access to housing, if needed, and to equipment, library, and mentors)?
- Are there processes in place by which students could file a complaint if they disagree with the decision on who is selected to participate, if they are not provided with the necessary resources to carry out their task, or if they experience discrimination or harassment?
- How will the success of the program be assessed?

Overall, having these basic questions in mind can serve as a guide when identifying programmatic needs that reflect the goals of the various stakeholders. In considering these questions, it might be helpful for URE designers to reflect on the various options discussed in Chapters 2 and 3 about the variety of types of UREs and the many interacting factors that influence them.

INITIAL DESIGN CONSIDERATIONS

For a designer of a URE, the initial steps in the process are to identify the goals that the URE will aim to achieve, recognize the key variables that may influence the URE, identify the types of programs available nationally that may serve as models, identify existing local programs that may be adapted or expanded to meet the goals, and determine what opportunities for innovation exist. Evaluating the programs that are already available can provide models and illuminate gaps. Considering the programs available locally may yield new partners or spark ideas that can be modified for use. Such investigations of the programs offered might point out a type of URE that is not in use but that could be added.

As described in the conceptual framework (see Chapter 3), UREs are affected by an interacting network of players (institutional and departmental policy makers and leaders, faculty, staff, and students) and by an institution's mission, goals, and resources. These interactions occur within the broader context of national policy (determined by funders, disciplinary societies, and government) that impacts decisions made on campus. Campus decisions on faculty roles, faculty rewards, space, and allocation of resources are of critical importance and directly affect UREs.

Goals and resources must be considered when choosing the type of program so that it will fit the needs of the student population while also working within the constraints of the available support structures (e.g., having space for the program, the necessary human and financial resources). Finding or creating the right program structure that can appropriately balance these various factors can result in a more manageable and sustainable program in which the intended benefits and outcomes are achieved. That is, if the program will not fulfill the needs of the students or cannot be supported institutionally in the long run, then the sustainability of the program will be in question. Table 8-1 provides a simplified view of the landscape of URE program types, illustrating various types to facilitate consideration of options. (See Chapter 2 for a detailed discussion with relevant examples.)

Alignment of a planned URE with a particular program's various goals and available resources is critical to offering academic experiences that will meet program goals for the students it targets. The types and specifics of UREs offered affect which of the *definitional characteristics* a student expe-

TABLE 8-1 Overview of the Variability of Attributes of UREs

Leadership	<ul><li>Professor</li><li>Lecturer</li><li>Senior researcher</li><li>Postdoctoral scholar</li><li>Industry researcher</li></ul>
Mentoring	<ul><li>Informal arrangements</li><li>Assigned mentor</li><li>Multiple mentors</li></ul>
Format	<ul><li>Apprentice-style URE</li><li>Course-based URE for academic credit</li><li>URE program that includes professional development</li><li>Industry URE</li></ul>
Duration	<ul><li>Several weeks to several years</li></ul>
Expectations for students	<ul><li>Learn discipline-specific procedures</li><li>Conduct an original investigation</li><li>Prepare poster or presentation on work</li></ul>
Student goals	<ul><li>Career awareness</li><li>Apprenticeship in a research environment</li><li>Insight into the nature of research</li><li>Contribution to a larger STEM discipline–specific goal</li></ul>
Value for student career trajectory	<ul><li>Prepare informed citizens</li><li>Strengthen likelihood of graduate school admissions</li><li>Helpful for industry employment</li><li>Useful for recommendations in general</li></ul>
Measured outcomes	<ul><li>Self-report survey</li><li>Interview</li><li>Assessment of knowledge</li><li>Journal</li><li>Research report or presentation</li></ul>
Populations(s) served	<ul><li>STEM majors/non-STEM majors</li><li>Historically underrepresented students</li><li>First generation students</li></ul>
Student funding	<ul><li>Unpaid (generally receive course credit)</li><li>Stipend</li><li>Full support</li></ul>

riences.[1] For example, joining an established research group could channel student work toward a predetermined problem using an already identified approach. A class that challenges students to pick a local environmental issue to investigate could provide many choices for a student to select a novel research question, while another course may have a set research paradigm that all students are expected to follow. Over time, an institution or program may offer more variety in the types of UREs available to their students, and this may enable students to choose UREs particularly tailored to their goals.

There is variability in terms of when the URE is offered—semester, academic year, or summer—as well as in the support systems (human and financial) required. Whereas many programs have the potential to offer students academic credit, summer programs are more likely to need to provide a stipend (and/or other forms of monetary support, such as providing room and board); this is more often available for apprentice-style programs that have financial resources specifically linked to such programs (e.g., external grant funding secured by the faculty mentor, institutional resources, or donor-funded endowments). Bridge and wrap-around programs, which have additional student support structures included such as peer mentoring and tutors, generally require additional financial resources.

Considering the many options of different types of UREs (e.g., apprentice-style, CURE, internship, co-op), it may seem daunting to decide, for a particular program, on the type that best aligns with the relevant stakeholder goals and resources in hand or that might be obtained. Each program will have constraints that will shape the offering and favor some types of UREs over others. If, for example, the goal of a URE is to increase the number of students matriculating into graduate school in STEM fields, then a key component of the program (in addition to experiencing research) may be test preparation and assistance with graduate school applications. Similarly, if a goal is to increase STEM knowledge and literacy, a URE may include not only working alongside a faculty member in a lab, but also assigned readings and periodic workshops featuring presentations on research across STEM disciplines.

Table 8-1 lays out many of the categories and choices for each category that need to be considered in planning and implementing a URE.

Faculty who decide to organize CUREs or expand other research opportunities for undergraduates may need help acquiring the mentoring and managerial skills required to do so effectively (Pfund, 2016). A key characteristic of most CUREs is a "parallel" research problem: one for which the mentor can teach students a common set of experimental approaches and

---

[1]The committee's set of URE definitional characteristics is specified in Conclusion 1 in Chapter 9.

common tools but within which each student has unique responsibilities. For example, in SEA-Phages (see Box 2-7 in Chapter 2) all students isolate a soil phage using a particular host bacterium; the isolated phages are related, but each will be unique, informing an analysis of phage evolution (Hatfull, 2015). Directing a CURE generally requires that faculty move beyond more traditional notions of "teaching" toward a more active mode of promoting student learning via the research framework, using pedagogies that are more aligned with active learning (e.g., shifting to a facilitator of student investigation rather than one who primarily imparts information).

Undergraduate research offices, created either as separate entities or as extensions of a college or university office of teaching and learning, can often provide a centralized resource for faculty, staff, and undergraduates engaged in UREs. In addition to helping undergraduates connect with appropriate experiences, they can facilitate general training (eg., how to keep a research notebook, research ethics), sponsor talks on STEM careers, manage paperwork, arrange summer housing for the undergraduates, or potentially even provide specialized instruction in research (see Box 8-1). At institutions that do not have an undergraduate research office to provide central support to those running or participating in UREs, an effort to create centralized procedures would be worthwhile; a part-time staff position could provide help with some of the needed features. Examples can be found in Appendix B and in the report from a convocation on integrating CUREs into the undergraduate curriculum (National Academies of Sciences, Engineering, and Medicine, 2015). The organizations described in the final section of this chapter may also serve as a source of ideas and

---

BOX 8-1
Entering Research Course for
Beginning Apprentice-Style Researchers:
University of Wisconsin–Madison

This two-semester seminar course for beginning researchers is taken concurrently with independent research credits by students from across the STEM disciplines. It provides structure and guidance for new undergraduate researchers and their mentors as they begin their research project together. It brings undergraduate students from across disciplines together to build a community that supports them as they navigate their first independent research experience and their first research mentoring relationship.[a]

---

[a]The course is described on the University of Wisconsin–Madison website; see https://www.biology.wisc.edu/Entering-Research [February 2017].

resources for faculty and administrators who are working to start or expand URE programs.

Another option to consider for developing highly effective UREs at many institutions is a "franchising" process. Under such a process, a well-designed URE (a CURE or program-based URE that has been thoroughly evaluated) could be adopted by many institutions. The process could be facilitated by having the initial sites develop tools and an evaluation procedure for other institutions to adopt and adapt. Identifying, encouraging, and funding dissemination of existing programs may accelerate the creation of effective UREs at many institutions and lead to evaluation efforts that can scale to tens or hundreds of institutions, hundreds of faculty, and thousands of students. Several examples of such consortia were discussed in Chapter 2. These consortia show particular promise in enabling institutions that have limited resources to successfully implement and sustain UREs (Blockus, 2016).

THE IMPORTANCE OF INCLUSION, ACCESS, AND EQUITY

Colleges and universities need to consider whether their approaches to offering UREs allow for equity of access. Emphasizing access and equity requires analyses and actions that are student-centered and focused. The *Engage to Excel* report of the President's Council of Advisors on Science and Technology (2012) describes many potential benefits of having students engage in some kind of research or other discovery-based experience in STEM and calls on higher education to make research opportunities available to as many students as possible, as early in their undergraduate careers as feasible. However, common practice has been to select the most advanced students (either in terms of length of matriculation, relevant coursework completed, or academic performance as determined by indicators such as grade point average) for preferred access, on the grounds that they will benefit most from such opportunities. Unless the number of research opportunities can grow substantially, such selection decisions likely will exclude many students, particularly those who do not choose to declare a STEM major. Unfortunately, this can include those who intend to become teachers, especially those planning to teach in the elementary or middle grades and who are likely to major in education or English, neither of which is a STEM discipline.

There also is a risk of unfairness if faculty members select students based on those who approach them seeking such opportunities, as ethnic/racial minority students and first generation students often are aware neither of URE opportunities nor of the benefits of a URE (Bangera and Brownell, 2014). Faculty or other mentors also may hold unrecognized, implicit biases that certain types or levels of students are more qualified than others or can contribute most to the research effort (Moss-Racusin et al., 2012). Both problems can restrict opportunities for disadvantaged students who might benefit the most from such experiences.

It may appear that requiring research and other discovery-based experiences through an apprentice-based program or CURE could address many of these issues of access and equity (Bangera and Brownell, 2014; Dolan, 2016). Accordingly, some colleges and universities are working to make a CURE part of the first-year experience. For example, the First Year Innovation and Research Experience (FIRE) program at the University of Maryland, College Park (modeled on the FRI program at The University of Texas at Austin described in Box 2-9) attempts to lower barriers to research and persistence.[2] If projects can be limited (for the most part) to hours for which a course or lab is scheduled, then more students who must work to support themselves and their families or who must commute to campus from long distances will be able to participate. However, requiring that most or all students engage in this kind of work presents its own set of problems, as there can be substantial logistical challenges to participating in research. In addition, if students feel that they are being compelled to participate in activities that they neither welcome nor appreciate, then they likely will not do so enthusiastically. Team structure, group work, and the quality of their URE work overall may suffer as a result, thereby diminishing the experience for all students involved in the URE.

Requiring undergraduate research can also present financial challenges. If a required CURE comes with extra fees, it may discourage some students' from choosing that major. CUREs that add extra fees for participation compared with traditional courses may place an insurmountable burden on some students, essentially blocking their enrollment. On the other hand, if students can be paid a stipend or hourly wage for participating in research with a faculty member, this may alleviate their need to find an off-campus job to cover their expenses and may serve to promote participation in a URE. Asking students to participate in off-campus symposia or meetings of disciplinary societies to present their work may preclude some students from participating, unless their costs for travel are provided by the institution. Too often, these kinds of special costs pose particular burdens for first generation, underrepresented, nontraditional, and socioeconomically disadvantaged students. Intentional recruiting of these subpopulations and dedicated funding sources to provide financial aid can counter many of these obstacles.

On the contrary, making a research experience optional can result in students opting out because they are concerned about the amount of time and effort required for the academic credits gained, and they may worry

---

[2] See http://www.fire.umd.edu/about.html [December 2016].

about how such programs or courses will be graded. Clear communication from the faculty, peer recruiting, and joining a CURE with friends are all conditions that may help ameliorate these challenges. For example, it might be necessary for faculty to talk to students about "failure" being commonplace in research and that in this course their grade will not suffer from an inability to get "the correct answer."

CONSIDERING THE GOALS OF ALL PARTICIPANTS

The design of UREs should consider the goals of all participants: students, faculty, department, and institution. Knowing who the various stakeholders are and paying attention to their goals and priorities can help shape and direct the design of a new URE or the refinement of an existing program. This is especially important when the stakeholders are at multiple institutions, such as in a National Science Foundation (NSF)-funded science, engineering, or technology center. Moreover, it is crucial to think about how the attributes of specific student populations (e.g., students of color, women, first generation students, community college transfers, commuter versus resident students, full-time versus part-time students, majors in the URE field versus nonmajors) affect the goals those students might have and how those goals will be addressed within the design (Blockus, 2016; Dolan, 2016).

As discussed in the conceptual framework, the committee has grouped the institutional goals for students participating in UREs into three major categories: (1) increasing participation and retention of students in STEM, (2) promoting STEM disciplinary knowledge and practices, and (3) integrating students into STEM culture (see Figure 3-1). This categorization was done to organize the outcomes that have been most frequently measured and documented in the literature. Although these categorical goals may not precisely mirror the motivations driving a particular URE design, they should be considered, along with the goals of the faculty and goals of the students.

Students themselves may not focus on the same goals, described above, that institutions and faculty may have for them. They may be focused on more practical goals, such as the potential for UREs to help them stand out more prominently in the sea of applicants to graduate or professional schools or for future employment. A student may be interested in learning more about a topic or a technique covered in a previous course or in working with a faculty member who taught the course; students may want to add to their resumes or get a strong letter of recommendation. It is important for faculty to share their goals for the students with the URE participants at the start of each experience. In an apprentice-style URE, mentors and students should take time to discuss the student's goals as well.

Students may choose to participate in a URE because of the topic of the research. For example, a particular URE may provide students with opportunities for community or civic engagement (such as a project related to environmental pollution) or opportunities to explore in depth an issue that has had an impact on the student's life or the lives of their families, friends, or communities (such as research on a specific disease or illness). Other students may be thinking of careers in a STEM discipline and see UREs as a chance to learn research skills and determine whether they find research interesting enough to want to pursue it further as a career option. Thus, some students might finish a URE with a solidified feeling that research is for them and go on to persist in a STEM degree (or seek a career), whereas others may benefit from the experience itself but might determine that research is not for them. Moreover, some students who never envisioned being a STEM researcher might discover a career path that suits them, although they had not considered it before. Further, as suggested in the conceptual framework, preparation for many career opportunities (perhaps most) can be enhanced by participation in a URE.

RESOURCES

The issue of resources for UREs is complex. Resources needed for research are as varied as the questions that drive the research and the disciplines that set the context for the research opportunity. A comprehensive list of resources needed for all forms of UREs across all STEM disciplines and research questions is beyond the scope of this report, so what follows is an illustrative compendium of resource issues and topics, which may be helpful to consider in the design of UREs. The success of UREs depends on supportive departmental administrators and interested faculty, along with the means to encourage and compensate faculty and to provide facilities so that the faculty have both the time and resources to engage undergraduates in research.

As departments and institutions consider expanding research opportunities for their undergraduates, a primary consideration and concern is cost. Can UREs be expanded by reallocation of current resources, or must new resources be identified and secured? Costs can be estimated based on current institutional budgets of colleges and universities that are currently engaged in providing UREs, as well as from public data on awards supporting such efforts by NSF, the National Institutes of Health, private foundations, and other funders. New costs will depend on the proposed program design (see the list of practical questions above in this chapter) and on what is already incorporated in the instructional budget.

The committee put together a set of questions to gather information about how this challenge is being addressed on a variety of campuses. See

Appendix B for excerpts from some of the institutional responses. These responses reveal considerable ingenuity as campuses move to exploit, repurpose, and conjoin current resources, even as they seek additional resources to expand or strengthen UREs.

Variations in Resources by Institution Type

Resources vary across institutions, but there are some commonalities that the committee observed within types of institutions. By their nature and mission, research-intensive universities include a large number of research-active faculty who potentially are available to design projects and participate in mentoring undergraduate students. Liberal arts schools and community colleges generally have a greater proportion of smaller classes, including smaller introductory classes, such that the transition from a "cook-book" lab course to a more research- or discovery-based lab course may be more easily accomplished within the existing infrastructure.

Institutions with an explicit mission to promote undergraduate research most often have resources already in place (e.g., budget, support personnel, space, equipment) and provide recognition and rewards to departments and faculty for achievement in this mission area. Some four-year colleges pride themselves on having all students engaged in research with a faculty member. For example, The College of New Jersey has reconfigured its entire curriculum to focus on undergraduate research, scholarship, and creative activity (Osborn and Karukstis, 2009). More information on this institution is available in Box 8-2. The culture of an institution with respect to innovation in pedagogy and support for faculty development can influence the extent to which UREs are readily introduced or improved. The physical resources available, including laboratories, field stations, engineering design studios and testing facilities, and the like can have an impact, as can the ability to access resources in the surrounding community (including other parts of a large university campus). In some cases UREs can be designed to take advantage of equipment that can be repurposed from pre-existing teaching laboratories. Faculty may be motivated by a desire to improve instruction, enrich an existing lab experience, or satisfy requirements necessary to receive funding (i.e., requirements aimed at furthering broader objectives of their home institution or funding sources). The intellectual traditions of the STEM field also have an impact. UREs appear to be more common in the life sciences and in geoscience, computer science, chemistry, and engineering than in physics and mathematics. UREs are increasingly more common in the social sciences than they were in the past and are even starting to appear in the humanities.

Some types of colleges and universities (community colleges, historically black colleges and universities, and others) generally expect faculty to

BOX 8-2
Campus Culture Change: The College of New Jersey

From 2004 to 2006, The College of New Jersey underwent a major overhaul to institutionalize undergraduate research as central to the mission of the college.[a] Following a CUR workshop in 1997, the college developed a series of strategic initiatives aimed at promoting and supporting a scholarly culture grounded in student engagement, undergraduate research, and the teacher-scholar model for faculty. The purpose of the initiative was to move undergraduate research from the periphery to the center of the college's mission. A first step was to develop a common language for undergraduate research that cut across the entire institution, so that the changes would not be limited to specific departments. As part of the transformation, the curriculum was modified, new courses were added, and the total number of courses offered was reduced. The curriculum was analyzed on both the macro level (e.g., all majors, first-year programs.) and micro level (i.e., every course syllabus). Equally important, changes were made to faculty teaching loads and the criteria used for tenure and promotion, to facilitate and reward scholarly work with undergraduates. In addition, a faculty council to support undergraduate research was created, along with the new position of Director of Faculty-Student Scholarly Collaboration. This reform did not involve a significant amount of resources but rather required a strategic allocation of existing resources. Outcomes included increased student retention rates, increased overall graduation rates, increased graduation rates of African American and Hispanic students participating in the URE program (compared to pre-program rates), strengthened faculty recruitment and retention, increased faculty proposal submission and funding rates, and increased support from donors.

We have striven to institutionalize undergraduate research in ways that weave it into the **fabric** of TCNJ's [the College of New Jersey's] learning environments through a range of synergistic connections. This is lived out fully in the School of Science, and benefits all of our students and faculty. Here, we highlight how we re-conceptualized and re-framed how we define the role and work of our students and faculty into an integrated and holistic model. By moving undergraduate research from the periphery to the center, our curricula and faculty workload structure were re-defined to incorporate undergraduate research (and other high-impact practices). This transformation of curriculum, faculty workload and rewards, and institutional identity was described in *Inside Higher Ed* as "a radical overhaul of the curriculum, centered on undergraduate research and the teacher-scholar model. . . . The faculty members say . . . they're credited for how much work they do, and what kind. That, in turn, encourages them to take risks in their research and teaching in ways that help students.

(Flaherty, 2014)

---

[a]See article on the Inside Higher Ed website at www.insidehighered.com/news/2014/10/16/how-college-new-jersey-rethought-faculty-work-student-success-mind [February 2017].

devote most of their time to teaching. Course-based research is more likely to be compatible with such expectations than one-on-one or one-on-few (mentor-to-mentee ratio) apprentice-style experiences.

The institutional and departmental requirements to support course-based research at community colleges will be similar to those noted throughout this report for four-year colleges. Given the increasing pressure to maintain already low tuition costs at the former, they will be under pressure to continue with traditional classroom instruction, which is less labor- and resource-intensive than research-based courses. In addition, it is harder for faculty to find time to develop UREs at institutions where they are required to teach many courses per semester. Faculty at community colleges generally have the heaviest teaching expectations, with little or no expectations or incentives to maintain a research program; they often have limited access to lab or design space and to a comprehensive collection of scientific or engineering journals, as well as few resources to undertake any kind of a research program. These conditions constrain the extent to which UREs can be offered to the approximately 40 percent of U.S. undergraduates who are enrolled in the nation's community colleges (which generally have high percentages of underrepresented students) for students' initial science training.[3]

Financial Costs and Benefits of UREs

The capital resources required for undergraduate research depend on the discipline, type of program, and topic under investigation. Availability of facilities and laboratories, access to field sites, and access to equipment are important considerations. Other financial considerations include staff available for coordination, lab supervision, and mentoring; funds for financial support of students and mentors; and faculty release time for research project development. Local resources, such as community field sites and the availability of business and industry representatives to mentor students, can also be considered as "capital" to support a URE program.

Due to the wide range of potential financial costs and the lack of publicly available information on these costs (Blockus, 2016; Dolan, 2016), the committee is unable to provide even range estimates for the cost of various URE formats. The costs for various components needed for URE programs will vary depending on the specific conditions on a campus and on campus policy on cost accounting. For example, faculty salaries paid for supervision of summer research vary dramatically at different locations. At some colleges, faculty are paid for teaching a summer course if they serve as a research mentor for a minimum number of students, whereas at other colleges such faculty are considered to be conducting summer research that

---

[3] See http://nces.ed.gov/programs/coe/indicator_cha.asp [February 2017].

is paid, if at all, through a grant they have secured. In the first case, the faculty salary is a URE program cost, whereas in the second case it is not. At many research universities, it is assumed that research-active faculty will absorb undergraduates into their lab year-round with no compensation, while in some cases supply money follows the student. Individual programs and institutions will need to consider their own circumstances, mission, and traditions in determining what sort of support can be provided. Will the potential value-added of providing UREs outweigh the costs in terms of dollars and institutional satisfaction? Programs that keep students on track to graduation have considerable value in maintaining institutional income from tuition, as well as supporting the long-term goals of the students.

Although in many instances funds can be repurposed to support UREs, particularly CUREs (see Box 8-3), institutions often will want to secure additional resources to start up or expand UREs. Funding avenues that can be explored include internal institutional resources and endowments, state-based funding sources, industry grants and partnerships, federal grants, and grants from private foundations. Many institutions have development offices that can provide information and guidance to those seeking funding, and some institutions have development officers who focus on securing funds for the undergraduate research mandate of the institution. Undergraduate research offices, present on many campuses, often post lists of potential funding sources online so that even those at other institutions can benefit from this information. Funding possibilities include federal agencies such as NSF, the National Institutes of Health, the Department of Education, the Department of Defense, and the National Aeronautics and Space Administration. There are also private sources of funding such as the

---

BOX 8-3
Leveraging Existing Resources

Malcolm Campbell at Davidson College, South Carolina, has switched the lab in his sections of the introductory biology course (64 students) to a research project using synthetic biology. Each student designs a gene promoter and predicts its function, then clones this promoter to test whether it works as predicted. For this CURE, regular teaching labs (equipped for molecular biology) and the regular teaching budget were adequate. No extra expenses or equipment were required. The only cost was faculty time to develop the module and the backbone plasmid that the students use. (The plasmid is now available through Carolina Biological Supply as pClone Red/Blue). Coupling this synthetic biology research module with other active learning strategies is reported to have had positive impacts on student retention and subsequent success (Campbell et al., 2014).

Howard Hughes Medical Institute and the American Chemical Society. The WebGuru Guide for Undergraduate Research[4] offers suggestions of possible funding sources, as well as providing information for undergraduates who are considering research. Individual undergraduate research opportunities with the federal government can now be searched in one location at the new website, http://STEMundergrads.science.gov. Many research-intensive universities provide summer research experiences for students from other schools; a strong undergraduate research office can help students identify and apply for such opportunities.

Opportunities for funding may come in various forms, and creative strategies can be used to generate the resources needed for UREs. Sometimes funds focused on other goals or programs can be supplemented to add support for undergraduate research. In other cases, multiple sources of funding can be combined to begin or sustain a program, or pre-existing resources can be repurposed or leveraged within and outside of the institution. For example, NSF's Advanced Technological Education program explicitly encourages colleges to partner with nonacademic entities in efforts to improve education in science and engineering.[5] The program's website suggests the National Network for Manufacturing Innovation as a potential partner; the network was set up with industry, academic, and federal partners to increase U.S. manufacturing competitiveness by promoting a robust and sustainable manufacturing research and development infrastructure.

One area in which opportunities for the low-overhead launch of new UREs would be particularly welcome is multidisciplinary UREs. These can be structured in multiple ways, one example is the VIP Program described in Chapter 2. Multidisciplinary experiences offer a logical way to exploit the most unique aspect of institutions of higher education, which is the presence of experts in many disciplines under one administrative roof and on one physically contiguous campus. A URE is generally much more flexible than a lecture-based class and can attract people who are passionate about some multidisciplinary topic. Enabling low-cost experiments in this area could unleash much creative activity from both faculty and students.

Such complexities related to costs also need to be recognized by organizations that wish to support UREs. Flexible grants that allow institutions to meet and overcome the often unique challenges for their students are likely to produce the greatest benefits. However, careful evaluation of what seems to work most effectively within and across institutions and among different kinds of student populations should be an integral component of any decisions about how to support such initiatives.

---

[4] See http://www.webguru.neu.edu/undergraduate-research/research-funding/possible-funding-sources [February 2017].

[5] See http://www.nsf.gov/funding/pgm_summ.jsp?pims_id=5464 [February 2017].

Human Resources

Ultimately, the success of a URE is tied to the personnel taking on the various roles required to design, implement, and sustain URE programs. The human resources include faculty advisors, mentors (if not the same as the faculty advisors), and others who provide support related to curricula, logistics, equipment, and supplies. In addition to identifying people who will play a crucial role in the operation of a URE, it is also important to identify experts (on and off campus) who can share knowledge that can support the design and evaluation of the program. These experts might include individuals with expertise in evidence-based teaching practices, curriculum development, learning sciences, and program evaluation, as well as current program directors and scientists with extensive experience supervising such programs. It may be appropriate to consider faculty from other departments or schools and individuals in business and industry with relevant expertise. Consulting or partnering with these experts can allow URE designers to build more easily on the work of others and to learn from the existing experience and evidence that have been gathered.

Those engaged in designing and running UREs can benefit from access to current professional development opportunities. Advisors and mentors participating in and supporting UREs can learn about pedagogy, facilitating group work, mentoring, and assessment, among other topics. As briefly described in Chapter 5, the quality of mentoring can have an impact on students' persistence in STEM (Johnson, 2002; Johnson and Huwe, 2003; Liang et al., 2002; Nagda et al., 1998; Pfund, 2016). In particular, a bad mentor can lead to a negative experience, which may motivate mentees to leave the program. Thus, professional development, especially for mentoring, can improve student participation and help faculty learn evidence-based practices that can lead to a more successful program.

Professional development is important for all of the key players involved in the URE, not just for faculty. Institutions can provide opportunities for postdoctoral fellows, graduate students, lab technicians, and even teaching assistants to develop their skills as mentors. These programs can occur at campus centers of learning; through participation in disciplinary society meetings, which now frequently hold workshops on these topics; and at related national conferences such as those organized by the Council on Undergraduate Research.

Space, Equipment, and Shared Resources

Implementing or expanding UREs will, by necessity, place competing demands on existing space; on purchase and maintenance of costly instrumentation, supplies, library and computing facilities; and on the personnel who must be associated with such enterprises. The problem may be exacerbated further in institutions where there is increasing pressure for individual faculty to find external funding to support some or all of their salaries, as well as the instrumentation and supplies that they need for their research programs. Departmental or institutional policies about use or sharing of space and research-grade instruments for both research and teaching are important considerations when seeking to implement or expand various kinds of UREs. As suggested above, revisiting the institution's stated vision and mission statements may help focus such discussions.

These discussions should include making plans to ensure that undergraduates have access to relevant journals and online resources as well as the necessary space and equipment. If research with students is not already part of the campus culture, identifying and motivating faculty to undertake such efforts can be challenging; doing so not only can involve large investments of time, but also necessitates re-examining current teaching practices.

However, lack of what are assumed to be required resources need not preclude the development of innovative and sometimes unorthodox opportunities for UREs. Such opportunities may include facilities and support from other parts of the campus and through local, state, and national entities, both public and private. Consortia can facilitate sharing of resources across disciplines and departments within the same institution or among different institutions, organizations, and agencies. Consortia that employ research methodologies in common can share curricula and other teaching/learning modules, research and technical data that students collect, and common assessment tools. Some consortia are able to organize scholarly venues for sharing research results as well (Blockus, 2016).[6] Such shared materials lessen time burdens for individual faculty and provide a larger pool of students to judge efficacy of the particular approach (Lopatto, 2015; National Academies of Sciences, Engineering, and Medicine, 2015, Appendix B).

Many schools have, or have access to, local field stations that can become the focus of a new or expanded research program (National Research Council, 2014). In other cases, students might use the campus or surrounding community itself as the research environment, taking up issues of conservation, efficient resource utilization, etc., which may be priority concerns of these potential partners. For example, the California State University (CSU) system has in place the "Campus as a Living Lab,"[7] which engages undergraduate students in research by providing funds for faculty to address basic and applied research questions that are essential and unique to individual CSU campuses, such as the energy efficiency of

---

[6]For another example, see the Phages DB website at http://phagesdb.org [December 2016].
[7]See http://www.calstate.edu/cpdc/sustainability/liv-lab-grant [February 2017].

a given building. Students need to travel only as far as the boundaries of their home campuses to engage in this kind of research-based work. At CSU schools, any cost savings that result from this research are directed back to the program on each campus, to encourage additional research. Similar innovative undergraduate research efforts are being developed through partnerships with campus entities such as dining services and physical plants, as illustrated by the work of Cathy Middlecamp at the University of Wisconsin–Madison (Kober, 2015, p. 47).

Sharing of research-grade instrumentation, often available through the U.S. national laboratories, can enable student investigations. Increasing numbers of these instruments can be operated remotely by faculty and students. In other cases, laboratories are willing to receive and process samples provided through UREs and return the assays or other results to student researchers (Kober, 2015). Sharing and support from local and regional URE networks and/or consortia is a possibility. As characterized in Chapter 2, there are URE programs that involve multiple institutions and leverage the sharing of resources to improve UREs. Numerous examples discussing some of these options are given by Elgin and colleagues (2016), and other examples appear in Appendix B.

DECISIONS ABOUT IMPLEMENTATION

There are many factors to consider when starting up a URE. Instructors and mentors need to consider information from the literature on UREs and use what is known about how people learn. They will need to assist undergraduates to integrate the experiences, activities, mentoring, and assignments they encounter as they participate in UREs so that the students can make connections to their broader experiences and education. Four principles for design are listed in Figure 3-2: (1) make STEM research accessible and relevant, (2) promote autonomy, (3) learn from each other, and (4) make thinking visible. Attention to these principles can enhance student learning.

In addition, the Council on Undergraduate Research (CUR) has outlined several best practices for UREs based on the apprenticeship model. CUR suggests that undergraduate research should be a "normal" part of the undergraduate experience regardless of the type of institution. It identifies changes necessary to include UREs as part of the curriculum and as part of the culture to support curricular reform, including modifications to the incentives and rewards for faculty to engage with undergraduate research. In addition, CUR points to professional development opportunities specifically aimed at improving the pedagogical and mentoring skills of instructional staff in using evidence-based practices as important for a supportive learning culture (Council on Undergraduate Research, 2012).

Learning from Experience and Evidence:
How Do UREs Fit into What Is Known About Student Learning?

UREs require students to make connections and to use the research literature to understand and contextualize their research findings. For students to understand the concepts and context for the research they are doing, they need to make sense of new knowledge by connecting it with prior knowledge and experience. To succeed in STEM, students need to learn how to organize their ideas, rather than holding a repertoire of fragmented, sometimes contradictory or disconnected ideas. Knowledge that is organized and coherent is easier to remember because there are multiple links between items that can aid in recall.

Encouraging students to both generate explanations and revise them as they make sense of their research can promote knowledge integration. These activities can set in motion a process of revisiting STEM-specific issues when they arise in new contexts, such as news articles or public lectures. UREs can foster the development of autonomous learners who sort out their existing ideas and integrate them with new ideas to continue to build coherent understanding. By practicing reflection regularly, students can develop the ability to monitor their own progress and to recognize new conflicts and connections as they arise. As this ability develops, students become more likely to use many of the reasoning strategies essential in STEM fields, such as drawing on evidence and forming arguments to reach conclusions.

The process of reflecting and explaining their reasoning can be crucial to student learning gains (Svinicki and McKeachie, 2011). Reflection is common when STEM professionals keep notebooks in which they record results and identify trends. Instructors and mentors can encourage students to maintain notebooks in which they ask students to include reflections about their struggles to conduct their project and the limitations of their work. In CUREs, instructors can include essay questions to instill a practice of reflection, rather than relying on multiple-choice questions. This approach has the advantage of being both part of the instruction and a source of insights into student progress (Lee et al., 2011).

Groups or teams of students working together can establish a community of learners and provide cognitive and social support for each other. Requiring students to be explicit about what they mean and to negotiate any conflicts that arise can foster metacognition. When instructors make their thinking explicit, it helps give students a sense of the process of conjecture, refinement, redesign, and reconceptualization involved in the research enterprise.

Engagement in UREs can enhance student learning over traditional instruction and improve retention of content knowledge (Cortright et al.,

2003; Johnson et al., 1998, 2007). Additional information about how students learn in UREs can be found in the Chapter 4 discussion of research studies and the Chapter 3 presentation of the committee's conceptual framework for UREs, which is based on research on how students learn.

Assessing Student Outcomes and Evaluating UREs

Proper assessment requires choosing goals and then designing UREs that target those goals through appropriate content and processes. Assessments should be designed so that they measure the extent to which a program's goals have been reached. A discussion of choosing goals and assessments can be found in Shortlidge and Brownell (2016). If, for example, the goal of a URE is increased matriculation into graduate programs, then a key component of the program (in addition to experiencing research) may be test preparation and coaching on graduate school applications. Measurement would need to track students over time to learn of their experiences with further education. Similarly, if a goal is to increase STEM knowledge and literacy, a URE may include not only working alongside one or more faculty mentors in a lab, but also additional assigned readings and periodic workshops featuring presentations on concepts and research across STEM disciplines. Measurement might include concept inventories and tests of disciplinary content. Overall, alignment of a planned URE with the various goals and available resources of the institution is a key strategy in offering academic experiences that succeed.

Faculty need to consider up front what type of evaluation will be completed, who will design the assessments, and how to ensure that the measurements are appropriate and informative. Information on evaluation and assessment of UREs can be found in numerous publications, including the following reports: *Knowing What Students Know* (National Research Council, 2001), *Reaching Students* (Kober, 2015), and *Vision and Change in Undergraduate Biology Education* (American Association for the Advancement of Science, 2011).

Another important aspect to consider when designing a URE is whether or not there is a specific intent to contribute to the extant literature on the efficacy of programs of undergraduate research. Although some level of evaluating the URE program is beneficial in all cases, to ensure that there is alignment between the objectives of the experience and the measurable outcomes, some programs are designed to address a specific research question about UREs (e.g., "Does the use of teamwork/collaboration in apprentice-style UREs lead to increases in the communication skills of students?"). In these instances, special considerations must be made during the design of the URE so that the type and quality of the evidence collected will be useful for drawing conclusions. (For a description of evidence type, see Chapters

1 and 7.) For programs designed to evaluate a particular outcome, it is important to identify the pre and post assessments that will be administered and to determine whether the measurements have been validated. In all cases, the local Institutional Review Board must be consulted and appropriate human subjects protections put in place before the assessment begins.

While it is clearly desirable for the design of new types of UREs to be well grounded in education and social science research, asking or requiring *every* new type of URE to be based upon or informed by education research before it can begin operation or receive funding could stifle creativity. Circumstances may be such that a short-term opportunity or collaboration makes it possible for faculty to quickly develop and test a new type of URE within a discipline, across two or more disciplines, or even across multiple institutions. If the experiment shows promising results, then the effort should be evaluated to understand how and why. After that, the approach can be tested for sustainability, transferability to other disciplines, and scalability.

NATIONAL ORGANIZATIONS THAT SUPPORT URES

This process of improvement can benefit from participation in collaborations and networks with others engaged in similar efforts. Sharing human, financial, and scientific or technical resources can strengthen the broad implementation of effective, high-quality, and more cost-efficient UREs. Strategically designed networks of faculty, institutions, regionally and nationally coordinated URE initiatives, professional societies, and funders can facilitate the exchange of evidence and experience related to UREs. These networks can help provide a venue for considering the policy context and larger implications of increasing the number, size, and scope of UREs. Such networks also could provide a more robust infrastructure to improve the sustainability and expansion of URE opportunities.

It may especially behoove community colleges, as well as geographically isolated and underresourced institutions, to engage in partnerships in order to expand opportunities for more undergraduates to participate in diverse UREs (see, for example, discussions in National Academies of Sciences, Engineering, and Medicine, 2015, and in Elgin et al., 2016). Faculty at community colleges and other institutions focused on teaching may be able to share pedagogical innovations with colleagues involved in these partnerships. Existing networks and consortia of faculty involved with UREs can serve as resources for those new to URE design or implementation (Blockus, 2016); for examples, see the text boxes in Chapter 2.

There are several organizations that focus directly on undergraduate research and cut across disciplines. CUR and the National Conference on Undergraduate Research promote and advocate for all types of UREs, across all disciplines in STEM and in the humanities.[8,9] CUR has developed an extensive description of Characteristics of Excellence for Undergraduate Research and a related web supplement with specifics on using these characteristics to assess undergraduate research. The Community College Undergraduate Research Initiative provides resources to 38 institutional partners; these resources include introductory workshops and start-up supplies, as well as faculty development opportunities.

Multiple groups focus on increasing opportunities for historically underrepresented students. The Annual Biomedical Research Conference for Minority Students[10] and the Society for Advancing Chicanos/Hispanics and Native Americans in Science[11] both sponsor opportunities and provide venues for underrepresented students to present the results of their scientific research and to network with each other, the scientists who mentor them, and other scientists who attend these gatherings. The National Action Council for Minorities in Engineering[12] performs a comparable role for underrepresented students in that discipline. The American Society for Microbiology's capstone program provides funding to undergraduates from underrepresented minority groups to enhance their ability to present their research.[13]

Societies of STEM research professionals traditionally have served as a platform for leaders and members from their respective STEM fields and subspecialties to present their research, discuss challenges, and scout opportunities in their field. These organizations provide opportunities for professional development and networking among members at regional and national levels. Many disciplinary society meetings invite undergraduate researchers to present their research during poster sessions or flash talks. The opportunity for undergraduates to communicate their research to a broader audience and engage with others aligns with many design characteristics of UREs (see Chapter 3). In addition to providing their meetings as platforms for undergraduate researchers to connect with peers, network with leaders of the field, and learn about other types of research, some disciplinary societies also are playing active roles to support the development and/or refinement of undergraduate teaching materials within their subject domains.

Although some societies have staff, standing committees, and policy

---

[8] See http://www.cur.org [February 2017].
[9] See http://www.cur.org/ncur_2015 [February 2017].
[10] See http://www.abrcms.org [February 2017].
[11] See http://sacnas.org/about [February 2017].
[12] See http://www.nacme.org [February 2017].
[13] See http://www.asm.org/index.php/component/content/article/25-education/students/142-asm-undergraduate-research-capstone-program-ur-capstone-2016?highlight=YToxOntpOjA7czo4OiJjYXBzdG9uZSI7fQ== [February 2017].

statements that focus on educational topics pertaining to preparing the next generation of STEM professionals, relatively few focus directly on the role of UREs in undergraduate education and how their society may influence the discussions, implementation, and expansion of such programs. Professional societies can act to support undergraduate research in many ways. For instance, many societies fund travel grants for undergraduates to attend professional conferences. Some societies engage in undergraduate research on a deeper level. The Committee on the Undergraduate Program in Mathematics of the Mathematics Association of America, for example, prepares and disseminates a curriculum guide that includes a chapter on Undergraduate Research in Mathematics.[14] The chapter provides guidance on building successful programs, mentoring, and communicating results. This association is also responsible for PICMath, a program to prepare mathematical sciences students for industrial careers by engaging them in research problems that come directly from industry.[15]

Other types of national groups have focused specifically on UREs. Some of these are discipline-specific, such as *On the Cutting Edge,* a program managed by the National Association of Geoscience Teachers that has held workshops for faculty on how to engage undergraduates in geosciences research. This association hosts a detailed website with many examples of UREs, as well as resources for learning about pedagogy and practice related to undergraduate research.[16] The Partnership for Undergraduate Life Science Education, which grew out of the report *Vision and Change in Undergraduate Biology: A Call to Action* (American Association for the Advancement of Science, 2011), consists of a network of biology faculty who work to improve undergraduate biology. This group has prepared a rubric to evaluate the progress of change, one section of which focuses on activities beyond the classroom—mainly undergraduate students participation in research.[17] Also in biology, CURENet is an organization whose stated mission is "a network of people and programs that are creating CUREs in biology as a means of helping students understand core concepts in biology; develop core scientific competencies; and become active, contributing members of the scientific community."[18]

---

[14] See http://www.maa.org/sites/default/files/pdf/CUPM/pdf/CUPMguide_print.pdf [December 2016].

[15] See http://www.maa.org/pic-math [December 2016].

[16] See http://serc.carleton.edu/NAGTWorkshops/undergraduate_research/index.html [December 2016].

[17] See http://api.ning.com/files/KFu*MfW7V8MYZfU7LNGdOnG4MNryzUgUpC2IxdtU mucnB4QNCdLaOwWGoMoULSeKw8hF9jiFdh75tlzuv1nqtfCuM11hNPp3/PULSERubrics-Packetv2_0_FINALVERSION.pdf [December 2016].

[18] See the CURENet website at http://curenet.cns.utexas.edu [February 2017].

CAMPUS CULTURE AND SYSTEMIC CHANGE

As institutional leaders consider the role of undergraduate research on their campus, they must consider how UREs fit into their institution's existing mission and culture. Faculty engagement in developing UREs requires significant time and effort and is not likely to be undertaken widely unless departmental and institutional reward systems recognize and reward faculty for the time required to initiate and implement UREs. Decisions to allocate limited funds to move courses, departments, and at times entire programs toward different outcomes may be required. For example, for some institutions it might be a good fit to have CUREs become more widespread and integral components of the departmental curricula. These types of changes will interact in multiple ways with the recognition and incentive systems and professional cultures to which individual faculty, departments, and interdisciplinary programs are accustomed. Changes to the systems and institutional culture might include policies for hiring, promotion, tenure, annual performance reviews, and compensation, along with potential changes in the institutional teaching/research balance. Changes in any or all of these areas can offer new pathways and incentives toward making UREs an integral component of a department's or institution's educational mission.

Regardless of institution type, focus of the research effort, and resources available, by emphasizing a student-centered approach, departments or institutions can increase their likelihood of success in improving existing UREs or in expanding the number and diversity of such learning opportunities to the greatest number of students possible. Campuses that cultivate environments that support continuous refinement of teaching programs, based on evidence of student learning and other measures of success, are more likely to be successful in cultivating and sustaining URE programs (for an example, see Box 8-2, above, on The College of New Jersey). Faculty and others who develop and implement such activities need support to be able to embed meaningful assessments into the design of their programs, to undertake the work involved with evaluating their courses or other types of UREs, and to analyze evidence to make decisions about URE design. Where they are available, centers for learning and teaching can provide guidance to URE developers on topics such as pedagogy and assessment. They can also be good venues for faculty to meet colleagues from other schools, departments, and disciplines for sharing education-related experiences and expertise.

To help projects for studying the mechanisms of UREs move forward more smoothly, partnerships can be formed that combine URE developers from the natural sciences and engineering with those engaged in disciplinary-based education research or with colleagues in the social sciences or schools of education who have appropriate expertise in designing experiments involving human subjects. Such partnerships should also include representatives of the campus Institutional Review Board. In addition, intercampus connections such as those between community colleges or other resource-limited institutions and research-intensive universities can improve the prospects for faculty in the former types of institutions to gain access to instrumentation and other resources, share student-generated research data and common assessments, collaborate with colleagues who are undertaking similar programs, and allow both faculty and students to benefit from interactions across more diverse student populations.

An equally important component of such efforts is recognition by departmental and institutional leaders that, as with any scientific research agenda, not all efforts to develop UREs will succeed, at least initially. Pedagogical efforts are more likely to succeed if they are encouraged and supported by academic leaders. Such support is particularly relevant and important for any untenured faculty member who chooses to take the risks associated with URE innovation. This can be done by acknowledging up front the potential for failure and establishing policies and procedures to accommodate initial failures, while simultaneously instilling expectations and pathways for continued improvements and success over time. Such proactive, supportive efforts will likely catalyze many kinds of innovations in the types of UREs that become available in a department or on a campus because they convey the important message that innovation is encouraged and risks will be managed. Similarly, policies must take into account the challenges that arise when efforts are made to scale up a pilot program or adapt a program begun at another institution.

Demonstrating that the leadership of an institution values UREs enough to engage the faculty and other stakeholders in discussions about changing reward systems to account positively for excellence in this realm also can be highly motivating to those who are, or wish to become, involved with such efforts. Allowing quality involvement with undergraduate research to have a role in decisions about tenure, promotion, or continuation of long-term employment contracts sends a powerful message. Restructuring reward systems in this fashion also may benefit the campus more broadly by broadcasting to the larger campus community (including prospective students who may be attracted to enroll and currently matriculated students who may remain because of such policies) about including such practices as an integral component of the institution's mission.

SUMMARY

This chapter provides many ideas that can be used by those designing or running UREs today. The information presented here is not grounded in the research literature as are other sections of the report; instead it builds on the knowledge and expertise of the committee and those they have heard about via their information gathering for this study and through their professional networks. The great variation in the types of UREs that can be offered and the groups of students who can participate mean that there are multiple factors to consider in choosing and designing a program. Goals and resources must be carefully considered when choosing the type(s) of URE to use on a given campus and when making decisions about how to implement, assess, and improve UREs. The culture of the campus and the incentives operating on faculty are key considerations, as are the interests and goals of the students. Every campus has a variety of resources that can be reconfigured and repurposed to support UREs, starting with current teaching laboratory facilities and budgets. Creative uses of the local site as the laboratory, exploiting online resources, and working with consortia can open up additional possibilities.

REFERENCES

American Association for the Advancement of Science. (2011). *Vision and Change in Under-graduate Biology Education: A Call to Action* (C. Brewer and D. Smith, Eds.). Washington, DC: American Association for the Advancement of Science.

Bangera, G., and Brownell, S.E. (2014). Course-based undergraduate research experiences can make scientific research more inclusive. *CBE–Life Sciences Education, 13*, 602-606.

Blockus, L. (2016). *Strengthening Research Experiences for Undergraduate STEM Students: The Co-Curricular Model of the Research Experience.* Paper commissioned for the Committee on Strengthening Research Experiences for Undergraduate STEM Students. Board on Science Education, Division of Behavioral and Social Sciences and Education. Board on Life Sciences, Division of Earth and Life Studies. National Academies of Sciences, Engineering, and Medicine. Available: http://nas.edu/STEM_Undergraduate_Research_Apprentice.

Campbell, A.M., Eckdahl, T., Cronk, B., Andresen, C., Frederick, P., Huckuntod, S., Shinneman, C., Wacker, A., and Yuan, J. (2014). Synthetic biology tool makes promoter research accessible to beginning biology students. *CBE–Life Sciences Education, 13*, 2285-2296.

Cortright, R.N., Collins, H.L., Rodenbaugh, D.W., and DiCarlo, S.E. (2003). Student retention of course content in improved by collaborative-group testing. *Advances in Physiology Education, 27*, 102-108.

Council on Undergraduate Research. (2012). *Characteristics of Excellence in Undergraduate Research.* Washington, DC: Council on Undergraduate Research

Dolan, E. (2016). *Course-Based Undergraduate Research Experiences: Current Knowledge and Future Directions.* Paper commissioned for the Committee on Strengthening Research Experiences for Undergraduate STEM Students. Board on Science Education, Division of Behavioral and Social Sciences and Education. Board on Life Sciences, Division of Earth and Life Studies. National Academies of Sciences, Engineering, and Medicine. Available: http://nas.edu/STEM_Undergraduate_Research_CURE.

Elgin, S.C.R., Bangera, G., Decatur, S.M., Dolan, E.L., Guertin, L., Newstetter, W.C., San Juan, E.F., Smith, M.A., Weaver, G.C., Wessler, S.R., Brenner, K.A., and Labov, J.B. (2016). Insights from a convocation: Integrating discovery-based research into the undergraduate curriculum. *CBE–Life Sciences Education, 15*, 1-7.

Flaherty, C. (2014). Faculty work, student success: How The College of New Jersey reimagined what professors can do. Available: www.insidehighered.com/news/2014/10/16/how-college-new-jersey-rethought-faculty-work-student-success-mind [February 2017].

Hatfull, G. (2015). Innovations in undergraduate science education: Going viral. *Journal of Virology, 89*(16), 8,111-8,113.

Johnson, D.W., Johnson, R.T., and Smith, K.A. (1998). Cooperative learning returns to college: What evidence is there that it works? *Change, 30,* 26-35.

Johnson, D.W., Johnson, R.T., and Smith, K.A. (2007). The state of cooperative learning in postsecondary and professional settings. *Educational Psychology Review, 19*(1), 15-29.

Johnson, W. (2002). The intentional mentor: Strategies and guidelines for the practice of mentoring. *Professional Psychology: Research and Practice, 33,* 89-96.

Johnson, W.B., and Huwe, J.M. (2003). *Getting Mentored in Graduate School.* Washington, DC: American Psychological Association.

Kober, N. (2015). *Reaching Students: What Research Says about Effective Instruction in Undergraduate Science and Engineering.* Board on Science Education, Division of Behavioral and Social Sciences and Education. Washington, DC: The National Academies Press.

Lee, Jr., J.M., Contreras, F., McGuire, K.M., Flores-Ragade, A., Rawls, A., Edwards, K., and Menson, R. (2011). *The College Completion Agenda: 2011 Progress Report.* New York: College Board Advocacy and Policy Center.

Liang, B., Tracy, A.J., Taylor, C.A., and Williams, L.M. (2002). Mentoring college-age women: A relational approach. *American Journal of Community Psychology, 30*(2), 271-288.

Lopatto, D. (2015). *The Consortium as Experiment.* Paper commissioned for the Committee for Convocation on Integrating Discovery-Based Research into the Undergraduate Curriculum. Division on Earth and Life Studies. Division of Behavioral and Social Sciences and Education. Washington, DC: The National Academies Press.

Moss-Racusin, C.A., Dovidio, J.F., Brescoll, V.L., Graham, M.J., and Handelsman, J. (2012). Science faculty's subtle gender biases favor male students. *Proceedings of the National Academy of Sciences, 109*(41), 16,474-16,479.

Nagda, B.A, Gregerman, S.R., Jonides, J., von Hippel, W., and Lerner, J.S. (1998). Undergraduate student-faculty research partnerships affect student retention. *Review of Higher Education, 22,* 55-72. Available: http://scholar.harvard.edu/files/jenniferlerner/files/nagda_1998_paper.pdf [February 2017].

National Academies of Sciences, Engineering, and Medicine. (2015). *Integrating Discovery-Based Research into the Undergraduate Curriculum: Report of a Convocation.* Washington, DC: The National Academies Press.

National Research Council. (2001). *Knowing What Students Know: The Science and Design of Educational Assessment.* J. Pellegrino, N. Chudowsky, and R. Glaser (Eds.). Committee on the Foundations of Assessment, Board on Testing and Assessment, Center for Education, Division of Behavioral and Social Sciences and Education. Washington, DC: The National Academies Press.

National Research Council. (2014). *Convergence: Facilitating Transdisciplinary Integration of Life Sciences, Physical Sciences, Engineering, and Beyond.* Committee on Key Challenge Areas for Convergence and Health, Board on Life Sciences, Division on Earth and Life Studies. Washington, DC: The National Academies Press.

Osborn, J.M., and K.K. Karukstis. 2009. The benefits of undergraduate research, scholarship, and creative activity. Pages 41-53 in M. Boyd and J. Wesemann (Eds.), *Broadening Participation in Undergraduate Research: Fostering Excellence and Enhancing the Impact.* Washington, DC: Council on Undergraduate Research.

Pfund, C. (2016). *Studying the Role and Impact of Mentoring on Undergraduate Research Experiences*. Paper commissioned for the Committee on Strengthening Research Experiences for Undergraduate STEM Students. Board on Science Education, Division of Behavioral and Social Sciences and Education. Board on Life Sciences, Division of Earth and Life Studies. National Academies of Sciences, Engineering, and Medicine. Available: http://nas.edu/STEM_Undergraduate_Research_Mentoring.

President's Council of Advisors in Science and Technology. (2012). *Engage to Excel: Producing One Million Additional College Graduates with Degrees in STEM*. Washington, DC: Executive Office of the President. Available: http://files.eric.ed.gov/fulltext/ED541511.pdf [February 2017].

Shortlidge, E., and Brownell, S. (2016). How to assess your CURE: A practical guide for instructors of course-based undergraduate research experiences. *Journal of Microbiology and Biology Education, 17*(3), 399-408.

Svinicki, M., and McKeachie, W.J. (2011). *McKeachie's Teaching Tips: Strategies, Research, and Theory for College and University Teachers*. Belmont, CA: Wadsworth, Cengage Learning.

9

Conclusions and Recommendations

Practitioners designing or improving undergraduate research experiences (UREs) can build on the experiences of colleagues and learn from the increasingly robust literature about UREs and the considerable body of evidence about how students learn. The questions practitioners ask themselves during the design process should include questions about the goals of the campus, program, faculty, and students. Other factors to consider when designing a URE include the issues raised in the conceptual framework for learning and instruction, the available resources, how the program or experience will be evaluated or studied, and how to design the program from the outset to incorporate these considerations, as well as how to build in opportunities to improve the experience over time in light of new evidence. (Some of these topics are addressed in Chapter 8.)

Colleges and universities that offer or wish to offer UREs to their students should undertake baseline evaluations of their current offerings and create plans to develop a culture of improvement in which faculty are supported in their efforts to continuously refine UREs based on the evidence currently available and evidence that they and others generate in the future. While much of the evidence to date is descriptive, it forms a body of knowledge that can be used to identify research questions about UREs, both those designed around the apprenticeship model and those designed using the more recent course-based undergraduate research experience (CURE) model. Internships and other avenues by which undergraduates do research provide many of the same sorts of experiences but are not well studied. In any case, it is clear that students value these experiences; that many faculty do as well; and that they contribute to broadening participation in science, technology, engineering, and mathematics (STEM) education and careers. The findings from the research literature reported in Chapter 4 provide guidance to those designing both opportunities to improve practical and academic skills and opportunities for students to "try out" a professional role of interest.

Little research has been done that provides answers to mechanistic questions about how UREs work. Additional studies are needed to know which features of UREs are most important for positive outcomes with which students and to gain information about other questions of this type. This additional research is needed to better understand and compare different strategies for UREs designed for a diversity of students, mentors, and institutions. Therefore, the committee recommends steps that could increase the quantity and quality of evidence available in the future and makes recommendations for how faculty, departments, and institutions might approach decisions about UREs using currently available information. Multiple detailed recommendations about the kinds of research that might be useful are provided in the research agenda in Chapter 7.

In addition to the specific research recommended in Chapter 7, in this chapter the committee provides a series of interrelated conclusions and recommendations related to UREs for the STEM disciplines and intended to highlight the issues of primary importance to administrators, URE program designers, mentors to URE students, funders of UREs, those leading the departments and institutions offering UREs, and those conducting research about UREs. These conclusions and recommendations are based on the expert views of the committee and informed by their review of the available research, the papers commissioned for this report, and input from presenters during committee meetings. Table 9-1 defines categories of these URE "actors," gives examples of specific roles included in each category, specifies key URE actions for which that category is responsible, and lists the conclusions and recommendations the committee views as most relevant to that actor category.

RESEARCH ON URES

Conclusion 1: *The current and emerging landscape of what constitutes UREs is diverse and complex. Students can engage in STEM-based undergraduate research in many different ways, across a variety of settings, and along a continuum that extends and expands upon learning opportunities in other educational settings. The following characteristics define UREs. Due to the variation in the types of UREs, not all experiences include all of the following characteristics in the same way; experiences vary in how much a particular characteristic is emphasized.*

TABLE 9-1 Audiences for Committee's Conclusions and Recommendations

Actor Category	Specific People in Category	Key URE Actions	Most Relevant Conclusions/ Recommendations
Education researchers	Those conducting discipline-based education research; researchers in education, sociology, psychology; and others	• Conduct well-designed studies on the effects of UREs. • Collaborate with URE designers on using evidence from the literature to improve URE design.	Conclusions 2, 3, 4, 5, 6, and 7 **Recommendations 1 and 3**
URE designers and implementers	STEM faculty and instructors; faculty in education	• Use appropriate methods to measure URE outcomes. • Base URE design on sound evidence. • Collaborate with education researchers on evaluation and design improvement.	Conclusions 1, 4, and 5 **Recommendations 1 and 3**
Mentors of students in UREs	STEM faculty, postdocs, graduate students, and experienced undergraduates	• Mentor students. • Take advantage of professional development opportunities.	Conclusion 8 **Recommendation 6**
Funders of UREs	Government agencies, private foundations, and colleges/universities	• Beyond resources to offer UREs, provide resources for well-designed studies on UREs.	Conclusions 2, 3, and 5 **Recommendation 2**
Professional and educational societies	Disciplinary societies, associations of colleges and universities, associations related to STEM education	• Provide resources and connections to URE designers/implementers. • Provide professional development; facilitate sharing of resources.	Conclusions 7 and 8 **Recommendations 3, 6, and 8**
Academic leadership	Presidents, provosts, deans, and department chairs	• Collect data to inform URE planning and improve quality and access. • Evaluate range of UREs offered (leverage resources and assess access). • Provide professional development opportunities to URE mentors. • Create policies to refine UREs based on evidence.	Conclusions 6, 7, and 9 **Recommendations 4, 5, 6, 7, and 8**

- *They engage students in research practices including the ability to argue from evidence.*
- *They aim to generate novel information with an emphasis on discovery and innovation or to determine whether recent preliminary results can be replicated.*
- *They focus on significant, relevant problems of interest to STEM researchers and, in some cases, a broader community (e.g., civic engagement).*
- *They emphasize and expect collaboration and teamwork.*
- *They involve iterative refinement of experimental design, experimental questions, or data obtained.*
- *They allow students to master specific research techniques.*
- *They help students engage in reflection about the problems being investigated and the work being undertaken to address those problems.*
- *They require communication of results, either through publication or presentations in various STEM venues.*
- *They are structured and guided by a mentor, with students assuming increasing ownership of some aspects of the project over time.*

UREs are generally designed to add value to STEM offerings by promoting an understanding of the ways that knowledge is generated in STEM fields and to extend student learning beyond what happens in the small group work of an inquiry-based course. UREs add value by enabling students to understand and contribute to the research questions that are driving the field for one or more STEM topics or to grapple with design challenges of interest to professionals. They help students understand what it means to be a STEM researcher in a way that would be difficult to convey in a lecture course or even in an inquiry-based learning setting. As participants in a URE, students can learn by engaging in planning, experimentation, evaluation, interpretation, and communication of data and other results in light of what is already known about the question of interest. They can pose relevant questions that can be solved only through investigative or design efforts—individually or in teams—and attempt to answer these questions despite the challenges, setbacks, and ambiguity of the process and the results obtained.

The diversity of UREs reflects the reality that different STEM disciplines operate from varying traditions, expectations, and constraints (e.g., lab safety issues) in providing opportunities for undergraduates to engage in research. In addition, individual institutions and departments have cultures that promote research participation to various degrees and at different stages in students' academic careers. Some programs emphasize design and problem solving in addition to discovery. UREs in different disciplines can take many forms (e.g., apprentice-style, course-based, internships, project-based), but the *definitional characteristics* described above are similar across different STEM fields.

Furthermore, students in today's university landscape may have opportunities to engage with many different types of UREs throughout their education, including involvement in a formal program (which could include mentoring, tutoring, research, and seminars about research), an apprentice-style URE under the guidance of an individual or team of faculty members, an internship, or enrolling in one or more CUREs or in a consortium- or project-based program.

Conclusion 2: *Research on the efficacy of UREs is still in the early stages of development compared with other interventions to improve undergraduate STEM education.*

- *The types of UREs are diverse, and their goals are even more diverse. Questions and methodologies used to investigate the roles and effectiveness of UREs in achieving those goals are similarly diverse.*
- *Most of the studies of UREs to date are descriptive case studies or use correlational designs. Many of these studies report positive outcomes from engagement in a URE.*
- *Only a small number of studies have employed research designs that can support inferences about causation. Most of these studies find evidence for a causal relationship between URE participation and subsequent persistence in STEM. More studies are needed to provide evidence that participation in UREs is a causal factor in a range of desired student outcomes.*

Taking the entire body of evidence into account, the committee concludes that the published peer-reviewed literature to date suggests that participation in a URE is beneficial for students.

As discussed in the report's Introduction (see Chapter 1) and in the research agenda (see Chapter 7), the committee considered descriptive, causal, and mechanistic questions in our reading of the literature on UREs. Scientific approaches to answering descriptive, causal, and mechanistic questions require deciding what to look for, determining how to examine it, and knowing appropriate ways to score or quantify the effect.

Descriptive questions ask *what* is happening without making claims as to *why* it is happening—that is, without making claims as to whether the research experience *caused* these changes. A descriptive statement about UREs only claims that certain changes occurred during or after the time the students were engaged in undergraduate research. Descriptive studies cannot determine whether any benefits observed were caused by participation in the URE.

Causal questions seek to discover whether a specific intervention leads to a specific outcome, other things being equal. To address such questions, causal evidence can be generated from a comparison of carefully selected groups that do and do not experience UREs. The groups can be made roughly equivalent by random assignment (ensuring that URE and non-URE groups are the same on average as the sample size increases) or by controlling for an exhaustive set of characteristics and experiences that might render the groups different prior to the URE. Other quasi-experimental strategies can also be used. Simply comparing students who enroll in a URE with students who do not is not adequate for determining causality because there may be selection bias. For example, students already interested in STEM are more likely to seek out such opportunities and more likely to be selected for such programs. Instead the investigator would have to compare future enrollment patterns (or other measures) between closely matched students, some of whom enrolled in a URE and some of whom did not. Controlling for selection bias to enable an inference about causation can pose significant challenges.

Questions of *mechanism* or of *process* also can be explored to understand *why* a causal intervention leads to the observed effect. Perhaps the URE enhances a student's confidence in her ability to succeed in her chosen field or deepens her commitment to the field by exposing her to the joy of discovery. Through these pathways that act on the participant's purposive behavior, the URE enhances the likelihood that she persists in STEM. The question for the researcher then becomes what research design would provide support for this hypothesis of mechanism over other candidate explanations for why the URE is a causal factor in STEM persistence.

The committee has examined the literature and finds a rich descriptive foundation for testable hypotheses about the effects of UREs on student outcomes. These studies are encouraging; a few of them have generated evidence that a URE can be a positive causal factor in the progression and persistence of STEM students. The weight of the evidence has been descriptive; it relies primarily on self-reports of short-term gains by students who chose to participate in UREs and does not include direct measures of changes in the students' knowledge, skills, or other measures of success across comparable groups of students who did and did not participate in UREs.

While acknowledging the scarcity of strong causal evidence on the benefits of UREs, the committee takes seriously the weight of the descriptive evidence. Many of the published studies of UREs show that students who participate report a range of benefits, such as increased understanding of the research process, encouragement to persist in STEM, and support that helps them sustain their identity as researchers and continue with their plans to enroll in a graduate program in STEM (see Chapter 4). These are effective starting points for causal studies.

Conclusion 3: *Studies focused on students from historically underrepresented groups indicate that participation in UREs improves their persistence in STEM and helps to validate their disciplinary identity.*

Various UREs have been specifically designed to increase the number of historically underrepresented students who go on to become STEM majors and ultimately STEM professionals. While many UREs offer one or more supplemental opportunities to support students' academic or social success, such as mentoring, tutoring, summer bridge programs, career or graduate school workshops, and research-oriented seminars, those designed for underrepresented students appear to emphasize such features as integral and integrated components of the program. In particular, studies of undergraduate research programs targeting underrepresented minority students have begun to document positive outcomes such as degree completion and persistence in interest in STEM careers (Byars-Winston et al., 2015; Chemers et al., 2011; Jones et al., 2010; Nagda et al., 1998; Schultz et al., 2011). Most of these studies collected data on apprentice-style UREs, in which the undergraduate becomes a functioning member of a research group along with the graduate students, postdoctoral fellows, and mentor.

Recommendation 1: *Researchers with expertise in education research should conduct well-designed studies in collaboration with URE program directors to improve the evidence base about the processes and effects of UREs. This research should address how the various components of UREs may benefit students. It should also include additional causal evidence for the individual and additive effects of outcomes from student participation in different types of UREs. Not all UREs need be designed to undertake this type of research, but it would be very useful to have some UREs that are designed to facilitate these efforts to improve the evidence base.*

As the focus on UREs has grown, so have questions about their implementation. Many articles have been published describing specific UREs (see Chapter 2). Large amounts of research have also been undertaken to explore more generally how students learn, and the resulting body of evidence has led to the development and adoption of "active learning" strategies and experiences. If a student in a URE has an opportunity to, for example, analyze new data or to reformulate a hypothesis in light of the student's analysis, this activity fits into the category that is described as active learning. Surveys of student participants and unpublished evaluations provide additional information about UREs but do not establish causation or determine the mechanism(s). Consequently, little is currently known about the mechanisms of precisely how UREs work and which aspects of UREs are most powerful. Important components that have been reported include student ownership of the URE project, time to tackle a question iteratively, and opportunities to report and defend one's conclusions (Hanauer and Dolan, 2014; Thiry et al., 2011).

There are many unanswered questions and opportunities for further research into the role and mechanism of UREs. Attention to research design as UREs are planned is important; more carefully designed studies are needed to understand the ways that UREs influence a student's education and to evaluate the outcomes that have been reported for URE participants. Appropriate studies, which include matched samples or similar controls, would facilitate research on the ways that UREs benefit students, enabling both education researchers and implementers of UREs to determine optimal features for program design and giving the community a more robust understanding of how UREs work.

See the research agenda (Chapter 7) for specific recommendations about research topics and approaches.

Recommendation 2: *Funders should provide appropriate resources to support the design, implementation, and analysis of some URE programs that are specifically designed to enable detailed research establishing the effects on participant outcomes and on other variables of interest such as the consequences for mentors or institutions.*

Not all UREs need to be the subject of extensive study. In many cases, a straightforward evaluation is adequate to determine whether the URE is meeting its goals. However, to achieve more widespread improvement in both the types and quality of the UREs offered in the future, additional evidence about the possible causal effects and mechanisms of action of UREs needs to be systematically collected and disseminated. This includes a better understanding of the implementation differences for a variety of institutions (e.g., community colleges, primarily undergraduate institutions, research universities) to ensure that the desired outcomes can translate across settings. Increasing the evidence about precisely how UREs work and which aspects of UREs are most powerful will require careful attention to study design during planning for the UREs.

Not all UREs need to be designed to achieve this goal; many can provide opportunities to students by relying on pre-existing knowledge and iterative improvement as that knowledge base grows. However, for the knowledge base to grow, funders must provide resources for some URE designers and social science researchers to undertake thoughtful and well-planned studies on causal and mechanistic issues. This will maximize the chances for the creation and dissemination of information that can lead to the development of sustainable and effective UREs. These studies can result from a partnership formed as the URE is designed and funded, or evaluators and social scientists could identify promising and/or effective existing programs and then raise funds on their own to support the study of those programs to answer the questions of interest. In deciding upon the UREs that are chosen for these extensive studies, it will be important to consider whether, collectively, they are representative of UREs in general. For example, large and small UREs at large and small schools targeted at both introductory and advanced students and topics should be studied.

CONSTRUCTION OF URES

Conclusion 4: *The committee was unable to find evidence that URE designers are taking full advantage of the information available in the education literature on strategies for designing, implementing, and evaluating learning experiences. STEM faculty members do not generally receive training in interpreting or conducting education research. Partnerships between those with expertise in education research and those with expertise in implementing UREs are one way to strengthen the application of evidence on what works in planning and implementing UREs.*

As discussed in Chapters 3 and 4, there is an extensive body of literature on pedagogy and how people learn; helping STEM faculty to access the existing literature and incorporate those concepts as they design UREs could improve student experiences. New studies that specifically focus on UREs may provide more targeted information that could be used to design, implement, sustain, or scale up UREs and facilitate iterative improvements. Information about the features of UREs that elicit particular outcomes or best serve certain populations of students should be considered when implementing a new instantiation of an existing model of a URE or improving upon an existing URE model.

Conclusion 5: *Evaluations of UREs are often conducted to inform program providers and funders; however, they may not be accessible to others. While these evaluations are not designed to be research studies and often have small sample sizes, they may contain information that could be useful to those initiating new URE programs and those refining UREs. Increasing access to these evaluations and to the accumulated experience of the program providers may enable URE designers and implementers to build upon knowledge gained from earlier UREs.*

As discussed in Chapter 1, the committee searched for evaluations of URE programs in several different ways but was not able to locate many published evaluations to study. Although some evaluations were found in the literature, the committee could not determine a way to systematically examine the program evaluations that have been prepared. The National Science Foundation and other funders generally require grant recipients to submit evaluation data, but that information is not currently aggregated and shared publicly, even for programs that are using a common evaluation tool.[1]

Therefore, while program evaluation likely serves a useful role in providing descriptive data about a program for the institutions and funders supporting the program, much of the summative evaluation work that has been done to date adds relatively little to the broader knowledge base and overall conversations around undergraduate research. Some of the challenges of evaluation include budget and sample size constraints.

Similarly, it is difficult for designers of UREs to benefit systematically from the work of others who have designed and run UREs in the past because of the lack of an easy and consistent mechanism for collecting, analyzing, and sharing data. If these evaluations were more accessible they might be beneficial to others designing and evaluating UREs by helping them to gather ideas and inspiration from the experiences of others. A few such stories are provided in this report, and others can be found among the many resources offered by the Council on Undergraduate Research[2] and on other websites such as CUREnet.[3]

Recommendation 3: *Designers of UREs should base their design decisions on sound evidence. Consultations with education and social science researchers may be helpful as designers analyze the literature and make decisions on the creation or improvement of UREs. Professional development materials should be created and made available to faculty. Educational and disciplinary societies should consider how they can provide resources and connections to those working on UREs.*

Faculty and other organizers of UREs can use the expanding body of scholarship as they design or improve the programs and experiences offered to their students. URE designers will need to make decisions about how to adapt approaches reported in the literature to make the programs they develop more suitable to their own expertise, student population(s), and available resources. Disciplinary societies and other national groups, such as those focused on improving pedagogy, can play important roles in

---

[1] Personal knowledge of Janet Branchaw, member of the Committee on Strengthening Research Experiences for Undergraduate STEM Students.

[2] See www.cur.org [November 2016].

[3] See (curenet.cns.utexas.edu) [November 2016].

bringing these issues to the forefront through events at their national and regional meetings and through publications in their journals and newsletters. They can develop repositories for various kinds of resources appropriate for their members who are designing and implementing UREs. The ability to travel to conferences and to access and discuss resources created by other individuals and groups is a crucial aspect of support (see Recommendations 7 and 8 for further discussion).

See Chapter 8 for specific questions to consider when one is designing or implementing UREs.

CURRENT OFFERINGS

Conclusion 6: *Data at the institutional, state, or national levels on the number and type of UREs offered, or who participates in UREs overall or at specific types of institutions, have not been collected systematically. Although the committee found that some individual institutions track at least some of this type of information, we were unable to determine how common it is to do so or what specific information is most often gathered.*

There is no one central database or repository that catalogs UREs at institutions of higher education, the nature of the research experiences they provide, or the relevant demographics (student, departmental, and institutional). The lack of comprehensive data makes it difficult to know how many students participate in UREs; where UREs are offered; and if there are gaps in access to UREs across different institutional types, disciplines, or groups of students. One of the challenges of describing the undergraduate research landscape is that students do not have to be enrolled in a formal program to have a research experience. Informal experiences, for example a work-study job, are typically not well documented. Another challenge is that some students participate in CUREs or other research experiences (such as internships) that are not necessarily labeled as such. Institutional administrators may be unaware of CUREs that are already part of their curriculum. (For example, establishment of CUREs may be under the purview of a faculty curriculum committee and may not be recognized as a distinct program.) Student participation in UREs may occur at their home institution or elsewhere during the summer. Therefore, it is very difficult for a science department, and likely any other STEM department, to know what percentage of their graduating majors have had a research experience, let alone to gather such information on students who left the major.[4]

---

[4]This point was made by Marco Molinaro, University of California, Davis, in a presentation to the Committee on Strengthening Research Experience for Undergraduate STEM Students, September 16, 2015.

Conclusion 7: *While data are lacking on the precise number of students engaged in UREs, there is some evidence of a recent growth in course-based undergraduate research experiences (CUREs), which engage a cohort of students in a research project as part of a formal academic experience.*

There has been an increase in the number of grants and the dollar amount spent on CUREs over the past decade (see Chapter 3). CUREs can be particularly useful in scaling UREs to reach a much larger population of students (Bangera and Brownell, 2014). By using a familiar mechanism—enrollment in a course—a CURE can provide a more comfortable route for students unfamiliar with research to gain their first experience. CUREs also can provide such experiences to students with diverse backgrounds, especially if an institution or department mandates participation sometime during a student's matriculation. Establishing CUREs may be more cost-effective at schools with little on-site research activity. However, designing a CURE is a new and time-consuming challenge for many faculty members. Connecting to nationally organized research networks can provide faculty with helpful resources for the development of a CURE based around their own research or a local community need, or these networks can link interested faculty to an ongoing collaborative project. Collaborative projects can provide shared curriculum, faculty professional development and community, and other advantages when starting or expanding a URE program. See the discussion in the report from a convocation on *Integrating Discovery-based Research into the Undergraduate Curriculum* (National Academies of Sciences, Engineering, and Medicine, 2015).

Recommendation 4: *Institutions should collect data on student participation in UREs to inform their planning and to look for opportunities to improve quality and access.*

Better tracking of student participation could lead to better assessment of outcomes and improved quality of experience. Such metrics could be useful for both prospective students and campus planners. An integrated institutional system for research opportunities could facilitate the creation of tiered research experiences that allow students to progress in skills and responsibility and create support structures for students, providing, for example, seminars in communications, safety, and ethics for undergraduate researchers. Institutions could also use these data to measure the impact of UREs on student outcomes, such as student success rates in introductory courses, retention in STEM degree programs, and completion of STEM degrees.

While individual institutions may choose to collect additional information depending on their goals and resources, relevant student demographics and the following design elements would provide baseline data. At a minimum, such data should include

- Type of URE;
- Each student's discipline;
- Duration of the experience;
- Hours spent per week;
- When the student began the URE (e.g., first year, capstone);
- Compensation status (e.g., paid, unpaid, credit); and
- Location and format (e.g., on home campus, on another campus, internship, co-op).

National aggregation of some of the student participation variables collected by various campuses might be considered by funders. The existing Integrated Postsecondary Education Data System database, organized by the National Center for Education Statistics at the U.S. Department of Education, may be a suitable repository for certain aspects of this information.

Recommendation 5: *Administrators and faculty at all types of colleges and universities should continually and holistically evaluate the range of UREs that they offer. As part of this process, institutions should:*
- *Consider how best to leverage available resources (including off-campus experiences available to students and current or potential networks or partnerships that the institution may form) when offering UREs so that they align with their institution's mission and priorities;*
- *Consider whether current UREs are both accessible and welcoming to students from various subpopulations across campus (e.g., historically underrepresented students, first generation college students, those with disabilities, non-STEM majors, prospective kindergarten-through-12th-grade teachers); and*
- *Gather and analyze data on the types of UREs offered and the students who participate, making this information widely available to the campus community and using it to make evidence-based decisions about improving opportunities for URE participation. This may entail devising or implementing systems for tracking relevant data (see Conclusion 4).*

Resources available for starting, maintaining, and expanding UREs vary from campus to campus. At some campuses, UREs are a central focus and many resources are devoted to them. At other institutions—for example, many community colleges—UREs are seen as extra, and new resources may be required to ensure availability of courses and facilities. Resource-constrained institutions may need to focus more on ensuring that students are aware of potential UREs that already exist on campus and elsewhere in near proximity to campus. All institutional discussions about UREs must consider both the financial resources and physical resources (e.g., laboratories, field stations, engineering design studios) required, while remembering that faculty time is a crucial resource. The incentives and disincentives for faculty to spend time on UREs are significant. Those institutions with an explicit mission to promote undergraduate research may provide more recognition and rewards to departments and faculty than those with another focus. The culture of the institution with respect to innovation in pedagogy and support for faculty development also can have a major influence on the extent to which UREs are introduced or improved.

Access to UREs may vary across campus and by department, and participation in UREs may vary across student groups. It is important for campuses to consider the factors that may facilitate or discourage students from participation in UREs. Inconsistent procedures or a faculty preference for students with high grades or previous research experience may limit options for some student populations.

UREs often grow based on the initiative of individual faculty members and other personnel, and an institution may not have complete or even rudimentary knowledge of all of the opportunities available or whether there are gaps or inconsistencies in its offerings. A uniform method for tracking the UREs available on a given campus would be useful to students and would provide a starting point for analyzing the options. Tracking might consist of notations in course listings and, where feasible, on student transcripts. Analysis might consider the types of UREs offered, the resources available to each type of URE, and variations within or between various disciplines and programs. Attention to whether all students or groups of students have appropriate access to UREs would foster consideration of how to best allocate resources and programming on individual campuses, in order to focus resources and opportunities where they are most needed.

MENTORING

Conclusion 8: *The quality of mentoring can make a substantial difference in a student's experiences with research. However, professional development in how to be a good mentor is not available to many faculty or other prospective mentors (e.g., graduate students, postdoctoral fellows).*

Engagement in quality mentored research experiences has been linked to self-reported gains in research skills and productivity as well as retention in STEM (see Chapter 5). Quality mentoring in UREs has been shown to increase persistence in STEM for historically underrepresented students (Hernandez et al., 2016). In addition, poor mentoring during UREs has been shown to decrease retention of students (Hernandez et al., 2016).

More general research on good mentoring in the STEM environment has been positively associated with self-reported gains in identity as a STEM researcher, a sense of belonging, and confidence to function as a STEM researcher (Byars-Winston et al., 2015; Chemers et al., 2011; Pfund et al., 2016; Thiry et al., 2011). The frequency and quality of mentee-mentor interactions has been associated with students' reports of persistence in STEM, with mentoring directly or indirectly improving both grades and persistence in college. For students from historically underrepresented ethnic/racial groups, quality mentoring has been associated with self-reported enhanced recruitment into graduate school and research-related career pathways (Byars-Winston et al., 2015). Therefore, it is important to ensure that faculty and mentors receive the proper development of mentoring skills.

Recommendation 6: *Administrators and faculty at colleges and universities should ensure that all who mentor undergraduates in research experiences (this includes faculty, instructors, postdoctoral fellows, graduate students, and undergraduates serving as peer mentors) have access to appropriate professional development opportunities to help them grow and succeed in this role.*

Although many organizations recognize effective mentors (e.g., the National Science Foundation's Presidential Awards for Excellence in Science, Mathematics, and Engineering Mentoring), there currently are no standard criteria for selecting, evaluating, or recognizing mentors specifically for UREs. In addition, there are no requirements that mentors meet some minimum level of competency before engaging in mentoring or participate in professional development to obtain a baseline of knowledge and skills in mentoring, including cultural competence in mentoring diverse groups of students. Traditionally, the only experience required for being a mentor is having been mentored, regardless of whether the experience was negative or positive (Handelsman et al., 2005; Pfund et al., 2015). Explicit consideration of how the relationships are formed, supported, and evaluated can improve mentor-mentee relationships. To ensure that the mentors associated with a URE are prepared appropriately, thereby increasing the chances of a positive experience for both mentors and mentees, all prospective mentors should prepare for their role. Available resources include the Entering Mentoring course (see Pfund et al., 2015) and the book *Successful STEM Mentoring Initiative for Underrepresented Students* (Packard, 2016).

A person who is an ineffective mentor for one student might be inspiring for another, and the setting in which the mentoring takes place (e.g., a CURE or apprentice-style URE, a laboratory or field-research environment) may also influence mentor effectiveness. Thus, there should be some mechanism for monitoring such relationships during the URE, or there should be opportunity for a student who is unhappy with the relationship to seek other mentors. Indeed, cultivating a team of mentors with different experiences and expertise may be the best strategy for any student. A parallel volume to the Entering Mentoring curriculum mentioned above, *Entering Research Facilitator's Manual* (Branchaw et al., 2010), is designed to help students with their research mentor-mentee relationships and to coach them on building teams of mentors to guide them. As mentioned in Chapter 5, the Entering Research curriculum also contains information designed to support a group of students as they go through their first apprentice-style research experience, each working in separate research groups and also meeting together as a cohort focused on learning about research.

PRIORITIES FOR THE FUTURE

Conclusion 9: *The unique assets, resources, priorities, and constraints of the department and institution, in addition to those of individual mentors, impact the goals and structures of UREs. Schools across the country are showing considerable creativity in using unique resources, repurposing current assets, and leveraging student enthusiasm to increase research opportunities for their students.*

Given current calls for UREs and the growing conversation about their benefits, an increasing number of two- and four-year colleges and universities are increasing their efforts to support undergraduate research. Departments, institutions, and individual faculty members influence the precise nature of UREs in multiple ways and at multiple levels. The physical resources available, including laboratories, field stations, and engineering design studios and testing facilities, make a difference, as does the ability to access resources in the surrounding community (including other parts of the campus). Institutions with an explicit mission to promote undergraduate research may provide more time, resources (e.g., financial, support personnel, space, equipment), and recognition and rewards to departments and faculty in support of UREs than do institutions without that mission. The culture of the institution with respect to innovation in pedagogy and support for faculty development also affects the extent to which UREs are introduced or improved.

Development of UREs requires significant time and effort. Whether or not faculty attempt to implement UREs can depend on whether departmental or institutional reward and recognition systems compensate for or even recognize the time required to initiate and implement them. The availability of national consortia can help to alleviate many of the time and logistical problems but not those obstacles associated with recognition and resources.

It will be harder for faculty to find the time to develop UREs at institutions where they are required to teach many courses per semester, although in some circumstances faculty can teach CUREs that also advance their own research (Shortlidge et al., 2016). Faculty at community colleges generally have the heaviest teaching expectations, little or no expectations or incentives to maintain a research program, limited access to lab or design space or to scientific and engineering journals, and few resources to undertake any kind of a research program. These constraints may limit the extent to which UREs can be offered to the approximately 40 percent of U.S. undergraduates who are enrolled in the nation's community colleges (which collectively also serve the highest percentage of the nation's underrepresented students).[5]

Recommendation 7: *Administrators and faculty at all types of colleges and universities should work together within and, where feasible, across institutions to create a culture that supports the development of evidence-based, iterative, and continuous refinement of UREs, in an effort to improve student learning outcomes and overall academic success. This should include the development, evaluation, and revision of policies and practices designed to create a culture supportive of the participation of faculty and other mentors in effective UREs. Policies should consider pedagogy, professional development, cross-cultural awareness, hiring practices, compensation, promotion (incentives, rewards), and the tenure process.*

Colleges and universities that would like to expand or improve the UREs offered to their students should consider the campus culture and climate and the incentives that affect faculty choices. Those campuses that cultivate an environment supportive of the iterative and continuous refinement of UREs and that offer incentives for evaluation and evidence-based improvement of UREs seem more likely to sustain successful programs. Faculty and others who develop and implement UREs need support to be able to evaluate their courses or programs and to analyze evidence to make decisions about URE design. This kind of support may be fostered by expanding the mission of on-campus centers for learning and teaching to focus more on UREs or by providing incentives for URE developers from the natural sciences and engineering to collaborate with colleagues in the social sciences or colleges of education with expertise in designing studies

---

[5] See http://nces.ed.gov/programs/coe/indicator_cha.asp [November 2016].

involving human subjects. Supporting closer communication between URE developers and the members of the campus Institutional Review Board may help projects to move forward more seamlessly. Interdepartmental and intercampus connections (especially those between two- and four-year institutions) can be valuable for linking faculty with the appropriate resources, colleagues, and diverse student populations. Faculty who have been active in professional development on how students learn in the classroom may have valuable experiences and expertise to share.

The refinement or expansion of UREs should build on evidence from data on student participation, pedagogy, and outcomes, which are integral components of the original design. As UREs are validated and refined, institutions should make efforts to facilitate connections among different departments and disciplines, including the creation of multidisciplinary UREs. Student engagement in learning in general, and with UREs more specifically, depends largely on the culture of the department and the institution and on whether students see their surroundings as inclusive and energetic places to learn and thrive. A study that examined the relationship between campus missions and the five benchmarks for effective educational practice (measured by the National Survey of Student Engagement) showed that different programs, policies, and approaches may work better, depending on the institution's mission (Kezar and Kinzie, 2006).

The Council on Undergraduate Research (2012) document *Characteristics of Excellence in Undergraduate Research* outlines several best practices for UREs based on the apprenticeship model (see Chapter 8). That document is not the result of a detailed analysis of the evidence but is based on the extensive experiences and expertise of the council's members. It suggests that undergraduate research should be a normal part of the undergraduate experience regardless of the type of institution. It also identifies changes necessary to include UREs as part of the curriculum and culture changes necessary to support curricular reform, co-curricular activities, and modifications to the incentives and rewards for faculty to engage with undergraduate research. In addition, professional development opportunities specifically designed to help improve the pedagogical and mentoring skills of instructional staff in using evidence-based practices can be important for a supportive learning culture.

Recommendation 8: *Administrators and faculty at all types of colleges and universities should work to develop strong and sustainable partnerships within and between institutions and with educational and professional societies for the purpose of sharing resources to facilitate the creation of sustainable URE programs.*

Networks of faculty, institutions, regionally and nationally coordinated URE initiatives, professional societies, and funders should be strengthened to facilitate the exchange of evidence and experience related to UREs. These networks could build on the existing work of professional societies that assist faculty with pedagogy. They can help provide a venue for considering the policy context and larger implications of increasing the number, size, and scope of UREs. Such networks also can provide a more robust infrastructure, to improve the sustainability and expansion of URE opportunities. The sharing of human, financial, scientific, and technical resources can strengthen the broad implementation of effective, high-quality, and more cost-efficient UREs. It may be especially important for community colleges and minority-serving institutions to engage in partnerships in order to expand the opportunities for undergraduates (both transfer and technical students) to participate in diverse UREs (see discussion in National Academies of Sciences, Engineering, and Medicine, 2015, and Elgin et al., 2016). Consortia can facilitate the sharing of resources across disciplines and departments within the same institution or at different institutions, organizations, and agencies. Consortia that employ research methodologies in common can share curriculum, research data collected, and common assessment tools, lessening the time burden for individual faculty and providing a large pool of students from which to assess the efficacy of individual programs.

Changes in the funding climate can have substantial impacts on the types of programs that exist, iterative refinement of programs, and whether and how programs might be expanded to broaden participation by more undergraduates. For those institutions that have not yet established URE programs or are at the beginning phases of establishing one, mechanisms for achieving success and sustainability may include increased institutional ownership of programs of undergraduate research, development of a broad range of programs of different types and funding structures, formation of undergraduate research offices or repurposing some of the responsibilities and activities of those which already exist, and engagement in community promotion and dissemination of student accomplishments (e.g., student symposia, support for undergraduate student travel to give presentations at professional meetings).

Over time, institutions must develop robust plans for ensuring the long-term sustained funding of high-quality UREs. Those plans should include assuming that more fiscal responsibility for sustaining such efforts will be borne by the home institution as external support for such efforts decreases and ultimately ends. Building UREs into the curriculum and structure of a department's courses and other programs, and thus its funding model, can help with sustainability. Partnerships with nonprofit organizations and industry, as well as seeking funding from diverse agencies, can also facilitate programmatic sustainability, especially if the UREs they fund can also support the mission and programs of the funders (e.g., through research internships or through CUREs that focus on community-based research questions and challenges). Partnerships among institutions also may have greater potential to study and evaluate student outcomes from URE participation across broader demographic groups and to reduce overall costs through the sharing of administrative or other resources (such as libraries, microscopes, etc.).

REFERENCES

Bangera, G., and Brownell, S.E. (2014). Course-based undergraduate research experiences can make scientific research more inclusive. *CBE–Life Sciences Education, 13*(4), 602-606.

Branchaw, J.L., Pfund, C., and Rediske, R. (2010) *Entering Research Facilitator's Manual: Workshops for Students Beginning Research in Science.* New York: Freeman & Company.

Byars-Winston, A.M., Branchaw, J., Pfund, C., Leverett, P., and Newton, J. (2015). Culturally diverse undergraduate researchers' academic outcomes and perceptions of their research mentoring relationships. *International Journal of Science Education, 37*(15), 2,533-2,554.

Chemers, M.M., Zurbriggen, E.L., Syed, M., Goza, B.K., and Bearman, S. (2011). The role of efficacy and identity in science career commitment among underrepresented minority students. *Journal of Social Issues, 67*(3), 469-491.

Council on Undergraduate Research. (2012). *Characteristics of Excellence in Undergraduate Research.* Washington, DC: Council on Undergraduate Research.

Elgin, S.C.R., Bangera, G., Decatur, S.M., Dolan, E.L., Guertin, L., Newstetter, W.C., San Juan, E.F., Smith, M.A., Weaver, G.C., Wessler, S.R., Brenner, K.A., and Labov, J.B. 2016. Insights from a convocation: Integrating discovery-based research into the undergraduate curriculum. *CBE–Life Sciences Education, 15*, 1-7.

Hanauer, D., and Dolan, E. (2014) The Project Ownership Survey: Measuring differences in scientific inquiry experiences, *CBE–Life Sciences Education, 13*, 149-158.

Handelsman, J., Pfund, C., Lauffer, S.M., and Pribbenow, C.M. (2005). *Entering Mentoring.* Madison, WI: The Wisconsin Program for Scientific Teaching.

Hernandez, P.R., Estrada, M., Woodcock, A., and Schultz, P.W. (2016). Protégé perceptions of high mentorship quality depend on shared values more than on demographic match. *Journal of Experimental Education.* Available: http://www.tandfonline.com/doi/full/10.1080/00220973.2016.1246405 [November 2016].

Jones, P., Selby, D., and Sterling, S.R. (2010). *Sustainability Education: Perspectives and Practice Across Higher Education.* New York: Earthscan.

Kezar, A.J., and Kinzie, J. (2006). Examining the ways institutions create student engagement: The role of mission. *Journal of College Student Development, 47*(2), 149-172.

National Academies of Sciences, Engineering, and Medicine. (2015). *Integrating Discovery-Based Research into the Undergraduate Curriculum: Report of a Convocation.* Washington, DC: National Academies Press.

Nagda, B.A., Gregerman, S.R., Jonides, J., von Hippel, W., and Lerner, J.S. (1998). Undergraduate student-faculty research partnerships affect student retention. *Review of Higher Education, 22*, 55-72. Available: http://scholar.harvard.edu/files/jenniferlerner/files/nagda_1998_paper.pdf [February 2017].

Packard, P. (2016). *Successful STEM Mentoring Initiatives for Underrepresented Students: A Research-Based Guide for Faculty and Administrators.* Sterling, VA: Stylus.

Pfund, C., Branchaw, J.L., and Handelsman, J. (2015). *Entering Mentoring: A Seminar to Train a New Generation of Scientists* (2nd ed). New York: Macmillan Learning.

Pfund, C., Byars-Winston, A., Branchaw, J.L., Hurtado, S., and Eagan, M.K. (2016). Defining attributes and metrics of effective research mentoring relationships. *AIDS and Behavior, 20*, 238-248.

Schultz, P.W., Hernandez, P.R., Woodcock, A., Estrada, M., Chance, R.C., Aguilar, M., and Serpe, R.T. (2011). Patching the pipeline reducing educational disparities in the sciences through minority training programs. *Educational Evaluation and Policy Analysis, 33*(1), 95-114.

Shortlidge, E.E., Bangera, G., and Brownell, S.E. (2016). Faculty perspectives on developing and teaching course-based undergraduate research experiences. *BioScience, 66*(1), 54-62.

Thiry, H., Laursen, S.L., and Hunter, A.B. (2011). What experiences help students become scientists? A comparative study of research and other sources of personal and professional gains for STEM undergraduates. *Journal of Higher Education, 82*(4), 358-389.

Appendix A

STEM Participation Rates

Table A-1 is reproduced from Eagan and colleagues (2014), which was commissioned for *Barriers and Opportunities for 2-Year and 4-Year STEM Degrees: Systemic Change to Support Students' Diverse Pathways* (National Academies of Sciences, Engineering, and Medicine, 2016). It analyzes data collected from the Cooperative Institutional Research Program's annual Freshman Survey, which surveys hundreds of thousands of students at four-year colleges and universities nationwide. The data presented are from the incoming students in Fall 2012.

Figure A-1 is from Estrada and colleagues (2016) and reflects the current percentages of science, technology, engineering, and mathematics (STEM) degrees for the following populations: underrepresented minority (including African American, Hispanic or Latino/Latina, American Indian, and Alaskan Native), white, and Asian/Pacific Islander. The data were derived from the data tables prepared by the National Center for Science and Engineering Statistics and based on data from the U.S. Department of Education's IPEDS 2010 Completions Survey.

TABLE A-1 Student Characteristics and Precollege Preparation Across STEM Disciplines and Social Sciences, as Percentages of Total Students by Discipline Category

Student Characteristics	Biological Sciences (15,338)	Engineering (15,727)	Math/ Computer Science (3,850)	Physical Science (4,140)	Social Science (20,763)
Gender					
Men	40	79	75	57	30
Women	61	21	25	43	70
Race					
American Indian	<1	<1	<1	<1	<1
Asian	14	13	16	10	7
Black	8	6	8	5	10
Latino	9	9	8	6	14
White	54	59	53	65	53
Other	15	13	15	14	15
Income					
Below $50K	30	25	32	26	38
$50K-$100K	30	32	31	34	29
Above $100K	40	43	37	40	33
Mother's education					
No college	26	23	27	22	31
Some college	16	15	16	16	17
College degree or higher	59	62	58	62	52
Precollege preparation					
HS GPA: A- or higher	62	62	55	64	45
Years of HS math: 4 or more	92	94	92	92	84
Years of HS physical science: 3 or more	29	39	33	50	28
Years of HS biological science: 3 or more	29	12	13	16	18
Completed calculus	39	51	45	45	24
Completed AP calculus	42	60	51	50	22

TABLE A-1 Continued

NOTES: Total student enrollment is shown under each discipline category. Numeric values are the percentage of this total. AP = advanced placement; GPA = grade point average; HS = high school.
SOURCE: Eagan et al. (2014, Table 2).

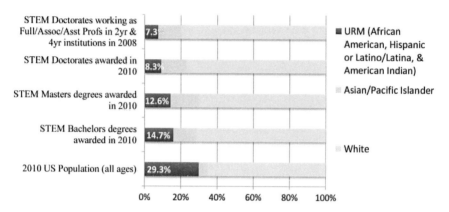

FIGURE A-1 Current percentages of underrepresented minority, white, and Asian/Pacific Islander populations with STEM degrees.
NOTE: URM (underrepresented minorities) includes African American, Hispanic or Latino/Latina, American Indian, and Alaskan Native. In this analysis, "STEM degrees" includes degrees categorized by the National Science Foundation as "Science & Engineering" (but excludes degrees in psychology and social sciences) in data tables prepared by the National Center for Science and Engineering Statistics and based on data from the U.S. Department of Education's Integrated Postsecondary Education Data System (IPEDS) 2010 Completions Survey.
SOURCE: Reproduced from Estrada et al., 2016, Figure 1, p. 2. Permission was granted by the authors.

REFERENCES

Eagan, K., Hurtado, S, Figueroa, T., and Hughes, B. (2014). *Examining STEM Pathways among Students Who Begin College at Four-Year Institutions.* Paper commissioned for the Committee on Barriers and Opportunities in Completing 2- and 4-Year STEM Degrees. Washington, DC. Available: http://sites.nationalacademies.org/cs/groups/dbassesite/documents/webpage/dbasse_088834.pdf [December 2016].
Estrada, M., Burnett, M., Campbell, A.G., Campbell, P.B., Denetclaw, W.F., Gutiérrez, C.G., Hurtado, S., John, G.H., Matsui, J., McGee, R., Okpodu, C.M., Robinson, T.J., Summers, M.F., Werner-Washrune, M., and Zavala, M. (2016). Improving underrepresented minority student persistence in STEM. *CBE–Life Sciences Education, 15*(es5), 1-10.

National Academies of Sciences, Engineering, and Medicine. (2016). *Barriers and Opportunities for 2-Year and 4-Year STEM Degrees: Systemic Change to Support Students' Diverse Pathways*. S. Malcom and M. Feder (Eds.). Committee on Barriers and Opportunities in Two- and Four- Year STEM Degrees. Board on Science Education. Division of Behavioral and Social Sciences and Education. Board on Higher Education and the Workforce. Policy and Global Affairs. Washington, DC: The National Academies Press.

Appendix B

Committee Questions to Undergraduate Institutions and Selected Responses

Questions about the Costs of Expanding Undergraduate Research Opportunities

1. School or program characteristics: Name of school and unit under discussion—is program for all students, all STEM majors (specify), or a particular department? Size of student pool?

2. Goals of the expansion: What are institutional goals for students undertaking this research experience? Please check all that apply:

_____ develop a better understanding of the scientific process
_____ improve a range of academic skills
_____ improve hypothesis generation and testing
_____ view oneself as a scientist
_____ produce work of interest beyond the classroom (to the community, scientists, etc.)
_____ contribute to work that will likely become a publication in a scientific journal

What are the goals for the institution? Please check all that apply:

____ increase retention in STEM
____ attract a stronger applicant pool
____ increase diversity in STEM
____ increase student/faculty satisfaction in STEM majors
____ providing such opportunities considered an important institutional characteristic

3. Type(s) of research experience(s) being utilized: Examples: are research opportunities being offered in scheduled courses (CURE); through group efforts during summer/winter break; or using the apprentice-style model, during summer or academic year, or both.

4. Resources available: What in-place resources were available for program expansion? What does the institution have? What is it known for? Examples: office of undergraduate research; research-active faculty willing to take undergraduates into their research groups, and/or develop CURE projects; on-campus undergraduate research symposium; teaching lab space available for summer research use; access to scientific journals; field stations; engagement with community problems; current budget for teaching cook-book lab assignments; budget for lab instructors; etc.

5. What resources needed to be added and/or modified? Over what time line and cost? Examples: new administrative staff to oversee/develop undergraduate research opportunities; new department staff to organize/teach/supervise students; lab space dedicated to undergraduate research; increased support for field station; increased supply budget; addition/expansion of on-campus undergraduate research symposium; conference travel budget for student presentations; expanded number of student stipends, etc. Give costs in general terms (ex. staff described as experienced educator with Ph.D. in X; supply budgets given as approximately X per student, or as a range per student, etc. Point out if needed resources came from re-purposing prior resources).

6. Outcomes to date, if known: Example: as your undergraduate research program has expanded, have you observed any of the following: increases in number of students participating in STEM research; increase in diversity of students participating; a shift in applications; a change in persistence in STEM or in STEM graduation rates, etc.

Excerpts from Responses

Amherst College (MA) excerpts from the response:

> *We are fortunate to have sufficient endowed funds to support a 10-week summer research experience for all chemistry majors embarking upon a senior thesis...*

> *We need to find ways of freeing up time for faculty to supervise research students. It is impossible to be a responsible or effective research supervisor if one is unable to spend uninterrupted time in the laboratory several days each week. Often it seems like research is an optional luxury.*

> *The greatest limitation for us is faculty time, and thus the greatest cost to pushing beyond our current limits would be to hire more faculty, or at minimum (especially for the STEM fields), more post-docs, postbacs (generally honors students continuing to work in the lab in which they did their honors thesis) or lab technicians in order to enhance the faculty member's capacity to mentor students.*

Anoka Ramsey Community College (ARCC) (in MN) *"is trying to infuse undergraduate research for all students in all disciplines"* based on plans developed through a Council on Undergraduate Research (CUR) workshop. The school currently has about 8,000 students and estimates that 30-40 percent are engaged in some sort of research or scholarly activity, primarily through course-based undergraduate research experiences (CUREs). Nine of 21 biology courses are providing novel undergraduate research experiences (UREs). ARCC has supported independent research students, often in partnership with other schools; at present student stipends for research work do not exist. Space is being repurposed and remodeled to create an Open Research Lab, which will need to be staffed. Faculty members are getting release credits to work on this program.

Austin College (TX) expanded its apprenticeship program during 2000-2008, and some departments also use research methods, CUREs, or scaffolded curriculum models to support that. A *"new strategic plan calls for every student to have two experiential learning experiences while an undergrad,"* and the Center for Research, Experiential, Artistic & Transformative Education (CREATE) was set up in 2015. The inaugural director is in the process of bringing all of the current campus programs together. An all-campus Austin College Student Scholarship Conference is held annually.

Chemistry and physics require research for the major; biology has grown from 23 percent participation in 2003 to 56 percent participation in 2015. Financial resources are being sought to expand and stabilize the program with student stipends, faculty stipends, supply money, and student travel awards in response to cited needs.

Central Washington University (WA) has expanded its Office of Undergraduate Research (OUR) in the past 2 years from one to two permanent staff positions (director and a support staff position) with funding from the provost. This expansion supports the institutional goal to provide opportunities for student scholarship/scholarly work. The addition of the second staff position frees up the OUR director to work on fund raising, raising campus profile of undergraduate research, etc. UREs are primarily apprentice-style during the academic year and summer. While a small amount of internal funds are available, funding for most projects comes from external faculty research grants, so most opportunities are for advanced students. A few introductory (first-year) and second-year students can get funding through a small fund for minority student research. A soon-to-be-sunseted grant funds approximately five STEM students and faculty for summer research. During the academic year, students receive academic credit and faculty receive teaching credit.

The **Community College of Rhode Island (CCRI)** has expanded the number of CUREs offered through its faculty training program. Two faculty attended a week-long CURE workshop and then ran a Faculty Learning Community to help others include undergraduate research in their courses. Three years ago, one faculty member (geology) included undergraduate research in her courses; this year six faculty members now offer UREs in courses (geology, oceanography, biology, microbiology, finance, psychology). To allow for the expanded efforts, a variety of resources were repurposed: existing lab supplies were used for CUREs as well as an expansion of an established URE symposium that was funded by the honors budget. There were also one-time additional resources to support this effort to include funds to compensate leader and participants in the Faculty Learning Community as well as travel costs covered for two faculty to attend a CURE workshop.

Faculty develop and implement their undergraduate research experiences at CCRI (both the CUREs and Honors Projects) without additional resources. Not only do faculty not get compensated for any additional time they have, they need to work within the current budget for materials and supplies. They also do not have separate research labs, since all labs are teaching labs or classrooms that

are used throughout the day. This limitation impacts the type and
scope of the research projects that can be done, and faculty take
that into consideration when deciding on research projects.

Delaware Technical Community College (Stanton Campus), a member
of the Community College Undergraduate Research Initiative (CCURI),
has been strengthening research in the Biotechnology and Biological Sciences programs. Both CUREs and apprentice-style models are being used.
Teaching lab space is available; National Institutes of Health and National
Science Foundation (NSF) grants have funded equipment purchases and
faculty development; lab fees are used to support supplies. Over the 5-year
period of the grant, there has been a 50 percent increase in the completion
rate. *"With the increased student success rate, the college has provided an
increased budget to support supply purchases for CUREs."*

Embry-Riddle Aeronautical University (ERAU) (FL) has a strong STEM
emphasis (heavy on engineering). Of the roughly 2,200 undergraduates,
about 40 percent participate in research/scholarship and approximately 250
are directly funded by the Undergraduate Research Institute. Students participate in academic and summer research in projects that are encouraged to
be multidisciplinary and multiyear. Current expansion of undergraduate research is into the introductory and intermediate-level courses. Some "study
abroad" classes have a research component. As part of the accreditation,
ERAU has chosen undergraduate research as its quality enhancement plan
(QEP; a QEP is currently required by the Southern Association of Colleges
and Schools for accreditation). With QEP funding, they have recently established an Undergraduate Research Institute (with two staff positions).

*QEP funding allowed for the establishment of the Undergraduate
Research Institute, basic/applied research and scholarship grants, a
program director (joint direction of Honors) and an administrative
assistant (joint with Honors).*

Everett Community College, Ocean Research College Academy (Everett,
WA) is a two-year, full time program for 120 students that includes an
embedded longitudinal research project on a local estuary. Students are
involved in data collection and analysis of biogeochemical metrics; training
in the first year enables students to test self-directed questions in the second
year. Students use a research vessel and a dedicated research lab funded by
NSF. CCURI funding provided initial faculty release time to initiate the
curriculum; maintaining that time (to mentor students) has been a struggle.
The faculty report that 70 percent of the research students matriculated

to a STEM major in university this past year and that they will continue to advocate for the program in the face of anticipated budget cuts.

At **Finger Lakes Community College** (NY), the departments of Science and Technology and Environmental Conservation are offering research experiences through scheduled academic year courses and as summer courses. Investments in faculty training and a small amount of equipment have been important; other resources have come from repurposing current resources. Before the recent expansion *"very few students were participating and now every student that takes general biology participates."*

Fort Lewis College (CO) is a *"non-tribal, native-serving institution and one of only two colleges [that] provide free tuition to qualified Native Americans."* Organizational changes in the college, increased internal funding, and an active undergraduate research symposium support increasing undergraduate research at Fort Lewis College. To promote undergraduate research, an associate dean position was redefined 6 years ago to support undergraduate research programs, teaching credits for labs and STEM teaching load were modified to accommodate time for undergraduate research, and internal funding was increased. The symposium, started 12 years ago for STEM students, advertised to nonparticipating faculty what could be done with student research. Subsequent changes to departmental senior seminars and assessment plans promote undergraduate research. Challenges to sustaining the program involve declining state budgets and rising research costs, while there has been an increase in STEM majors and graduates between 2010 and 2015.

> *Within the STEM disciplines, reorganization of senior seminar courses happened after the undergraduate research symposium began. I think the departments began to see what undergraduates could accomplish, and wanted their students to have those experiences. Some of the changes were driven by external accreditation (Engineering); others were tied to revision of the departmental assessment plans. (When departments wrote learning outcomes involving the process of science, they started thinking about how they could improve those learning outcomes by having students do science themselves.) The dean has also been encouraging departments to involve students in research, partly because it benefits students, and partly as an encouragement to faculty to be more active in their fields.*
>
> *The costs of undergraduate research, especially in the sciences, is high. Even when faculty/departments economize (i.e., group proj-*

ects, less diversity of projects), it is not clear that costs are sustainable without some type of permanent funding (i.e., an endowment). Although our administration is encouraging undergraduate research-like experiences in all departments, the budget that they are applying to this mandate is not likewise rising to meet the increased needs.

The **Gonzaga University** (WA) Biology Department uses a combination of CUREs and apprentice-style research opportunities. The Phage Hunters course has been adapted to include isolation of new phage as the lab for the introductory biology course (BIOL 105: Information Flow in Biological Systems) and phage annotation in the lab for sophomore-level genetics. Faculty received training on how to develop a CURE through a collaborative Howard Hughes Medical Institute (HHMI) grant that supported seven colleges and universities; this helped the faculty and accelerated implementation of CUREs. Supply costs are managed by charging a $95 lab fee. Faculty efforts are supplemented by two lab coordinators and undergraduate teaching assistants, who receive course credit for their efforts. A research coordinator oversees the apprentice-model research program, which involves approximately 30 students per semester and about 65 students per summer, up from 20 in 2006.

Hope College's (Holland, MI) Division of Natural and Applied Science is initiating a program called "Day1 Research Communities" for first-year students; capacity in five communities is about 170 students of 400 eligible. This program also emphasizes developing a "community of scholars." Hope also has a significant apprentice model program and CUREs for upper-level students. Two of the five tracks are two-semester programs ("Phage Discovery" and "Watershed") that demand more time investment by students and faculty and are thus more expensive to run. "Watershed" students come to campus a week early for fieldwork and live together during the year. A post baccalaureate lab director involved in both courses helps to lessen demands on faculty, as do upper-level students who serve as teaching assistants. Funding from HHMI has helped to expand course-based research experiences in general, but this has been done with an eye on sustainability. Unfortunately, cutting-edge techniques tend to require more expensive consumables and up-to-date equipment. If needed, the college will tap endowed funds.

Ivy Tech Community College (IN) *"has come to appreciate the value of a URE for community college student"* and offers both CUREs and summer UREs to students in biotechnology and nanotechnology. Students can participate in the NSF Community College Innovation Challenge and in the iGEM competition. The faculty make use of a wide range of support organizations, including CCURI, CUR, CUREnet, the Cold Spring Harbor Laboratory DNA Learning Center, CyVerse, and local industrial partners. A mix of internal and external resources is available for supply costs, etc., but need remains for a dedicated lab and for funds for high tech expenditures. No stipends are available to students. Students who participated in UREs have presented posters at a variety of meetings and are reported to exhibit significant personal gains. Local industry is now requesting job applications from these students.

The **Kapiolani Community College** (HA) Math and Sciences Department is using a wide range of URE platforms, including bridge programs, grant-supported UREs, research-intensive courses that are part of the associates degree, elective CUREs, internships, and collaborative projects. In spring 2016, 49 of 391 registered students were in the elective CURE courses. A mix of institutional resources and grant funds are being used to support new staff in a STEM Center to support the new lab courses. There has been steady growth in enrollment and graduation numbers.

Lincoln University of Pennsylvania's Department of Biology provides academic year undergraduate research both via a CURE (biotechniques course) and apprentice-style research (funded through an HBCU-UP grant that provides $500/student for supplies). Funding comes from research-active faculty with external grants and some departmental supply budget. The school is establishing an undergraduate research office with funding via Title III. Undergraduate research has been showcased at a campuswide symposium for the past 15 years.

At **Longwood University** (Farmville, VA), faculty are bringing research into the biology curriculum using both national CUREs (Genomics Education Partnership, synthetic biology) and a local CURE (*Pilobolus* distribution in nature). About 10 percent of the biology students participate per year, and plans are under way to expand this. A summer apprentice-style URE is also available at Longwood. While an Office of Student Research was initiated 8/2015, "*[the] classroom related research programs typically are not recognized by University programs and exist solely at the discretion of faculty using course lab fees to support the project.*" The Genomics Education Partnership, a national CURE, "*provides essential resources that are outside of the expertise and budget of our faculty*"; both small grants from GCAT and contributions from industry have also helped support the genomics CURE.

Loyola Marymount University (Los Angeles, CA) has an undergraduate student body of about two-thirds of the 9,500 students enrolled. About a year ago, the Office of Undergraduate Research went from a faculty director with administrative support to two permanent staff positions (three-quarter time associate director and half-time administrator coordinator). A research symposium started 8 years ago. UREs for all fields of study are primarily through apprentice-style experiences offered in both the summer and academic year. In the academic year, students are compensated via work-study funds, academic credit arranged through departments, or as volunteers. During the summer, students receive stipends, housing costs, academic skills workshops, and social gatherings through a university program. Some students are funded through outside grants to faculty. Faculty mentors receive no compensation from the university but receive recognition that may help toward tenure and promotion. The symposium participation has increased over the years. The cycle of increased URE participation spurred interests in staffing increases. Increases in staffing raises undergraduate research on campus, which starts the cycle again.

The **Moreno Valley College** (CA) Department of Natural Sciences and Kinesiology has expanded research experiences for biology and chemistry students. A major goal is to increase the transfer rate to four-year institutions, including top schools. The primary vehicle is class-based projects, but a few students are working on individual projects. Resources are very limited: only one biology lab, faculty (no lab instructors or teaching assistants), and the budget for the cook-book labs. Growing recognition by administrators and faculty of the importance of UREs is cited as the most valuable resource. The faculty report that increased participation in STEM research leads to students being more engaged, enthusiastic, and persisting in STEM.

At **North Carolina Central University** (Durham, NC), laboratories for the three introductory biology courses (required of all majors) have been transformed into research-infused labs. Participation in the research version is voluntary, and over the past 3 years 39 percent of the 440 eligible students have participated. The research experiences are organized in 5- to 10-week-long modules, and they maintain a continuity of practice using *S. cerevisiae* as the model system. Labs are designed to require only the scheduled lab times. This system seems to work well for the university's students, who are 29 percent first generation, 65 percent Pell-grant supported, with little or no prior research experience. While this is a research-active campus "*there are not enough labs to accommodate the large number of STEM majors. . . . CURE courses are essential for our university to expose large numbers of STEM students to a research experience.*" A grant from HHMI has supported the introductory biology courses, including hiring a lab coordinator and supporting Science Education Post-Docs; the latter program will be lost when the grant ends, as state funding is extremely tight.

Penn State Brandywine, with around 1,600 students, is primarily a two-year college in which the majority of students transfer to complete their baccalaureate degrees. They have recently added four-year degrees in biology and in engineering (these have not been in place long enough to have graduates), and anticipate a program in environmental science. The campus is working toward expanding degree programs, with the goal of becoming a stand-alone four-year degree campus in the Penn State system. All types of undergraduate research are available ("engaged scholarship"): CUREs, apprentice-style during academic year and summer. Community-based research and service learning are available. There are challenges to the undergraduate research between terms due to liability issues for students who are not currently enrolled in credits. The recent formation of a faculty Undergraduate Research Committee centralizes funding efforts (the committee has a budget), and a new mini-grant program for students can cover research expenses. Two recent additions to undergraduate research on campus are awards for outstanding student researcher and outstanding faculty mentor (given annually). A quote on how the college does this:

> *What we needed to do was start having campus-wide conversations about how we as a campus define undergraduate research. . . . Once we came together across disciplines for at least one campus-wide meeting a semester, we immediately grew as a community and had more faculty buy-in. . . . Our campus also has an institutional membership to CUR, and that has shown us faculty that the administration is also serious about undergraduate research and "branding" us as a campus that engages students and takes the research process seriously as a student learning outcome.*

At **St. Edward's University** (Austin, TX), the Biology Department faculty are participating in the Genomics Education Partnership and in the HHMI Phage Hunters program, and they are now starting to convert the freshman series labs to a local CURE.

> *While an institution-specific CURE has advantages with regard to focusing on local scientific questions, . . . they lack several benefits that come with participation in national CUREs . . . quality of infrastructure (project materials, databases, resources), and the resources to develop these; possibility of publication (education and scientific literature) for students and faculty; high impact on students career aspirations based on exposure/participation with a national collective; presentation at national venue—students see themselves as part of the scientific community.*

Trinity University has built on a long history of undergraduate research in STEM fields. Undergraduate research has been expanded into the social sciences and humanities in the past 3 years. Both apprentice-style UREs and CUREs engage students. CUREs are primarily in upper-division courses, but are beginning to be part of introductory biology courses through a CURE on pollination. Engaged learning occurs in the social sciences through CUREs. Observed outcomes, whether or not related to undergraduate research, are increases in the number of entering students interested in STEM, the number of STEM majors, and the number of first generation and minority students at Trinity.

The **University of Maryland, College Park** initiated FIRE (First-Year Innovation & Research Experience) in 2014-2015 to provide inquiry-based experiences and broad mentorship for non-honors freshmen from all academic disciplines. The goal is to help students (about 400 this year) to view themselves "as a professional," help them select a major, and increase academic success, as well as to integrate the education and research missions of the university. The program is modeled after the Freshman Research Initiative at University of Texas at Austin (see Box 3-9), with a similar three-semester structure. But FIRE also supports students in their transition during their fourth semester to the next step—whether an apprentice-style research experience, an internship, etc. Each research stream is led by a Ph.D.-level Research Educator, who plays a critical role for the success of the program. Assessment plans include participation in a HHMI-funded collaboration with Duke University, University of California, Santa Barbara, and others to use a new core assessment to measure student growth, satisfaction, self-efficacy, confidence, and motivation.

At the **University of Pittsburgh,** there has been a significant increase in CUREs targeted at first- and second-year students in biology, with some CUREs in chemistry as well. Both national efforts (SEA-Phages [Science Education Alliance Phage Hunters; see Box 3-7] and the Small World Initiative) and local CUREs based on research interests of individual faculty are being implemented. The goal is to enroll all introductory biology students (freshmen and sophomores) in either a one-semester or two-semester CURE by 2018. Costs are being managed by charging a lab fee for supply costs (currently $75, but may rise to around $150) and by using undergraduate teaching assistants, who do not get paid, for the majority of teaching assistant positions. Senior-level staffing remains an issue; there are about 1,200 introductory biology students per year, presenting challenges in terms of scale. The school reported on a *"Persistence in The Sciences (PITS) survey, that links variables such as Project Ownership, Science Identity etc. with a self-reported interest in continuing in STEM. The PITS data show very* *strong impacts in this area in all of the CREs we have assessed . . . in contrast to traditional labs that score very poorly....*"

At the **University of Wisconsin–Eau Claire**, undergraduate research has long been important to institutional identity. Expansion of UREs has been continuous, with punctuated growth in 1997 and 2010 due to a differential tuition program to support experiential learning. Differential tuition provides expansion in student and faculty stipends and funds for student travel to professional conferences. Funds from this source approach $1 million. Programming efforts to support expansion of UREs target underrepresented students, first-year students, and international research. Current efforts focus on mentoring support, CUREs, community-based research, and first-year student participation. *"These are being tackled during significant budget cuts, so [the efforts] are using human resources rather than funding."* Revising the curriculum supports a faculty research track, and CURE development is funded by an NSF grant with University of Wisconsin–Milwaukee. The on-campus symposium is now a week-long celebration with increased participation by students and faculty.

Appendix C

Committee and Staff Biographies

James Gentile (*Chair*) is emeritus dean for the natural and applied sciences and Kenneth G. Herrick professor of biology at Hope College in Holland, Michigan. He is also a past president of Research Corporation in Tucson, Arizona, a foundation dedicated to science since 1912. He has conducted extensive research on metabolism and the conversion of natural and xenobiotic agents into mutagens and carcinogens with funding from the National Institutes of Health, the National Science Foundation (NSF), the U.S. Environmental Protection Agency, and the World Health Organization. He is the author of more than 150 research articles, book chapters, book reviews, and special reports in areas of scientific research and higher education, and he is a frequent speaker on issues involving the integration of scientific research and higher education. He serves on the Biosphere2 Governing Board and the boards of the Science Friday Foundation, and American Association of Colleges and Universities Project Leap Initiative. He received his Ph.D. in genetics from Illinois State University and undertook postdoctoral studies in the Department of Human Genetics at the Yale University School of Medicine.

Ann Beheler is executive director for emerging technology grants at Collin County Community College, near Dallas, Texas. She has been involved in the information technology (IT) industry for more than 30 years. She is the principal investigator for an NSF National Center that focuses on IT and communications as well as other NSF grants. She also led a large national Trade Adjustment Assistance Community College and Career Training Grant (Department of Labor). She has corporate experience through leading her own consulting firm and managing IT-related divisions and grants in community colleges in Texas and California. She created and taught in one of the first networking degree programs in Texas. She is known for bringing together business and industry effectively, using a streamlined process to identify with them the knowledge, skills, and abilities they predict will be needed by "right-skilled" job candidates in the future. She then works with faculty to align curriculum such that those who complete certificates and degrees in IT have the knowledge, skills, and abilities that will make them readily employable in high-paying IT positions. She holds an M.S. in computer science from Florida Institute of Technology and a Ph.D. in community college leadership from Walden University.

Janet Branchaw is assistant professor of kinesiology at the University of Wisconsin–Madison. She is also the director of the Wisconsin Institute for Science Education and Community Engagement and associate director of the Mentor Training Core of the National Research Mentoring Network. She is chairperson of the Leadership Committee for NSF's Biology Research Experiences for Undergraduates and directs an NSF-funded Research Experience for Undergraduates on integrated biological sciences. She developed training curricula for research mentors and for undergraduate research mentees. She led a project to develop a common assessment tool for use across NSF's Research Experience for Undergraduates programs. Her research focuses on the development, implementation, and evaluation of innovative approaches to undergraduate science education, with an emphasis on undergraduate research, assessment of student learning, and broadening participation in science among underrepresented groups. She received her Ph.D. in physiology from the University of Wisconsin–Madison.

Kerry Brenner (*Study Director*) is a senior program officer for the Board on Science Education. In addition to directing this study on Strengthening Research Experiences for Undergraduate STEM Students, she recently coordinated a workshop on service learning in undergraduate geosciences education and collaborated with the Board on Life Sciences (BLS) on a convocation on Integrating Discovery-Based Research into the Undergraduate Curriculum. In past work with BLS, she served as study director for the project that produced *Bio2010: Transforming Undergraduate Biology Education for Future Research Biologists*. As an outgrowth of that study, she participated in the founding of the National Academies Summer Institutes for Undergraduate Education. She has led a standing committee for the Department of Defense on Medical Technologies, multiple studies related to microbiology and biosecurity, and a study of the decision-making process for reopening facilities contaminated in biological attacks. Her bachelor's degree is from Wesleyan University (Middletown, Connecticut) and her Ph.D. in molecular biology is from Princeton University.

Deborah Faye Carter is associate professor of education in the School of Educational Studies at Claremont Graduate University. Previously she was an assistant professor of higher education at Indiana University, where she also was program chair of the Higher Education and Student Affairs program. While at the University of Michigan, she was an associate professor in the Center for the Study of Higher and Postsecondary Education and then became the center's director. She was awarded the Bobby Wright Dissertation of the Year Award from the Association for the Study of Higher Education and the Harold Johnson Diversity Award from the Univeristy of Michigan. She has been a member of or has chaired several committees in national organizations inluding the American Educational Research Association, the Association for the Study of Higher Education, and the American College Personnel Association. Her areas of research include the impact of college on students, especially students of color or low-income students; students' degree aspirations; students' transition to college; and the effects of undergraduate research on students' major choices and graduate school attendance. She received her Ph.D. in higher education from the University of Michigan.

Melanie Cooper is the Lappan-Phillips professor of science education and professor of chemistry at Michigan State University. Her research has focused on improving teaching and learning in large-enrollment general and organic chemistry courses at the college level, and she is a proponent of evidence-based curriculum reform. She has also developed technological approaches to formative assessment that can recognize and respond to students' free-form drawings, such as the beSocratic system. She is a fellow of the American Chemical Society and the American Association for the Advancement of Science (AAAS). She was on the leadership team for the Next Generation Science Standards. She has received a number of awards including the American Chemical Society award for achievement in research on teaching and learning in chemistry, the Norris award for outstanding achievement in teaching chemistry, and the Outstanding Undergraduate Science Teacher Award from the Society for College Science Teaching. She received her Ph.D. in chemistry from the University of Manchester, England.

Edward J. Coyle is the John B. Peatman distinguished professor of electrical and computer engineering at Georgia Institute of Technology and a Georgia Research Alliance Eminent Scholar. He is the founder and director of the Vertically Integrated Projects (VIP) program, which integrates research and education by embedding teams of undergraduates in the graduate research groups of faculty. He is also the founder and director of the VIP Consortium, a group of 15 universities committed to growing and disseminating the VIP program. He was a co-recipient of the National Academy of Engineering (NAE) 2005 Bernard M. Gordon Prize for innovation in engineering and technology education and a co-recipient of the American Society for Engineering Education's 1997 Chester F. Carlson Award for innovation in engineering education and the IEEE Signal Processing Society's 1986 Best Paper Award. He was elected a Fellow of the IEEE in 1998 for his contributions to the theory of nonlinear signal processing. His current research interests include undergraduate education, signal and image processing, and wireless sensor networks. He received a B.S. degree in electrical engineering from the University of Delaware and M.S. and Ph.D. degrees in electrical engineering and computer science from Princeton University.

Sarah C.R. Elgin is Viktor Hamburger professor of arts and sciences and a professor of biology, professor of genetics, and professor of education at Washington University in St. Louis. Her research on fruit flies focuses on epigenetics, gene regulation, and heterochromatin formation. In 2002, she became a Howard Hughes Medical Institute Professor with the goal of integrating primary research in genomics into the college curriculum. This project has been expanded and disseminated as the Genomics Education Partnership (GEP), a consortium of more than 100 college and university faculty. GEP undergraduates participate in gene sequence improvement and annotation projects, with the goal of publishing the results in primary research journals; more than 900 undergraduates are co-authors on GEP papers. She has awards for contributions to science education from the Genetics Society of America and other professional societies. She is a fellow of AAAS and the American Academy of Arts & Sciences. She serves on the editorial boards of *Chromatin & Epigenetics* and *CBE–Life Science Education*, on the science advisory board for CyVerse, and on the advisory board for CourseSource. She earned her B.A. in chemistry from Pomona College and her Ph.D. in biochemistry from the California Institute of Technology.

Mica Estrada is an assistant professor in the Department of Social and Behavioral Sciences and the Institute of Health and Aging at the University of California, San Francisco, School of Nursing. Her expertise is in social influence, including the study of identity, forgiveness, intergroup relations, and integrative education. She is leading longitudinal, theory-driven research and evaluation for several interventions designed to increase persistence of historically underrepresented students in STEM fields. Her publications from these studies assess how students' orientation toward the scientific community predicts their perseverance in and commitment to that community. She is co-principal investigator on a NSF Climate Change

Education Partnership grant that provides educational tools and learning opportunities to San Diego regional leaders and residents regarding the changing climate. Her work in the local community includes promoting the Quince Project for Latina teens. She received a Leadership Institute Graduate Award from the Society for the Advancement of Chicanos and Native Americans in Science in 2013 and the Adolphus Toliver Award for Oustanding Research in 2016. She earned her B.A. in psychology from the University of California, Berkeley, and her Ph.D. in social psychology from Harvard University.

Eli Fromm is Roy A. Brothers university professor and professor of electrical and computer engineering at Drexel University. He has been principal investigator on bioengineering research projects involving implantable transmitters and sensors for physiologic measurements and on initiatives for undergraduate research. At Drexel, he was vice president for educational research, vice provost for research and graduate studies, interim dean of engineering, and interim head of the biosciences department. He held positions with General Electric and E.I. DuPont and was a NSF program director, Congressional Fellow on the U.S. House of Representatives Science Committee staff, and visiting scientist with the Legislative Office of the Research Liaison, Pennsylvania House of Representatives. He is a fellow of multiple professional societies in engineering and engineering education, a member of the National Academy of Engineering (NAE), and the inaugural recipient in 2002 of the NAE's Bernard M. Gordon Prize for significant contributions to engineering and technology education. He has received numerous other awards and honors from professional societies in engineering, from the Accreditation Board for Engineering and Technology, and from multiple universities. He holds a B.S. in electrical engineering and an M.S. in biomedical engineering from Drexel University and a Ph.D. in physiology and bioengineering from Thomas Jefferson University.

Ralph Garruto (NAS) is research professor in biomedical anthropology at the State University of New York, Binghamton. He is a human population biologist whose research focuses on natural experimental models of disease, using both field and laboratory approaches. His cross-disciplinary research include studies of neurodegenerative disorders including amyotrophic lateral sclerosis and Parkinson's disease, as well as food chain disorders, health transition studies, obesity and bionutrition, malaria, Lyme and other tick-borne diseases, and prion diseases, especially chronic wasting disease. He has field research projects in Micronesia, Vanuatu, Ukraine, China, Siberia, and upstate New York. His laboratory focus is on cellular and molecular mechanisms of neuronal degeneration, host-pathogen interactions, experimental modeling, use of mitochondrial DNA in biomedical and evolutionary studies, and the study of gene-environment interactions in health and disease. He currently has 50 undergraduates associated with his laboratory. They work in teams with graduate students, and he meets with each at least weekly. The undergraduates typically stay for several years working in the field or laboratory or modeling risk of infection. He received his B.S. in zoology, M.A. in anthropology, and Ph.D. in anthropology (human population biology) from Pennsylvania State University.

Eric Grodsky is associate professor of sociology at the University of Wisconsin–Madison. His expertise is the sociology of education and quantitative methods. His research is on understanding the pathways students take into and through higher education, including the changes over time in the effects of grades, test scores, and course-taking on college attendance and completion. He has also evaluated the relationship between STEM course-taking, degree completion, and labor market outcomes for students who complete sub-baccalaureate degrees or who start but fail to complete their postsecondary credential. He serves on the editorial board of *Educational Evaluation and Policy Analysis*, is the deputy editor for *Sociology of Education*, and is an incoming associate editor for the *American Educational Research Journal*. He served as chair of the Sociology of Education Special Interest Group for the American Educational Research Association and as president of the Sociology of Education Association. He chaired the Sociology of Education section of the American Sociological Association in 2015-2016. He received his B.A. in anthropology and sociology from Kenyon College, his M.S. in sociology from the University of Wisconsin–Madison, and his Ph.D. in sociology with a minor in education policy from the University of Wisconsin–Madison.

James Hewlett is a professor of biology at Finger Lakes Community College, where he also serves as director of Biotechnology/Biomanufacturing. He is the New York Hub Director of the Northeast Biomanufacturing Center and Collaborative and serves on the editorial board of the National Center for Case Study Teaching in Science, the editorial board of *CBE–Life Sciences Education*, the advisory board for Rochester Institute of Technology's Center for Bioscience Education and Technology, and the steering committee for the University of Georgia's Course-based Undergraduate Research Experiences (CURE) Network. His areas of research include molecular and macro-level indicators of stress in corals and coral reef ecosystems, biomarkers for early detection of symbiotic breakdown in corals, and employment of noninvasive DNA-based mark-and-recapture methods in studying populations of the eastern red-tail hawk and North American black bear. He leads the Community College Undergraduate Research Initiative, which uses inquiry-based teaching to expose students to scientific investigation in introductory biology courses and provides resources for 26 institutional partners throughout the United States and a portfolio of support services to institutions and faculty. He earned a B.S. in biology from Bucknell University and an M.S. in physiology/marine science from the University of Connecticut.

Laird Kramer is director of the STEM Transformation Institute and professor of physics in the College of Arts & Sciences at Florida International University. His work focuses on facilitating institutional change through implementation of, and research on, evidence-based educational practices. He led transformation of the undergraduate physics experience at the university, creating more well-prepared majors by implementing modeling instruction–based studio physics courses, establishing student-centric methodologies, and establishing a high school–university research and learning community. He fostered a community that enables future teachers to implement their instructional craft, built by operating more than a decade of intensive, summer professional development in modeling instruction for high school teachers. He earned a B.A. in physics from George Washington University and a Ph.D. in physics from Duke University.

Jay B. Labov is Senior Advisor for Education and Communication for the National Academies of Science, Engineering, and Medicine. He has directed or contributed to 25 National Academies reports focusing on undergraduate education, teacher education, advanced study for high school students, K-8 education, and international education. He directed the National Academy of Sciences and Institute of Medicine committee that authored *Science, Evolution, and Creationism*. He oversees the NAS efforts to confront challenges to teaching evolution in the nation's public schools, coordinates NAS efforts to work with professional societies and state academies of science on education issues, and oversees the work of the BLS on improving education in the life sciences. An organismal biologist by training, he was on the biology faculty at Colby College for 18 years. He is a Kellogg National Fellow, Fellow in Education of AAAS, Woodrow Wilson Visiting Fellow, 2013 recipient of the Friend of Darwin award from the National Center for Science Education, and current chair of the AAAS Education Section. In 2014 he was named a Lifetime Honorary Member by the National Association of Biology Teachers and received a National Academies Staff Award for Lifetime Achievement.

Marcia C. Linn is professor of cognition and development, specializing in education in mathematics, science, and technology, in the Graduate School of Education at the University of California, Berkeley, where she investigates science teaching and learning, gender equity, and design of learning environments. She leads the Technology-Enhanced Learning in Science Community and is a member of the National Academy of Education and fellow of AAAS, American Psychological Association, Association for Psychological Science, and Center for Advanced Study in Behavioral Sciences. She was chair of the AAAS Education Section and president of the International Society of the Learning Sciences. She received the first award in educational research from the Council of Scientific Society Presidents, as well as rewards from the National Association for Research in Science Teaching and the American Educational Research Association. She twice won the Outstanding Paper Award of the *Journal of Research in Science Teaching*. She was a Fulbright Professor at the Weizmann Institute (Israel) and visiting fellow at University College, London, and the Institute J. J. Rousseau (Geneva). She served on the Science Board of AAAS, Graduate Record Examination board of the Educational Testing Service, McDonnell Foundation Cognitive Studies in Education Practice board, and NSF Education and Human Resources Directorate. Her B.A. in psychology with emphasis on statistics and a Ph.D. in educational psychology are from Stanford University.

Linda A. Reinen is an associate professor of geology at Pomona College. She uses field, laboratory, and numerical modeling methods to explore the mechanical behavior of crustal rocks in tectonically active regions. Through apprentice-style and classroom research experiences, her students investigate the surface deformation associated with active faulting in the San Andreas Fault system and the active margin in New Zealand. A long-time proponent of teaching through student research, she codeveloped a Research Methods CURE that for two decades has been central to the Pomona College geology curriculum. She led workshops on engaging undergraduate students in research for the National Association of Geoscience Teachers, American Geophysical Union, Geological Society of America (GSA), Council on Undergraduate Research, and Project Kaleidoscope. Her community outreach includes discussions of the Great California ShakeOut and other earthquake-related topics with grade school, college, local business, and community group audiences. She was a National Association of Geoscience Teachers Distinguished Speaker, Geosciences Counselor for the Council on Undergraduate Research, and 2003 recipient of GSA's Biggs Award for Excellence in Earth Science teaching. She was a Visiting Research Scholar (University of Auckland, New Zealand) and a Visiting Assistant Research Geophysicist (University of California, Riverside). She holds a Ph.D. from Brown University.

Heidi Schweingruber is director of the Board on Science Education and has been involved in many of its major projects since its formation in 2004. She co-directed the study that wrote *A Framework for K-12 Science Education* (2011), which became the first step in revising national standards for K-12 science education. She was study director for a review of NASA's pre-college education programs and co-directed the study that produced *Taking Science to School: Learning and Teaching Science in Grades K-8*. In addition to editing National Academies reports on education, she co-authored two award-winning books that translate findings of National Research Council reports for practitioners: *Ready, Set, Science!: Putting Research to Work in K-8 Science Classrooms* and *Surrounded by Science*. She previously was a senior research associate at the Institute of Education Sciences in the Department of Education, director of research for the Rice University School Mathematics Project, and faculty member in psychology and education at Rice University. She has served on advisory boards for the Merck Institute for Science Education, the Discovery Learning Research Center at Purdue University, and Building Capacity for State Science Education. Her Ph.D. in developmental psychology and anthropology is from the University of Michigan.

Amy Stephens is a program officer for the Board on Science Education and an adjunct professor for the Southern New Hampshire University Psychology department, where she teaches online graduate-level courses in cognitive psychology and statistics. Her background is in behavioral and functional neuroimaging techniques, and her research has examined a variety of student populations, spanning childhood through adulthood. Her prior work at Johns Hopkins University (JHU) Center for Talented Youth focused on characterizing cognitive profiles of academically talented youth, to develop alternative methods of identifying and aiding talented students from under-resourced populations. Her research has also explored the effectiveness of spatial skill training on performance in math and science classes, as well as overall retention rates in STEM-related fields for students entering the JHU engineering program. She holds a Ph.D. in cognitive neuroscience from JHU and continued as a postdoctoral fellow jointly in the Center for Talented Youth and the School of Education.

Heather Thiry is a researcher at the Ethnogaphy and Evaluation Research Center of the University of Colorado Boulder. She conducts research and evaluation studies on underrepresentation of women and minorities in STEM disciplines, the professional socialization of graduate students, and pedagogical reform initiatives in STEM education. Her research interests include the social and cultural factors that enhance or hinder educational reform, scientific career paths and career decision making, and the underrepresentation of women and minorities in the sciences. She has published on the professional development of education-engaged scientists and the overrepresentation of women scientists in teaching and outreach. Her current work focuses on learning progressions, exploring when students are most receptive to learning certain skills along the path from novice to experienced researcher. She has taught educational foundations and policy courses for preservice teachers, directed a service-learning program at a community college in California, and served as a counselor in an urban elementary school. She has run programs at the K-12 and community college levels to provide case management and social services for low-income and first generation students. She received her Ph.D. in educational foundations, policy, and practice from the University of Colorado Boulder.